Creating Stable Foster Placements

Creating Stable Foster Placements

Learning from Foster Children and the Families Who Care For Them

Andy Pithouse and Alyson Rees

Foreword by Freda Lewis

Jessica Kingsley *Publishers*
London and Philadelphia

First published in 2015
by Jessica Kingsley Publishers
73 Collier Street
London N1 9BE, UK
and
400 Market Street, Suite 400
Philadelphia, PA 19106, USA

www.jkp.com

Copyright © Andy Pithouse and Alyson Rees 2015
Foreword © Freda Lewis 2015

Front cover image source: Shutterstock®.

Library of Congress Cataloging-in-Publication Data
Pithouse, Andy.
Creating stable foster placements : learning from foster children and the families who care from them / Andy Pithouse and Alyson Rees.
    pages cm
Includes bibliographical references and index.
ISBN 978-1-84905-481-2 (alk. paper)
1. Foster children--Great Britain. 2. Foster parents--Great Britain.
I. Rees, Alyson. II. Title.
HV887.G7P58 2014   362.73'30941--dc23
                2014015603

British Library Cataloguing in Publication Data
A CIP catalogue record for this book is available from the British Library

ISBN 978 1 84905 481 2
eISBN 978 0 85700 865 7

Printed and bound in Great Britain

CONTENTS

Foreword

As someone with many years' experience working in foster care, in policy development as the fostering policy manager for the Welsh Government, then as the director of The Fostering Network, it is with much enthusiasm that I write this forward to a book that captures in rich detail the often overlooked home world of foster carers, their children and the children they care for. The research presented in this book and the messages it gives are a timely reminder to all of us, who work to improve outcomes for looked after children, that it is attention to day to day living in a caring family home that can make the biggest difference to helping a child.

Across social care we increasingly encourage practitioners to work with the users of services to build on their strengths and focus on what they can do, not what they can't. Yet all we seem to read from research in the field of looked after children is the poor outcomes of this group. Thankfully, this book is very different, with the research taking a strengths-based perspective to explore the ways children in care and foster families can together create meaningful, stable and mutually enriching home environments.

The Care Inquiry of 2013 published the results of an extensive investigation on how best to provide stable and permanent homes for vulnerable children. The report into the inquiry's findings, *Making not Breaking,* presents evidence from parents, relatives, adopters, special guardians, foster carers, residential workers, academics, policy people and managers and practitioners at all levels. Children and young people provided evidence via focus groups, online surveys and presented their views via film and in person to the inquiry.

The main conclusion was that 'permanence' for children means 'security, stability, love and a strong sense of identity and belonging'.

The strong message to the inquiry was that it is the *relationships* with people who care for and about children that are the golden threads in children's lives, and that the quality of a child's relationships is the lens through which all in the sector should view what we do and plan to do. It is precisely this hidden domain of the child becoming part of the foster family that the book reveals, in the way it captures those everyday events, activities and attachments that underpin caring relationships that deepen over time.

The research conducted by the authors is focused 'solely on the home setting and relationships therein' and explores the everyday interactions that all families experience. For example, it looks at eating together and the social value of shared mealtimes, often an experience that looked after children have not had with their birth families. Indeed, I remember a foster carer telling me that several adults that she had fostered as children returned for a traditional lunch on Sunday and she regularly had a dozen people attending, continuing the ties made in her family. This book examines how such ties are first made and sustained. It addresses key issues around the child's sense of self and how clothing, bodily care, touch, private space, trusting relationships, tolerance and commitment, all in different ways, and at different times, shape and define the often invisible world of foster care.

From my own professional experience working for The Fostering Network[1] in the UK I have long recognised the strong relationships that are made within foster families. The Fostering Network has a history of highlighting the valuable role that men, and sons and daughters of foster families play in foster care. Men can be foster carers alone or as a couple and have a huge role to play in demonstrating positive role models for children who may have had very little contact with men or may have only had negative experiences. The families in this study recognised the value of the male's role and where there was no adult male partner often a son in the family would ensure they were involved with the fostered child.

Sons and daughters of foster carers also have a crucial role to play in fostering families. They share not only their home with a stranger but their parents too. A 13-year-old son in a fostering family once said to me:

---

1   The Fostering Network is the UK's leading fostering charity. By working with foster families and the services that support them, it helps those fostered to achieve the very best they can.

> When your mother is pregnant you have months to get used to the idea. I've come home from school and there is a [fostered] baby here, who wasn't here in the morning and then I have disturbed nights because it wakes up crying. I try not to mind because I know we are helping that baby, but I just wish we had a bit more notice!

If birth children are not happy then it can be difficult for foster carers to continue to foster.

Throughout the book we glean insights into motivations to foster and the values that people bring to the role. This makes for valuable reading and finds similarity with recent research undertaken on behalf of the Welsh Government by The Fostering Network, *Fostering in Wales: Who cares and why?* This identified that most foster carers share a common set of values. That is, they are principally motivated by an intrinsic desire 'to do the right thing' and to contribute to society.

The book gives a clear voice to children throughout. Foster care is about children and an extract from a diary entry of Stuart, a looked after child, sums up successful foster care:

> And now I am waiting for tea to be ready, which is good then we sit down and talk about what happened today...

This conjures up for me an 'ordinary' family scene, Stuart is experiencing something that is replicated in millions of homes around the world, giving children respect, a chance to be heard in a warm loving environment. Through my work at The Fostering Network I have developed enormous admiration for foster carers and the role they choose to take on. For me, the authors sum up foster care perfectly:

> It is difficult not to see effective foster families as impressive, able to repeatedly offer authentic warmth, communicate acceptance, and be authoritative but also flexible in response to the needs of the child.

I fully recommend the book to those who want to understand more about what contributes to effective fostering.

Freda Lewis
Former Director of The Fostering Network (Wales)

ACKNOWLEDGEMENTS

We wish to express our sincere thanks to all those children and adults participating in the study and the fostering agencies that facilitated our research. We very much hope our findings will be of use to other foster families and children and those agencies that support them. If so, we hope this may repay in some small way the adults and children who gave so very generously of their time, wisdom and hospitality. Without their enthusiastic help, this book would not be possible. Additionally, we would like to thank Philippa Williams who has a wealth of direct experience in fostering and adoption, and who advised us in developing our key messages for practice, we are much indebted.

Any errors in omission or presentation and interpretation of the views of participants and similarly in regard to our treatment of the large body of research in this field remains our responsibility alone.

Introduction

Foster care is increasingly the chosen option for children in public care, with 75 per cent of those who are looked after by local authorities in England and Wales being fostered (BAAF 2014; Welsh Government 2013). Given this overwhelming reliance on foster care it is perhaps surprising there has been only a limited amount of research into the day-to-day experiences of those adults and children who make up these remarkable families that foster. This much has been noted by fostering expert Linda Nutt (2006, p.1) who observes 'qualitative research focusing on foster carers is scant. We know little about their day-to-day lives'. Similar authoritative views have been expressed by leading families researcher Pauline Erera (2002, p.56) who states:

> The foster family itself has received little research attention. The family's structure, dynamics and stage of development, as well as its boundaries and the roles and relationships among family members and with the birth family, all merit further study.

Hence, we aim in this book to offer an 'inside' view of the everyday lives of foster carers and their children and of course the children and young people who are fostered. This is based upon an intensive and extended period of fieldwork research with a small number of families, as we indicate below. The field research was conducted primarily by Alyson Rees (AR). We have crafted the book so that it may appeal to a wide range of readers such as students, trainers, front-line professionals and other researchers in children's services who are likely to have some direct engagement with fostering. Also, and just as importantly, we intend it to be accessible to those professional foster carers who in their busy lives may find time to keep abreast of relevant research, amongst which we very much hope this text will find a place.

Our book is unavoidably 'academic' in that it draws upon theories in social work, sociology and psychology; it also draws on other recent research into fostering in the UK. Together, these will help us understand better the family practices we describe in later chapters. We aim to reveal to a diverse readership what seems to make for success in the usually hidden domain of foster care. Our book is based upon close and intimate engagement with a small number of families, ten in all, who were deemed to be successful in providing durable stable care. We examine that care from the different viewpoints of children and adults and seek to identify what it is about the activities, meanings, values and relationships within these families that makes for effective fostering. In doing this we have paid special attention to the voice of the child and have sought to follow the advice of Winter (2006, p.61) who urges that research involving children should:

> encourage participation by focusing on their perspectives in and of themselves and, whatever their age, giving them a direct, unfettered voice and bringing these voices in to the public domain to bring influence to bear on policy, procedure and practice.

While our commitment to the child's voice is central to the study design, this has to be seen as contexualised in the lived experience of the foster family overseen by adults and through them to kin, friends and neighbours in the wider community. Such an inclusive approach to the usually unobserved world of family life is not unique, after all reality television has increasingly focused on the lives of families, based on 'fly on the wall' type programmes (e.g. *The Family*, BBC 1974; *The Family: Teen Stories*, Channel 4 2008; *The Family*, Series 1–3, Channel 4 2013–2014).

We have attempted something similar in that we have tried to capture key features of the private world of fostering but through the exacting discipline of a qualitative research design, as we outline later. What this has given us is a rare glimpse into the inner workings of the foster family from which we have identified lessons about what works well and, as importantly, what young people appreciated most about being in foster care. To this end, we do not address wider aspects of their care careers, past or future, with social services departments, nor their engagement with education or health services. Such areas, together with the views of related professionals, have been the subject of detailed attention elsewhere as we outline in Chapters 1 and 2. Instead we focus solely on the home setting and relationships therein.

To repeat, our research design was based upon a desire to focus on foster families that were thought to be successful and to analyse the reasons for this success. Like Chase *et al.* (2006), we did not want to add to a familiar and long-trodden path about the negative aspects of the care system and thereby repeat much of what is already known about shortfalls in support for looked after children and young people (see Harber and Oakley 2012; Rowe and Lambert 1973). In short we wanted to focus on the positives and in doing so we have utilised a 'strengths-based' perspective. This is best understood as a conceptual framework which adopts a different way of looking at individuals, families and communities, seeking to recognise, improve and sustain capacities, rather than focusing on the inadequacies that, to varying degrees, we all possess (Saleeby 1996, 2006). Happer *et al.* (2006, p.55) make this very point in regard to their study into children in care:

> We know that looked after children can overcome early experience of trauma and adversity. Our participants demonstrate that children's histories do not have to predict their future, and that journeys through childhood to adulthood can be changed. We are learning that being looked after should be a time at which there is real opportunity for change.

We endorse this perspective and have sought to illuminate how effective foster families can nurture children in a safe, caring environment so as to build on their strengths and thereby extend or build new capacities. The poem below captures something of this experience. It is voiced by a foster child and reveals the poignancy of loss of what was before but also speaks of the welcome safety of a new home and, potentially, a better future:

Me

My feelings are true.
We rely on you
When I am sad
When I am lonely.

Here I am safe at a foster home.
I feel very happy.
Sometimes I am snappy,
Sorry to say
I'm on my way
To a new life.

(Lauren, aged 9 – *Taking Care*, BBC Books 2004)

Capturing this rarely glimpsed experience of an often unhappy child or young person entering the home of strangers, and gradually coming to feel safe and wanted, requires careful attention both to research methods and to research ethics in order to gather authentic insights while ensuring anonymity for all involved. With this in mind we devised the following study design.

Methods and sample

Our study comprised a mixed methods qualitative exploration of ten foster families deemed 'successful' by their fostering agency in providing durable good care. Hence our core research aim was to locate those activities, meanings, forms of participation, relationships and settings that underpinned the quality of care that contributed to these stable placements.

Small-scale intensive studies can yield valuable insights into fostering as we shall see in Chapter 1 (e.g. Buehler, Cox and Cuddeback 2003; Gaskell 2010; Madigan *et al.* 2013; Pugh 1999). Thus we sought a purposive sample of foster families, that is, a sample containing pre-defined characteristics likely to yield 'information rich' material to address our core research aim (see D'Cruz and Jones 2014). The sample was located through our professional links with fostering agencies. In brief, ten families were identified that were deemed to provide lasting stable care according to the following minimum criteria (see also Sinclair 2008). We defined these as: where a child or young person had been placed without disruption for over 12 months and where the adults had been foster carers for at least one year. (We do not assume that placements which disrupt lack the care elements that we describe in the book; there are many reasons why placements do not last as planned as we note in Chapter 1).

We wanted a sample that varied by type of fostering agency, family structure, carer background, age and needs of the foster child, and which included birth children of the foster family. Using our contacts we approached three types of providers of mainstream foster care likely to be found across much of the UK. These comprised a large voluntary sector fostering agency with families located across England and Wales; an urban local authority where there were no additional external support services on offer to carers; and a local authority with a more dispersed population and rural hinterland with an extra support service for carers provided by a small voluntary sector organisation. For reasons of strict confidentiality we do not identify the local authorities nor the voluntary agencies, nor location of the families. At occasional points in the book we draw comparison between these agencies and the families they support but only where clear distinctions derive from the data and merit comment. In any event, our small sample does not allow us to claim that the carers in this book are somehow typical of others connected to local authorities or the independent sector. However, insofar as our findings enjoy some congruence with other relevant studies, we can, with caution, infer some wider relevance for our interpretation of the data. For a more developed account of our qualitative techniques and methodology see Pithouse and Rees (2011).

The lead researcher in the field, AR, visited the ten families over a 12-month period, spending between eight and 30 hours with them to undertake interviews, conduct informal observation, and to collect other data via family exercises and audio diaries. Meeting the families over this extended period helped generate acceptance and trust and allowed us to learn much about the dynamic and unfolding world of fostering. The families were jointly selected by AR and social work staff in the three participating agencies who approached the families on our behalf. All those approached agreed to participate.

Amongst the ten families there were 18 adults comprising eight heterosexual couple carers and two single female carers. Their ages ranged from 39 to 61 (average age 50.2) and all were White British. They had been carers for an average of 9.5 years. Eight of the families had at least one birth child living at home, some nine children in all. One family in the study had no children placed with them. It is often the case that foster families will have no child placed at some point but they are nonetheless valid participants in a study that seeks out reflective judgements about the foster care experience (see also Sinclair *et al.* 2005a). At the start of the study there were 16 foster children aged 9–16 (whom we refer to interchangeably as children or young people) living with these families. Six of the young people were Black British and ten were White British. Of these, some nine agreed to participate in the study. We introduce these families and the children in more detail in Chapter 3.

We now turn to the qualitative research methods we used. These were deployed in the following sequence which together yielded a richly layered dataset that allowed us to grasp the subtle ways in which the host family and fostered child began to learn about each other and to establish meaningful and caring relationships. Our methods included:

1. A postal questionnaire sent prior to interviews to gain demographic data from carers in order to construct a profile of each family. The questionnaire included a Likert scale to scope carers' attitudes to fostering; in doing this we drew on research by Buehler *et al.* (2003) to generate comparison with other foster families.

2. In-depth interviews undertaken with adult carers about their motives, role and experiences in fostering. This included a challenging behaviour questionnaire developed from fostering research by Quereshi and Alborz (1992) which helped establish the knowledge and capacities of carers in dealing with children with complex needs.

3. In-depth sensitive exploratory interviews utilising a clear ethical stance (e.g. Best 2012) undertaken with the children of the carers and the young people in the foster placement, which explored

multiple themes around the day-to-day fostering experience in the family.

4. Birth children and foster children were asked to construct an eco-map (see Holland 2011) of the people closest to them in order to identify the strengths and location of key relationships.

5. A group exercise was undertaken with carers, birth children and children in placement which involved looking at vignettes about family problems. This was developed from the work of Padbury and Frost (2002) and required participants to seek an agreed solution to the issues raised, thereby revealing something of the problem-solving capacities across the families.

6. Carers and young people were asked to record an audio diary of their thoughts and reflections about ordinary family events over a chosen period of seven consecutive days. As in other studies where creative digital methods are used to facilitate freer communication and reflection (Arthur *et al.* 2014), this proved to be a fertile element of the research design providing thoughtful and unprompted illuminations of daily life at home.

7. Home visits to each family by AR were undertaken across the fieldwork period to engage in interviews, deal with the arrangements to complete the audio diaries and to talk to children about their eco-maps. This often entailed the researcher being invited by children to different parts of the home including the child's own bedroom, seeing the children play in the garden and indoors, meeting their friends and pets, and seeing photos of holidays and significant others in their lives. Such visits were also an opportunity for unobtrusive observations (O'Leary 2014) about which the participants were aware.

In using this mixed methods approach, we aimed to gain some 'purchase on the shifting realities' (Edwards and Talbot 1999, p.188) of foster home relationships and lifestyles that we were trying to capture. The research relationships with adults and children might best be typified as 'co-productive' whereby the university researcher AR (qualified and experienced social worker) and participants jointly explored and constructed richly detailed understandings about family life. Children were treated as experts in their own lives and active explorers of their home and external environments. They were able to influence the focus and topics of the interviews and the audio diaries. In this sense the researcher was an 'adult as enquirer' rather than an adult as 'expert' and somehow 'in charge' of the encounter (Clark 2014; Elden 2013). However, there was not sufficient time to engage the families in data analysis nor in the crafting of the findings.

Research into children's lives at home can be difficult in terms of gaining access to a privatised social space (Atkinson *et al.* 2001), particularly as children rarely occupy positions of power within the domestic arena. This is also the case for foster children whose position within the host family can be precarious. While there were few difficulties in gaining access to the families and children it was nonetheless important to keep in mind matters of safeguarding. These were a conscious aspect of the research encounter and all participants (and agencies) were made aware by AR that disclosure of concerns of a child protection nature would entail operation of the appropriate procedures.

A clear ethical approach to the study was sought using guidance from the British Sociological Association (2002). Accessible information sheets were produced for all adults and children participating. Children were interviewed one to one and were made aware that their comments would not be shared with carers or parents. Pseudonyms have been used throughout and permissions granted from all participants to use their comments in any published materials. They gave these consents freely in the hope that their views and experiences may be of use to other carers and children. Due to the rich data and small scale of the study, other potential identifiers have been either omitted or amended to preserve full anonymity.

Themes and issues in stability – the content of the book

We now turn briefly to a synopsis of the book chapters in order to outline how the rare and revealing insights we discovered will be themed and ordered. This may assist readers in selecting areas of more pressing interest. However, we would urge a preliminary reading of the first two chapters which provide much of the conceptual underpinning for our findings and analysis in Chapters 3 to 7.

Chapter 1: Fostering in the UK: Key Characteristics and Challenges

This chapter provides a brief introduction and background to fostering with particular reference to the UK context. The chapter summarises key research and considers the types and purposes of foster care and the elusive notion of 'success'. Evaluation studies of fostering outcomes are selectively reviewed. The chapter notes the importance of involving children in foster care planning and preparation. Issues of challenging behaviour and foster care training are also outlined and the chapter concludes with a discussion of foster families as caring systems.

Chapter 2: Ways of Thinking about Children and Families in Foster Care

In this chapter we outline different but complementary approaches to theorising foster care and related aspects of child development. We consider familiar but important psychological issues of attachment and stability. We next address the crucial matter of resilience in childhood and its connections to social and psychological wellbeing and the importance of a 'strengths' approach. The chapter then turns to an area relatively less applied to fostering, that of the sociology of childhood and the family. Here, notions of individualisation and its impact on the care relationship are discussed in relation to fostering. We pay special attention to what has been termed in social work literature as the 'ethic of care', and how this helps us understand the motives and meanings that might underpin fostering.

Chapter 3: Meet the Families

This chapter introduces the ten families and gives an overview of key participants. The chapter presents basic demographic material regarding the sample and compares this to other relevant research.

The chapter then outlines aspects of family structure and composition and relates this to key social science literature on UK families. Issues of gender are briefly considered together with recent sociological commentary on family practices.

Chapter 4: Tough Job Fostering: Why Do It?

This chapter looks at care as pivotal for child development and explores how this relates to the ways foster carers look after children. The chapter focuses on the family practices of the foster carers, what it is that carers actually 'do'. Parenting 'style' is considered, particularly in the way it appears to demonstrate a very different care experience for most of the looked after children. We explore the backgrounds of these foster families, their motivation to care, their biographical and cultural histories and examine the roles of both female and male carers. The chapter briefly considers the sociological notion of the 'gift relationship' as a way of understanding fostering. The nature of the 'gift' is explored in relation to providing stable long-term care. The implications of this for foster agencies in delivering durable placements are also noted.

Chapter 5: Food, Fostering and Family Life

This chapter considers the ceremony and the symbolism of food as an expression of intimacy, care and belonging. The chapter looks at food and mealtimes to illustrate aspects of the parenting approach adopted by adult carers and the birth children. Issues of food choice and access to food by the fostered young people are considered together with the impact of the routines surrounding the preparation of food and regularity of mealtimes. The enactment of the family through these routines is examined, particularly the significance of the 'Sunday Lunch' as a means of family celebration and communing. The chapter concludes with a summation of food and mealtimes as a vital ingredient of family association and an everyday means to display care.

Chapter 6: Foster Care and the 'Body'

This chapter starts by noting that the human 'body', while often discussed within a sociological framework, is much less considered within fostering literature, social work assessments, or social work standards and codes of practice. The chapter focuses on issues of intimacy and the body, particularly as foster care typically involves the child as stranger entering a new family home. The chapter explores the boundaries that the families put in place to manage these encounters and goes on to look at gender, bodily care and bodily comfort in foster care. The chapter considers the importance of touch as a demonstration of care and affection. The chapter concludes by reference to matters of bodily boundary and taboo in fostering.

Chapter 7: Space and Place in the Foster Home: Views from the Young People

This chapter seeks to give a distinct 'last word' to the foster children and the birth children in this study. Their perspectives are presented in relation to their experience of space and place that reveals important insights into the fostering process. The views of fostered children on the space provided to them in the foster home are explored. The question of place in relation to the home and its links to kinship networks, leisure activities and the community is considered briefly in regard to resilience building. The impact of fostering on sibling relationships and positioning within the family is explored with birth children, as is the role of the birth child in the family business of fostering and their responsibilities. The chapter concludes by reference to the importance of extended family networks and community support.

Following Chapter 7, there is a brief section that summarises the key themes and issues in the book and their implications for practice and research.

CHAPTER I

Fostering in the UK

Key Characteristics and Challenges

We do not address here a large literature on fostering laws, policies and copious procedures across the four UK countries – these being the subject of very different interpretations, if not contested viewpoints, and a study in their own right (see BAAF 2014; Cosis Brown 2014; Mehmet 2005; Smith *et al.* 2004). Indeed, some would argue that foster care in England and Wales is in urgent need of reform in order to deliver safer care, a fast response to placement matching, better recruitment, higher fees and more training (see Harber and Oakley 2012). Fostering is not without its critics; however, our focus here is on what seems to work from the viewpoints of carers, the fostered children and the birth children. In doing so, we address the activities, meanings, relationships and dynamics that bear upon stability and success in foster care. First, however, we set out some brief contextual background in which to situate our study.

In the UK the concept and development of foster care began in Scotland in the mid nineteenth century (Triseliotis *et al.* 1995), although different forms of boarding-out existed as far back as the seventeenth century and beyond (see Cosis Brown 2014; Hidden Lives Archive 2014; Nutt 2006). The historical role of foster care was to provide a substitute parent, so very often contact between the child and the birth family was discouraged in an attempt to strengthen the fostering relationship. Short-term care and reunification with family came to be seen as complementary goals after the 1948 Children Act (Triseliotis *et al.* 1995). Different skills were required as the role migrated from foster parent to foster carer, that is, a role often involving work with birth families and contributing to care planning. These changes were reinforced by the move from residential care towards community-based care in the 1980s, when increasingly specialist foster carers were recruited as an alternative to institutional care (Berridge, Biehal and Henry 2012).

Rowe and Lambert's classic study (1973) highlighted the plight of many children lingering in residential care and this was part of the impetus to move children away from such institutions. As a consequence of these changes, children entered foster care with diverse needs and frequently with difficult behaviour. Bullock (2002) argued that if foster carers were needed to look after children with challenging behaviour they would have to be partners rather than agents of social workers. The role of partner however has often been seen as difficult to achieve (Kirton *et al.* 2007; Peake 2009). Colton and Williams (1997) reviewed international trends and developments in the purpose, definition and practice of foster care; they noted that the term 'foster carer' had been instituted specifically to avoid the suggestion that a child's biological parents have been replaced by foster carers and their families. Understandably, this is not always easy for carers to accept given the emotional commitment required of them and the often long-term nature of some placements (see Blythe *et al.* 2012). Quite simply, the foster care role is not reducible to some bounded and more distant professional persona because it takes place within the intimate enclave of a family and the physical space of their home (Nutt 2006; Schofield *et al.* 2013).

The idea of fostering as a family support service with the aim of family reunification was given further legislative impetus by the Children Act (1989). Alongside the decrease in residential care provision, the aim of returning children to their birth parents created an increased need for foster care, especially short-term foster care. Research suggests (Sinclair 2010; Sinclair *et al.* 2000) that this trend had in some instances (older children in particular) led to numerous failed attempts at reunification with birth families resulting in damaging consequences for the young people concerned. Children's difficult behaviour can cause stress for carers (Biehal *et al.* 2010; Farmer *et al.* 2004) who often require increased support to fulfil their role (Farmer 2010).

Most carers remain volunteers and receive an income to cover expenses, and most children enter short-term care and return home quickly (BAAF 2012; Berridge 1999, p.241; Cousins 2009). A move toward fee paying especially in the independent sector has developed markedly in recent decades and a more 'professionalised' approach has been taken towards the role and identity of carers and their relationships with fostering and other agencies (Wilson and Evetts 2006). In short, fostering is increasingly viewed as a skilled and effective intervention, but many argue that it remains a service that has yet to be properly funded, supported and researched (Fostering Network 2007). A summary of the profile of UK foster carers by McDermid *et al.* (2012) found that carers were typically over 35 years of age, although the age for commencing caring was between 30 and 40 years. While there seems to be no official retirement age for carers there is of course a loss of provision when they decide to withdraw from fostering. Also the increasing demand for long-term placements reduces the pool of available carers (Clark 2009). It was found by McDermid *et al.* (2012) that approximately 75 per cent of carers were married or cohabiting. Most then were part of couples and the main carer was typically the female. In Farmer *et al.* (2004) 10 per cent of main carers were male and this was likely to be associated with fostering adolescents.

Some of the most comprehensive longitudinal research in the UK has been done by Sinclair *et al.* (2000) and Sinclair (2010), who found there were few foster families with young birth children, or where the female in the family worked full time. They also found that 46 per cent of the young people in foster care were female and 54 per cent male. Some 18 per cent of carers had no child placed with them at the point of the research. This under-utilisation could play a part in tackling supply shortages of placements. Their study revealed that each carer had on average 1.8 children placed with them at any one time. The ethnicity of carers and looked after children, according to Ofsted's (2011) examination of English local authorities, was respectively 89 per cent white and 81 per cent white. By contrast, in independent fostering agencies (IFAs) it was 78 per cent and 71 per cent respectively. IFAs would seem to be marginally more successful at recruiting black foster carers.

The proportion of foster carers without educational qualifications would seem to be slightly higher than the national average (Collis and Butler 2003; McDermid *et al.* 2012). In McDermid *et al.* the majority of carers were educated to GCSE or A-level standard, but fewer were educated to degree level than in the general population. There appear to be few if any major studies which explore the impact of qualifications held by foster carers upon the quality of support offered to the foster child in regard to their achievements in education. We too have created similar profiles of the carers involved in our study and these are introduced to the reader in Chapter 3.

IFAs were first set up in the UK in 1987, with 'the intention of offering a better service to foster carers and the children for whom they cared' (Collier 1999, p.189). Independent agencies tend to offer round the clock support, regular respite care, and additional health and educational services provided to the children being looked after by carers. They also tend to offer carers more financial support. A survey of IFAs in Britain by Sellick and Connolly (2002) challenged conventional wisdom that these were predatory enterprises poaching local authority foster carers. Their study found that only 33 per cent of foster carers were directly recruited from local authorities. Additionally, in a contemporary climate of public sector austerity, local authorities may well seek to secure as many placements as they can 'in-house' and only commission independent providers as a last resort (Sellick 2013). While the strengths and weaknesses of independent provision have been considered by Selwyn *et al.* (2010a), the outcomes for children placed in either local authority or independent foster care have rarely been compared and there appears little known about whether IFAs 'make a difference to children' (Sellick and Connolly 2002, p.119). Indeed, Sinclair (2010, p.193) in his study of foster care suggests that he 'failed to find any difference in outcomes between foster care by independent and local authority sectors'.

Attempting to meet the increased demand for foster care has not been achieved without considerable strain for those involved, nor has it occurred with sufficient attention to resourcing and regulation. Colton *et al.* (2008) noted a worldwide shortage of foster carers, and difficulties over recruitment and retention. These and related issues have long been emphasised by the National Foster Care Association (NFCA 1997) whose report *Foster Care in Crisis* pulled few punches. The lack of foster carers and the consequences of this were summarised thus by NFCA:

1. Most foster households are likely to be full and do not have immediate vacancies.

2. Limited or little choice is available for new admissions.

3. The range of carer competences and preferences does not necessarily correspond with the range of needs of children.

4. There are marked variations in the levels of carers across the country.

The situation may not have altered markedly since the NFCA report, as more recently Tapsfield (2012, p.1) notes that the 'fostering system is on the brink as the number of children in care soars'. Notably, the Looked After Children Strategic Implementation Group in Scotland (2013) acknowledged similar problems and considered ways in which carers with no current placement could be used to better effect. Similarly, Fostering Network (2013) highlighted the shortfall of foster carers and the need for increased recruitment of foster families. The findings from research by Norgate et al. (2012) emphasise the lack of placement options and the contribution of this to placement instability, as does a study by Gaskell (2010) in relation to the way children's views factor into (or not) placement selection. We know from Sinclair et al. (2000) and Sinclair (2010) that there is a lack of placement choice, particularly for minority ethnic groups (see also Selwyn et al. 2010b) and teenagers (Farmer 2010).

Conditions of scarcity and a service under pressure are not untypical of findings in much research into contemporary fostering (Harber and Oakley 2012). Indeed, in 2006 Nutt stated that the proportion of children in public care placed in foster homes had more than doubled over the previous 20 years (Nutt 2006). At March 2013, Fostering Network (2013) noted that almost 63,000 children lived with 52,500 foster families in the UK. They estimated that there was a need to recruit in the next 12 months (April 2013 to March 2014) a further 9000 foster families to keep up with the demand for foster care.

Types and purpose of foster care

It is important when reviewing and evaluating fostering to consider the types and purposes of foster care. Many of those who enter the care system spend little time there and it has been the view of many that foster care should be a short-term option (Forrester *et al.* 2009). Bullock *et al.* (2006) found that most children go home very quickly and relatively easily; others return after long separations and a few go home by default or accident. These trends suggest a basic distinction between short- and long-term care. Further distinctions can be made according to the purpose of the stay; for example, a short-term placement may occur while a parent is hospitalised or in some instances remanded to court. By contrast, we are witnessing an increase in a type of concurrent planning whereby carers are willing to become adopters if attempts at reunification are unsuccessful (Borthwick and Donnelly 2013). The following is adapted from the still-relevant classification developed by Rowe *et al.* (1989):

- short term – emergency, assessment, remand, roof over head
- shared or support care – regular short 'respite'-type breaks
- medium term – task-centred treatment, bridging placements, preparation for independence, adoption (sometimes by carers)
- long term – upbringing, 'forever home' in some instances.

While these categories still broadly apply, the characteristics of those fostered in each type may have changed (see Wilson *et al.* 2004). Additionally, terminology about the aims and duration of placements does vary across local authorities and fostering agencies which further complicates any attempt to provide a clear picture of contemporary fostering (Biehal *et al.* 2010). Bullock *et al.* (2006) call for better integration between local and national policies so that care systems can become more consistent in best practice and quality. In brief, the field remains complex and a definitive picture of what foster care looks like across the UK remains elusive. But what of the impact of fostering: is it successful – or is this an elusive aspect of the service too?

Success in fostering? Issues of definition and measurement

In order to establish those features and attributes that contribute to a successful placement, it is necessary to first define 'success'. A satisfactory placement is usually seen as one which lasted as long as it was intended to, usually prior to reunification or movement on to a planned longer-term placement (Leathers 2006). A successful foster placement that has not broken down and which has had identifiable positive repercussions has typically been measured by the improved outcomes for the young person and the level of satisfaction for the host family. For Leathers (2006) a placement breakdown is defined as a disrupted placement that was then terminated and followed by another *non-permanent* placement.

Berridge and Cleaver (1987) noted however that a breakdown in itself is not as clear an outcome as we might expect, as it depends on a perception of how long the placement was *intended* to last and there may be different views on this. Thus the aspect of 'breakdown' may be a matter subject to varying interpretations. Wilson, Petrie and Sinclair (2003) worked on the premise that a breakdown occurred when the foster carer, the child's social worker and/or family placement social worker defined it thus. Similarly, a placement was defined as successful when these participants agreed that it had gone well from a viewpoint of child wellbeing. Such an approach does not seem to prominently involve the child's perspective as a defining criterion.

One particular difficulty in measuring success, notably in long-term care, is that there seems to be no singular universally agreed definition of 'permanence' and the means by which this can be evaluated to demonstrate what has been achieved. Schofield *et al.* (2012, p.244) explain the point thus:

> The goal of permanence for children separated from their birth families and in the care of the state has dominated child care policy in the UK, the USA and Canada since the 1980s, but the meanings of permanence in terms of stability, emotional security and family membership into adulthood are complex and the placements and legal status thought best able to achieve permanence are contested.

Boddy (2013, p.1) expands on this:

> A meaningful definition of permanence must recognise the key qualities of family relationships for children and adults across generations – including a sense of belonging and mutual connectedness and of continuity between past, present and future.

Again we can see how difficult it is to gauge success in fostering if we are not listening to all the voices and especially those of the children (James and James 2004). Boddy (2013, p.2) further asserts that permanence depends on 'securing the right placement for the right child at the right time'. It follows that a placement may discontinue in order to locate a better fostering option for a child. It may also be that some early disruptions result in a placement in which the child finally becomes settled and attached. The setting in fostering guidance of an upper threshold of placement moves such as no more than three in 12 months (see Sinclair 2008) may well deter some providers from trying to find the ideal option if it means breaching the limit; children may be discouraged by service providers from seeking a change of placement for the same reason (see Harwin and Owen 2003; Minnis and Walker 2012). That said, the number of placement moves is noted as rising to an average of four in 2010 and five in 2011 (OFSTED 2012). Children's experiences within the care system vary considerably, depending on factors including age, ethnicity and reasons for placement. What we can deduce from these important studies is that there can be no easy generalities encompassing what success might mean in such a diverse service field.

If we are to grasp 'success' in fostering by measuring the outcomes of the placement then we have to recognise that outcomes may vary at any point in time and that fostering is often part of a wider care plan that will bear upon events. That the effects of these variables are difficult to capture is noted by Sinclair *et al.* (2005a). They argue that foster care offers a 'time-limited form of permanence', and suggest that it should not be evaluated solely on its own but seen as part of a wider care career of a child. This raises the question whether foster care should and can be evaluated at all in its own right and there is little evidence of the outcomes of foster care being monitored systematically by the professional community in order to guide the development of policy and practice (Kelly and Gilligan 2000).

A key challenge around outcome measurements in foster care is in (i) agreeing the range of factors to be assessed as likely determinants of success or failure and (ii) agreeing what or who the fostering outcomes should be compared against. It was noted for example by Sinclair *et al.* (2005b) that those children in their sample who returned home showed little, if any, educational improvement. Thus should outcomes be measured against what the child might have achieved (or not achieved) if returned to birth parents, or against children who have never experienced any disruptions in their lives? The few studies which have sought a comparative analysis found that children who stayed in the care system longer appeared to be less psychologically and physically damaged than those returned to disruptive homes (Sinclair *et al.* 2005b). A review of literature on fostering outcomes by Forrester *et al.* (2009) suggests that children who return home may do worse on a range of measures, including health, education and behavioural difficulties. It was also the case that even after positive care experiences children who are looked after are still likely to have more difficulties in their lives than those in the general population. The impact of early adversity and harm can have a lasting impact that may not easily be remedied by later exposure to care services.

That children in care are likely to have significantly more difficulties than those in the general population points us immediately to the high expectations we should have for foster care to help moderate the harms and disadvantages already experienced by the child. In attempting to grasp how this might be addressed by foster care we cannot rely solely on the perspectives of professionals alone (Kelly and Gilligan 2000) but must enlist and listen closely to the voices of those children and adults directly involved (Sinclair 2010). Hence we now turn to a growing body of UK research into the way foster care is delivered and how it is understood, particularly by the different participants in the foster family. We will draw on these studies in later chapters in order to explore how our families compare with others, particularly in relation to matters of attachment, challenge, failure and success.

Fostering success – Key messages from research

Sinclair *et al.* (2003), when analysing key elements of fostering success, identified three core factors: (i) the foster child wanting to be fostered and/or having attractive characteristics, (ii) carers who demonstrated warmth and were child-centred, (iii) sympathetic interaction between the two parties whereby they 'clicked'. It follows that early intervention to prevent spirals of negative interaction between carer and child is essential to restore stability. It has long been known that breakdowns can occur as a build up of events whereby termination is due more to the 'last straw' rather than some specific single cause (Aldgate and Hawley 1986; Berridge and Cleaver 1987). Clearly, there are subjective issues here in that one carer may reach a breaking point before another. Likewise, there are interpersonal factors whereby a child and carer will 'click' and where that same 'chemistry' might not be reproduced between that same child and a different carer and either may intuitively know the placement won't work. Sinclair *et al.* (2005a) reveal how children in their study stressed the importance of compatible expectations in relation to discipline. However, if a child accepts the carer they are more likely to accept the carer's rules.

Clearly, such subjectivities cannot easily be factored into placement planning if at all (Wilson *et al.* 2004) and reveal little of the effort and forbearance brought by adults and children that underpin the gradual building of trust and attachment. In short, effective planning, matching, and the role of time and the testing of relationships is part of a critical pathway. The stakes can be high given the transformational power of foster family relationships and the negative consequences for all of placement failure. Schofield and Beek (2009) describe in their longitudinal study of long-term placements the way children, over time, develop attachment and acquire resilience through fostering and the significant positive changes this brings. We address these issues of time, attachment and resilience-building throughout the book but turn now to the connected theme of acceptance by the family (Sinclair 2010) and a sense of belonging (Biehal *et al.* 2010) by young people in foster care.

A sense of belonging

Government policy has for many years highlighted the importance for children of 'a sense of security, continuity, commitment and identity' and the need for a 'secure, stable and loving family to support them through childhood and beyond' (DfE 2010, p.12). Studies of long-term care (Biehal *et al.* 2010; Schofield *et al.* 2012) have identified the need for a sense of belonging and mutual connectedness as 'part of a family' as being vital and therefore must feature in any understanding of successful care. A sense of belonging has to be felt and experienced by the children and their views are therefore essential. Much research in foster care has not managed to incorporate the voice of the child (Elden 2013). This might be because of the approach of welfare professionals and researchers 'who fail to acknowledge sufficiently what being a child means in terms of that child's experience, agency and personhood' (James and James 2004, p.201).

Advocates of children's participation and citizenship have argued that 'taking account of children's perspectives also requires a fundamental change of ethos and culture, and a move away from an adult driven approach to the accepted ways of dealing with issues' (Rose 2006, p.287). This shift has evidently been difficult to achieve because relatively few foster care studies have engaged both the birth children and the foster children, as in our study. Much research has of course been carried out with foster children and separately with birth children and some landmark studies are now outlined.

Biehal *et al.* (2010) report on longitudinal findings that those who remained in long-term foster care appeared to do no worse than those who had been adopted. They report that children's sense of belonging was impacted on, sometimes negatively, by contact with birth family. They also note that birth parents were often psychologically present even when there was no physical contact. One contributory factor to success was seen to be 'children's willingness to fit in' (2010, p.203). The children who were still being fostered reported a variable sense of 'belonging'. Those who had no contact with birth parents felt they were more 'quasi adopted' and claimed a strong sense of belonging. A second group who maintained a positive contact with their birth family felt an 'inclusive' sense of belonging to both families. A third group with a more difficult history with their birth family had a more provisional sense of belonging.

They note, as others have (Boddy 2013; Farmer 2010; Rock *et al.* 2013; Sinclair *et al.* 2007), that the age of child at entry to placement is closely linked to disruption, with the older the child the more likelihood of instability. Biehal *et al.* (2010, p.268) also note that this may have been intensified by the 'late separation from birth parents, which in some ways had been the consequence of delay on the part of social workers'. It has also been observed that entering care over the age of 11 years may be accompanied by more challenging conduct, possibly because 'those who have lived with significant harm for many years carry the effects of abuse with them' (Brandon *et al.* 2008, p.104).

Much research (Gaskell 2010; Minnis and Walker 2012; Timms and Thoburn 2006) reveals that young people want a choice of placement and that their voices should be heard. Children sometimes feel that they are being moved to new placements for bureaucratic or resource management reasons. This may occur when, for example, a placement intended as short-term only works very well for the child who wishes to stay there longer but the fostering provider requires the placement for other short-term admissions (see Minnis and Walker 2006). Young people also want their identity as 'in care' to be handled carefully according to a small qualitative study (Madigan *et al.* 2013) that found children were uncomfortable about their foster care status and thought they would be viewed differently by others because of this. The NSPCC's (2011) small study of looked after young people revealed their limited access to sensitive information and personal advice regarding their emotional, physical and sexual wellbeing; such intimate aspects of care are normally the province of birth parents and family. We address some of these critical issues of personal intimacy in Chapter 6 when we look at foster care and the 'body'. It is however to the voices of birth children that we now move.

Birth children

Relatively little attention has previously been paid to the experiences of birth children in the foster family. Doobar (1996) found that birth children felt that their views were not listened to and that they wanted to be involved in the planning stages of a placement. Likewise, Fox (2001) found that (i) birth children wanted to be included in all stages of the planning of the foster care process, (ii) birth children can be put at risk by inappropriate placements and (iii) birth children need preparation for a forthcoming placement. It is often risk of or actual harm to birth children that contributes to placement breakdown. Birth children sometimes have to cope with disturbing behaviour and may feel they are left to their own devices to manage negative feelings caused by some hurt, rejection, anger, shock, and a sense of being let down by parents who they perceive as focusing more on the foster child than them (see also Hojer *et al.* 2013). Indeed, Farmer (2002, 2010) reveals it is often the case that adult carers get much support from their own children, even from older children who no longer live in the family home, and that this is beneficial to placement harmony. Farmer (2010, p.156) notes that far 'more recognition is needed of the important role played by carers' children in supporting children'.

Twigg and Swan (2007) suggest that birth children have an enhanced awareness of social issues and gain satisfaction from seeing foster children develop and grow (see also Part 1993, 1999 and Pugh 1999). When they become young adults they may well consider fostering themselves. By contrast, some birth children wondered whether it was worth it and viewed the positives of fostering as overstated. Birth children often found it difficult to complain for fear of being seen as selfish and undermining of their parents' choices; they wanted to support and protect their parents. Birth children sometimes have to deal with aggression and become recipients of violence and/or threats from the fostered child. Twigg and Swan (2007) noted that in some cases, if similar treatment had been experienced by a looked after child, it could well be the subject of a planning meeting or even a child protection conference.

There have been mixed findings regarding the presence of the foster carers' own children who are near to the age of the foster children. This significantly increased the likelihood of breakdown in Berridge and Cleaver's study (1987). Sinclair *et al.* (2003) found in their study that birth children being in the household did not have an adverse effect upon placement disruption. Farmer (2002) however found that if there was a birth child in the home who was between two and five years younger than an adolescent foster child, placements were at increased risk of disruption, possibly because these younger children were more vulnerable to any behavioural difficulties of the fostered young person. While young people with histories of aggressive or difficult behaviour experienced higher levels of disruption, Farmer (2002) found that the converse was sometimes true; young people who had shown emotional distress in the past had fewer placement breakdowns, possibly because they had turned their difficulties inwards rather than acting these out. In later chapters we give voice to both the birth child and foster child in the same placement in order to glean more of these sometimes testing relationships.

Placement with siblings

Some studies have found that being placed in foster care with siblings is associated with favourable outcomes (Fratter *et al.* 1991; Wedge and Mantle 1991; Wilson 2004). Berridge and Cleaver's (1987) classic study of foster home breakdown is still pivotal in this matter. They found that sibling and peer support were key ingredients in placement stability. There were fewer breakdowns where (i) young people with other siblings had at least some of those siblings living with them, (ii) the children did not change school and (iii) other foster children of a similar age were placed together and where they were able to offer each other support. This seemed to promote resilience in children who were mutually supportive of each other, highlighting the caring qualities of children in foster care. The ability of a young person to build and sustain relationships with their peers is a useful barometer of emotional health (Schaffer 2008).

There is some evidence that children placed together with their favourite siblings appeared better adjusted than children separated and placed in different foster homes but those who were not close seemed unaffected by separations (see Wilson *et al.* 2004). There is not much in the way of highly definitive findings regarding sibling placements and stability (see Dance, Rushton and Quinton 2002; Head and Elgar 1999; Mullender 1999) and there are many factors involved which make it difficult to predict outcomes. Helgar's (2005) analysis of international studies on sibling placements found that joint sibling arrangements were 'as stable or more stable' than those of separated siblings. Nevertheless, she concludes that as ever there is a need for individualised and contextualised approaches to the needs of the child in question. Studies by Schofield (2002) and Dance *et al.* (2002) concluded that children found it particularly difficult to cope when they had been placed in care and when their siblings had remained with their family. This impacted on the children's behaviour due in part to a sense of feeling rejected and believing they were unlovable.

Foster carers' perceptions

Buehler *et al.* (2003) examined carers' perceptions of fostering in order to help understand what they found rewarding and thereby what might motivate them to cope successfully with the demands and stresses of fostering. The most cited rewards in their small sample were 'making a difference in a child's life and seeing a child grow and develop'. Sinclair, Gibbs and Wilson (2004) also found that having an impact on other people's lives is a rewarding aspect of fostering. By contrast, the most common stressors cited by Buehler *et al.* (2003) were the behavioural, emotional and health problems of the children; the age and number of children and the child leaving or being removed. Reimer's (2010) study of carers notes common themes with regard to successful fostering which centred around the structure of family patterns and daily life. Carers noted the need for clear organisation and set routines to family living. Carers also believed that consistency over clear rules and expectations facilitated successful fostering.

Such themes resonate with other literature (see Orme and Buehler 2001) on key characteristics of effective parenting, which we address in more detail in Chapters 3 and 4. Research on family functioning suggests that successful foster families are likely to be characterised by routine and structural clarity (Reimer 2010; Seaberg and Harrigan 1997). The importance of clear and consistent structure must be counterpoised with the need for foster family flexibility, acceptance, patience and empathy. These not altogether compatible elements suggest something of the complex and subtle nature of the effective foster family (see Golding and Hughes 2012), particularly in responding to any difficult behaviour, as we discuss next.

Challenging behaviour and foster carer training

The characteristics of the child being placed in foster care will undoubtedly have an impact on success rates. Teenagers for example are often 'on the move' even in 'ordinary families' and most studies of teenage placement schemes show quite high rates of breakdown. Studies have long found that foster placements of older children are more at risk of breakdown and that placement aims are more difficult to achieve (Berridge and Cleaver 1987; Biehal *et al.* 2010; Rowe *et al.* 1989). Young people's behaviour can be critical to the disruption of a placement and the foster carer's ability to deal with these challenges is crucial (Rock *et al.* 2013). With the reduction of residential facilities, foster carers are being expected to cope with young people displaying increasingly more challenging behaviour and they require additional support and training. They also have to engage more with the family of the fostered child and need training on this too (Biehal *et al.* 2010; Farmer 2010).

In regard to carers coping with challenging behaviour, Pithouse *et al.* (2002) looked at behaviour modification training to see if this resulted in a change in the young person's conduct. While the training was well received by carers, the research could not identify any change in the child's behaviour. It was thought likely that, consequent to training, the carers perceived that they were understanding and coping better with the behaviour rather than modifying it to any significant extent. A study by Macdonald (2002) was designed to test whether training foster carers in managing challenging behaviour would have benefits for looked after children and foster carers. This study too had some disappointing results. Sinclair (2010, p.202) found no clear evidence that training or support affected placement success but that 'both training and support from local authorities could improve morale and retention of carers, but not necessarily impact on outcomes'.

In short, it is difficult to ascertain just how effective foster care training programmes are in moderating challenging behaviour. However, we do know from studies of attachment training that foster carers find the theory valuable and applicable to their thinking and interaction with children and young people (see Golding *et al.* 2006;

Golding and Hughes 2012; Laybourne *et al.* 2008; Schofield and Beek 2005). A study of a parenting group by Holmes and Silver (2010) focused on helping carers to understand attachment theory; the group also addressed the impact of early maltreatment on behaviour and helped the foster carers to develop empathy. Attendance at the group led to an improvement in child–parent relationships and importantly an 'attunement' of carers to the complex needs of some children (see also Ironside 2012 about ways to empathise with the child's perspective). The group work programme led to a significant decrease in stress for carers, and also allowed them to reflect on attachments in their own childhood. Carers were clear that they would have benefited from this training prior to looking after a child.

Lipscombe *et al.* (2004) found that whilst parenting skills are important it is essential to recognise that these are based on two-way interactions, whereby the carers influence the foster child and vice versa. Thus the foster child will impact on the family and there will be some reciprocity of caring from the child. The contribution that foster children make to a family is an important dynamic and caring should not be seen as a one-way process. Here we can see the importance of considering relationality, interdependence and connectivity (Williams 2004;Boddy 2013). In a study by Sinclair *et al.* (2003), children commented on the dynamics and workings of the family around discipline and the differences between the cultures of foster homes and their own families. Each family has its own culture and routines (Reimer 2010). Much of this may be taken for granted by the family and only becomes apparent when a newcomer joins. Sinclair *et al.* (2003) revealed that the most important aspect of caring is responsive parenting, with carers being able to adapt to the child. The pre-conditions which allow for this are the characteristics of the child, the skills of the carer and the compatibility between them.

The level of strain experienced by carers can diminish their capacity to parent. Strained carers may be more likely to dislike the young people placed with them and, as Sinclair *et al.* (2003) found, liking the child is a significant factor that helps for a successful placement. Interestingly, in Farmer's study (2002), carers appeared to like less those young people who had been scapegoated and singled out for rejection by their own family. Possibly the young people felt less worthy of love and had come to expect rejection; such a belief may be self-fulfilling and impact negatively upon placement relationships (see Rushton 2003). Farmer (2002, 2010) also found that many of the young people in placement had a lower emotional/developmental age than their chronological years, and it was important for the carers to be able to provide activities, learning and play that recognised their current developmental stage. She also found that some single carers were receiving less help, partly because they had no means of child-care cover to attend group support meetings or training (Farmer 2002, 2010). Having briefly considered issues of behaviour and training, we now move on to the dynamics of the foster family itself.

Foster families

Foster families are often seen as nuclear families hosting an additional member. The fact is that the temporary addition of a foster child significantly alters the structure of the family. Foster families however are neither temporary nor permanent. If the family have a succession of foster children this renders their status as relatively permanent, yet in the current climate with many couples in nuclear families divorcing, foster families too, statistically, can be seen as a 'temporary' structure (see Thomson and McArthur 2009). Popular positive stereotypes of carers cast them as 'saints' or 'martyrs', dedicated altruistic and idealised parent figures who are able to cope with burdens that 'ordinary' parents are not capable of bearing. Erera (2002) suggests that this stereotyping can be an isolating factor for foster carers, because if they are so gifted and giving, then it follows they may not need support from outside. It is expected that they will somehow resolve the child's problems, expending unusual effort in tutoring, mentoring and helping the child function in school and in interpersonal relations. They are not expected to voice their own needs or complain about children, like other parents do. Thus foster carers feel that others will be disappointed if they behave like other parents. This idealised stereotype has its polar opposite which views foster carers as surreptitiously motivated by financial gain, or seeking to adopt by the back door. Neither of these stereotypes can ever capture the more complicated and subtle realm of day-to-day living through which care and support is provided, as later chapters will reveal.

The foster family is seen by Erera (2002) as a unique 'family system' in which members need to make sometimes complex adjustments to their relationships when a foster child joins (Seaburg and Harrigan 1997; Thomson and McArthur 2009). A key issue here is that carers are not the foster child's parents and if they act as if they are they may well experience conflict with the child. Yet if they do not act in a parenting capacity then they are, implicitly at least, acting outside the basic mandate of pursuing the child's best interests, as would anyone with parenting responsibilities (see Erera 2002). In principle, the primary status is that of 'professional carer' but inevitably emotional relationships don't conform to some 'official' identity. Hence, a carer will often have to straddle the roles of both parent and foster carer, emphasising one or other depending upon circumstance and the needs of the child (see Schofield *et al.* 2013).

While it is the case that the foster family, more than any other family type, is shaped by laws, policies and procedures, it is also true that there is no 'blueprint' to work from, thus it is a system that is rarely without challenge. For example, as the child is not usually expected to be permanent, she or he may be regarded as a short-term 'outsider'. This may create disequilibrium in the family especially in the early stages until the child becomes 'known' and accepted (Hojer *et al.* 2013; Seaburg and Harrigan 1997). If the foster relationship is defined as temporary, then it is possible that affection and caring for the child could be provisional and less likely to deepen compared with those who stay long term.

Where foster children have become closely attached over time and then move on there is likely to be a sense of loss for the family, yet they are rarely given the legitimacy to grieve (see Carroll *et al.* 2007; Riggs and Willsmore 2012). This paradox of an emotional attachment built between carer and child only to be ruptured when a child leaves the foster home is now increasingly recognised (see Kjeldson and Kjeldson 2010). Thomson and McArthur refer to this as a form of 'ambiguous loss'; one which is not marked by significant rituals or indeed publicly acknowledged. In their study, carers described how their hearts felt broken, how children were seemingly erased from their lives, of not being informed about a child's subsequent progress and, in that context, not knowing 'whether they made a difference' (Thomson and McArthur 2009, p.73). While Buehler *et al.* (2006) note that being able to handle the ambiguity of the parent/carer role and deal with loss are important skills for foster carers, it is likely that some carers and their children will need support and training in 'letting go' (see Farmer 2010; Hojer *et al.* 2013).

Extending foster care

Increasingly, studies of long-term foster care have shown that it has the potential to deliver stability, permanence and belonging for young people through to adulthood and thus it should not be viewed as some 'last resort' but an authentic part of the care repertoire (Biehal 2012; Biehal *et al.* 2010; Schofield and Beek 2009; Sinclair 2010; Sinclair *et al.* 2007). Schofield *et al.* (2012) found that children in long-term foster care had a sense of permanence and were enjoying the sorts of rights and expectations that birth children had for a safe passage to adulthood. Stein (2012) reported better outcomes for young adults who sustained positive ties with previous carers. Stein argues that people need resources across the life course and that parental responsibility extends far beyond childhood and the period of transition around leaving home. Young people need continuity in supportive relationships from childhood to adult life and there is no obvious reason why this sort of commitment could not be provided by long-term foster carers too.

If long-term care is now an increasing and key element of care provision then leaving care has equally become a topic of increasing if not pressing concern. For example, Rees *et al.* (2014) note that there is a need for a more gradual transition from adolescence to adulthood for those looked after and a need to 'equalise the playing field' for children in foster care. It has been claimed that the average age of leaving home in the UK is around 27 years (Saga 2013). Those young people leaving the care system do so at a much earlier age, with no open door through which to return. Young care leavers have described the transition to independence and self-sufficiency as 'harsh, shocking and characterised by insecurity' (Rees *et al.* 2014, p.11). Indeed, the very term 'care leaver', which we have used here and elsewhere without much reflection, should perhaps be used with some reluctance. It carries something of a stigma, of being a special category – a former public care child, a 'poor relation' in the canon of happy childhoods. We do not speculate upon a more appropriate terminology but think it high time that such be considered to denote children whose care status changes. Most of 'us' never leave the care of those we are cherished by, at least not simply by reaching a particular birthday in our relatively early years. A more thoughtful phrasing to capture this transition is overdue.

There is now much policy commitment to extending the age at which young people can stay with foster carers (see Boddy 2013; Munro *et al.* 2011) and at the time of writing there is legislation being passed in Wales and England to give effect to this. In December 2013 the English Government announced they would put an amendment in the Children and Families Bill giving all fostered young people the right to remain with their foster carers until the age of 21. In January 2014 the Scottish Government announced that they would be extending the opportunities for young people to stay in foster care into early adulthood. Similarly, the Welsh Government in March 2014 agreed an amendment to extend the period young people could stay in foster care to the age of 21 (Fostering Network 2014).

Conclusion

Throughout this chapter we have concentrated on key studies about foster care in the UK. Each study has added valuable insights to a developing body of knowledge about fostering. We will draw on these sources again in later chapters when we present our own findings about the day-to-day activities, meanings, relationships and family dynamics that generate successful foster care. Finally we summarise below important messages from research.

STABILITY IN FOSTER CARE: KEY MESSAGES

- Foster carers need to be warm, child-centred, responsive and thoughtfully 'attuned' to the individual child's needs.

- Foster carers cope better when they have training about attachment and about the likely causes of children's difficult behaviour.

- The 'click' or 'chemistry' between the carer and child can be a decisive factor in stability and needs to be understood better when planning placements.

- Better matching and stability is gained by consulting foster and birth children over options regarding placement choice.

- Better understanding of the role of birth children in supporting placements is needed. The age of a birth child as older or younger than a foster child can, for different reasons, be a factor in stability.

- Clarity and consistency around rules and boundaries in the foster home are important but patience and flexibility are also necessary.

- Sibling connections and peer support can be important ingredients in placement stability.

- Foster breakdowns are more of a risk when children enter care at a later age, particularly teens when exposure to harm or adversity has led to entrenched behaviours.

- Breakdowns in placement are often to do with a series of events (last-straw scenario), hence early intervention by support services to help restore stability is essential.

- Young people who remain in foster care for longer and through the transition to adulthood have improved outcomes.

- Long-term foster care has the capacity to provide permanence and a sense of belonging for young people.

- Conditions of scarcity and services under pressure mean that placement options are limited and there remain insufficient carers for the diversity of looked after children.

CHAPTER 2

Ways of Thinking About Children and Families in Foster Care

Introduction

While we may believe that fostering is in essence a practical activity informed by the caring instincts of well-meaning adult foster carers – and their own children too – this would only be part of a much more complicated explanation of what goes on between those directly involved. Fernandez and Barth (2010) note that internationally there has been a shift in foster care toward 'child well-being' and it is the fundamental building blocks of attachment and resilience that contribute to wellbeing and which will be addressed in this chapter. In doing so we draw briefly upon key psychological theories about child and adult attachment and stability and also about a child's resilience and capacity to cope with adversity. Also, we need to consider childhood and caring from a sociological perspective (see Holland and Crowley 2013) to get a sense of how parenting and family life is performed today in ways so very different to a generation or two ago and the implications of this for contemporary fostering. Throughout this and later chapters the unifying thread that runs through our thinking is an approach which focuses upon why and how we care *for* and *about* others. This in turn brings to our attention ideas and questions around intimacy and relationships, reciprocity and interdependence, and the private world of emotions. With this in mind, we start with a brief outline of infant and adult attachment – that most profound and foundational aspect of care and development.

Attachment and stability

When thinking about the foster care experience it is vital to consider first the impact of separation from the birth family upon the child and the implications of this for placement planning and stability (Cairns 2006; Schofield and Beek 2014a). Attachment theory finds its early exposition in the classic work of Bowlby (1951). This maintains that in order for infants to develop emotionally, they require a close, consistent and durable relationship with an adult who provides protection, care and comfort (Berridge 2002). More recent contributions to this theory suggest that a child's network is likely to have many relationships where attachment is also significant and likely to bear upon emotional development and which requires consideration when thinking about a child's needs (Aldgate and Jones 2006). In addition there can be a range of other positive relationships in a child's (and later adult) experiences which can help modify negative early patterns of attachment and which give cause for some optimism in regard to caring for the looked after child (see Aldgate and Jones 2006). Ideas about attachment are an essential element in the way we understand the needs of looked after children (Golding and Hughes 2012). Clearly children cannot put down lasting attachments if they are constantly changing placements and losing or loosening friendship patterns and destabilising their roots in schooling (Holmes and Silver 2010; Osborne *et al.* 2010). Health care too is likely to be affected by placement disruptions (Harwin and Owen 2003).

For looked after children, separation from close attachment figures, however unsatisfactory these may be, can often generate a sense of fear and insecurity (Aldgate and Jones 2006). That said, young people with little or no prior positive attachment to an adult are known to experience disruption at the beginning of a placement because of their difficulties in establishing trust and accepting boundaries (Farmer 2002, 2010). Foster children may also have unrealistic expectations if not fantasies about a placement that may never marry with the home in question. They may also experience difficulties in settling, through blaming themselves for their removal from their home of origin. Thus, as is widely recognised, planning and preparation are vitally important for young people in making effective transitions and new placement relationships with carers (see Norgate *et al.* 2012; Owen 1989). Clearly it is important for carers (see Schofield and

Beek 2014a) and professionals (see Schofield and Beek 2014b) to be aware of attachment theory in considering the behaviour of the young people being placed. We have mentioned in Chapter 1 that foster carers find training around attachment theory both valuable and applicable to their thinking and interaction with children and young people (see Golding and Hughes 2012; Holmes and Silver 2010).

Using attachment theory, Schofield *et al.* (2000) delineated four main categories of children who enter placements and who have experienced poor or disrupted attachment. These categories in Table 2.1 are illustrative only of possible broad behaviour patterns and in reality children may display a mix of these and may move across categories too. The typology below if simplistically applied could risk stereotyping children; rather it is intended here to capture something of the experience of carers when children come to their family and the challenges this may represent in developing warm and meaningful attachment over time.

Table 2.1 Categories of children

Open Book	Shows feelings, hungry for love, eager to please, restless, loud and impulsive.
Closed Book	Reluctant to share feelings, worries and fears. Difficult to get close to. Can be well behaved.
On the Edge	Frightened, frightening, fragile, distrustful, helpless, sad, could be violent, without remorse.
Rewarding	Pleasant to carers, makes friends easily, causes no problems at school.

Given the likely attachment difficulties of children who are being looked after, the skills of the foster carer are paramount. Studies have shown that carers providing the greatest stability are likely to:

- enjoy being with children
- be family-centred

- be flexible but firm
- be emotionally resilient
- communicate openly and honestly
- be amenable to outside support.

(SCIE 2004)

Other success factors in fostering that help build attachment identified by Sinclair and Wilson (2003) were the thoughtful use of empathy which helped demonstrate understanding and care, handling challenging behaviour proportionately and consistently, and promoting the child's self-esteem. Additionally, as any foster carer will know, the importance of reflection, patience and time in building attachment is critical if difficult to quantify (Ironside 2012). Schofield and Beek (2005) argue that the quality of care is key to attachment in foster care, with effective foster carers being able to place themselves in the shoes of the child. Attachment theory is a reflective lens through which to 'see' the child's needs and in doing so the foster carer or other care professional also requires a sense of the child's resilience and coping capacities (Guerney-Smith *et al.* 2010). Acquiring coping strategies and resilience is part of basic human development but particularly so in our more vulnerable early years. How to manage adversities in childhood is particularly relevant to those who are looked after, as we explore next.

Resilience

Notions of resilience are prominent within social care literature (Cairns 2006; Gilligan 2009) and there are various definitions. For example, Gilligan (2001), defines resilience as 'comprising a set of qualities that helps a person to withstand many of the negative effects of adversity'. Howe *et al.* (1999) define resilient people as those who when under stress and adversity are able to maintain psychological integrity and remain able to draw on a range of personal strengths to cope with those difficulties. Resilience can also be defined more straightforwardly as 'normal development under difficult conditions' (Fonagy *et al.* 1994, p.233). Thus a resilient child has more positive outcomes than might perhaps be expected given the level of adversity threatening her or his development (see Flynn *et al.* 2004). Resilience can also be seen in families, some of whose members may be more adept at managing difficulties than others (Dolan 2008; Hill *et al.* 2007; Sinclair 2010). In contrast to adults, stressful life events can affect not only child and adolescent health and welfare but the developmental process itself (Smith and Carlson 1997).

Notably, the internationally renowned Resilience Research Centre hosted at Dalhousie University, Canada, have refined their definition of resilience to include being able to negotiate and access resources: 'Resilience is the capacity of people to navigate to the resources they need to overcome challenges and their capacity to negotiate for these resources so that they are provided in ways that are meaningful'. However, trying to work out just how resilient a child might be under adverse conditions is not straightforward and most studies have been carried out retrospectively to identify how and why it was some particular children coped and others did not. Checklists have been devised that aim to measure capacity for resilience (see Resilience Research Centre 2014) but as yet there is no reliable way to routinely predict with accuracy what sorts of people will overcome which sorts of adversities in life.

Research generally has been unable to isolate with any precision those factors that generate resilience against specific risks and stressors in life. In short, resilience is not something that we can simply 'measure' as we do with cognitive and physical developmental milestones. Much will depend upon our reactions to specific circumstances in which there are likely to be a range of external and internal factors that affect how we respond, as we discuss below. In consequence we need to think about resilience more systemically in order to capture a number of variables that may enhance or reduce our capacity to handle adversity (Ungar 2008). In doing so we also ask ourselves how fostering can help promote a child's resilience to the typically difficult circumstances that surround their leaving home and entering foster care. However, if we also think of resilience as an ability to navigate and access meaningful resources the possibilities for how foster care can help become clearer.

In essence, a resilience-based approach to foster care would focus on maximising the likelihood of better emotional and social outcomes for looked after children by building a protective network around them. The concept of resilience offers us a useful framework for intervention based upon the assessment of potential areas of strength within the ecology of the child – that is, within the child's whole system (physical, intellectual, emotional and social) – and building on those areas. This systemic or ecological approach does not assume that the foster placement will meet all of the child's needs. Instead the emphasis is on building a web of support for the child as Farmer (2010, p.161) elaborates:

> Foster carers with substantial social networks and local professional support offered more warmth to young people, were more satisfied with the placements and the young people they fostered showed improved well-being.

The resilience perspective in fostering thus relates closely to an ethic of care (warmth and commitment of the carer), to resources, and particularly to interdependent relationships whereby both carer and child and a wider network give and receive support (Schofield *et al.* 2012). We explore this notion of interdependence later in the chapter. Daniel and Wassell (2002) developed the following schema which outlines a systemic approach to resilience incorporating key factors and resources:

Biological and individual factors:
genetic disposition and temperament.

Close family or substitute family
relationships, with secure attachments.

The wider community, for example,
extra familial and friendship support.

Here, people are seen to acquire capacities in resilience in two ways, by their inherited genetic disposition to stress and by the effects of life challenges that have stimulated their experiential learning for handling adversity. This ecological notion of individual, family, friendship, community and wider societal effects means that resilience is never just located at the individual level. The environment beyond the family provides multiple opportunities for positive growth and development in children (Farmer 2010). Also, supportive initiatives at a national policy level have been associated with protection (Smith and Carlson 1997). For example, the Framework for Assessment (DoH 2000) is an instrument of policy that provides tools employed by social workers in Wales and England to assess children. It is based heavily on systems thinking that looks to the strengths within the child, family and wider environment and ways to build on these to enhance resilience.

Put simply, positive home experiences, positive school experiences, positive leisure time experiences and their combination are factors that play a part in enhancing resilience (Haggerty *et al.* 1996). Within this, the familiar issues of culture and social class (Reimer 2010) and the ways in which these are likely, or not, to harmonise and help build resilience and protection in regard to the foster child, foster family and community are important aspects of care planning (see Ungar 2008). Promoting the above factors as a core aim of a foster care plan requires a 'team' approach to intervention by professionals, carers and significant others in the child's life. And the team requires a shared understanding of how resilience is to be nurtured across the different domains of a child's life. Clearly, this cannot be left to the carers alone.

To reiterate an earlier point, resilience does not denote some notion of a fixed 'quantity'. We don't possess either 'lots of' or 'little' resilience; instead we need to think about resilience in more dynamic ways, as something that varies in relation to the situations we are exposed to and the protective factors that we can draw upon. When we think about the risks we are exposed to in life it is often their accumulation rather than a single event that causes us the most difficulty; and it is this cumulative clustering which is likely to create negative outcomes for vulnerable children (see Fraser *et al.* 1999; Smith and Carlson 1997). Thus we need to conceive of resilience in terms of both risk and protective factors. In doing so, we need to understand that a child's adaptive behaviour emerges from the interplay of combinations of risks that may be predictive of negative development outcomes, and combinations of counteracting factors that may reduce or ameliorate these risks (Whittaker 2001).

Important examples of counteracting factors that moderate risk can be seen in the work of Schofield and Beek (2005, p.12) who observe:

'hopefulness is in itself a resilience characteristic, perhaps as necessary for agencies, workers and carers as it is for looked after children they seek to help'. Thus personal qualities can help children respond adaptively to stressors such as neglect, criticism, family violence and other risks. Wolin and Wolin (1993) discovered a range of protective influences that are largely to do with personal attributes such as insight, independence, fulfilling relationships, initiative, creativity, humour and the capacity to distinguish good from bad. Berridge and Cleaver (1987) found that sibling and peer support were important factors in promoting resilience and preventing placement breakdown. Happer *et al.* (2006) and Farmer (2010) note the importance of a foster child's contact with extended family members and friendship networks of the foster family. Such contact was seen to enhance a sense of belonging, providing attachments across generations and access to experiences which were seen as potentially enriching. Oosterman *et al.* (2007) analysed a wide body of international research to detect the key factors impacting on resilience and found that foster children in highly motivated, involved and nurturing foster families experienced less placement breakdown. They also found additional factors that yielded significant influence were family resources (material and emotional), support from relatives and support from caseworkers. These factors exert their protective effects through a process of time, close proximity and quality of care giving.

Interventions to promote resilience

The research on protective factors suggests that there are four general categories of interventions to promote resilience and coping: enhancing self-esteem, improving academic achievement, promoting social skills and strengthening families and social supports (Fraser *et al.* 1999). Sources of support for children and adolescents, particularly those in care settings, should therefore include: building esteem and reinforcing that one is a person of value; informal support such as problem-solving advice; instrumental support, that is providing specific resources or services that assist in problem solving; companionship support and the opportunity to engage in activities with others (Smith and Carlson 1997). Gilligan's (2007) important analysis (of mainly US evidence) revealed that taking part in extra-curricular and out-of-school activities improved academic performance.

Flynn *et al.* (2004) provide valuable insights from research into resilience among Canadian children in foster care. They found a relatively high percentage with good outcomes on health, self-esteem and pro-social behaviour. There were more moderate outcomes for relationships with friends, and for managing anxiety and emotional distress. However, they found particularly low outcomes with regard to academic performance which, as in the UK, 'remains poor' (Osborne *et al.* 2010, p.17). This may not be surprising given that many young people experience placement moves that disrupt an often already fragile schooling experience (Davey and Pithouse 2008; Jackson and Martin 1998; Jackson and Sachdev 2001). In regard to academic performance, Jackson and Martin's (1998) seminal study found that the protective factors most strongly associated with educational success were:

- stability and continuity
- learning to read fluently at an early age
- having a parent/carer who valued education
- having friends outside care who did well at school
- developing out-of-school hobbies
- attending school regularly.

Osborne *et al.* (2010) undertook a study and found that carers lacked training on the value of education and they suggest that carers undertake regular reading with foster children. Similarly, Flynn *et al.* (2004) found that key protective factors for the child that would help promote achievement at school and in the community were a close relationship with the adult care giver, an authoritative style of parenting that was characterised by warmth, monitoring and expectations, a family climate where there was little conflict between parents, an organised home environment, parental post-secondary education and, critically, parental involvement in the child's education. On a community level they found that protection was afforded by effective schools and pro-social organisations (e.g. school clubs, church groups), neighbourhoods possessing high levels of social cohesion and social control, and a high level of public safety with good health and social services.

In summary, children in foster care will have experienced and may still be experiencing particular stresses at what is considered to be a vulnerable period in the lives of all young people. Thus it will be imperative to focus on a range of factors that will help to develop protective strengths in order to change or moderate any negative trajectory of development. This in turn calls for an inter-agency and multi-disciplinary approach to foster care to increase the likelihood of a more positive and systemic impact for the child.

Facilitating communication skills and the role of social pedagogy

The National Children's Bureau along with partners facilitated 'Relationships Matter' groups in three pilot sites which ran for 8–12 weeks. The groups provided a safe environment for looked after young people to learn about and practise communication skills and reflect on the impact of these on their relationships (Ryan 2012). Looked after young people will often not have had many positive role models to follow in order to develop their own communication skills. Learning how to deal with strong emotions, be reflective, and be more successful in getting on with others is essential in negotiating resources and garnering mutual friendships and the support this brings. The groups were not therapeutic but activity based and centred on communication skills. The groups were positively evaluated as building self-esteem and resilience and the project developed a handbook and guidance (see Ryan 2012).

Linked to this notion of communication is the developing field of 'social pedagogy' in the UK which can offer foster care a new mode of practice and training (see Cameron and Petrie 2011). The term denotes a way of working that recognises children think, feel, have a physical, spiritual, social and creative existence, and that all of these characteristics are in interaction in the person. This approach stands in some contrast to more procedural methods used by child-care professionals in the UK (Munro *et al.* 2011; Petrie *et al.* 2006). Pedagogues seek to work with the whole child and they also bring themselves, as a whole person, to their practice. Social pedagogy acknowledges the ethical and emotional facets involved in working in a caring capacity and recognises how these can affect relationships and communication with children. The perceived strengths of the pedagogic approach for foster care include that it provides a more rounded strengths approach to thinking about children and their upbringing and which focuses on their everyday activities (Cameron and Petrie 2011). This is an area that has considerable potential for fostering and further research would be beneficial.

Stress buffering for carer and child

It is of course the case that foster carers and their children also need to be resilient to cope with looking after young people who are vulnerable, at risk and may often exhibit challenging behaviour (Sinclair 2010). When recruiting foster carers, social workers will assess many facets of the applicants including their abilities and resilience to cope with the inherent stresses of the job, yet there has been relatively little research into how to promote resilience in foster families. That said, how adults can buffer or handle stress and cope with adversity has been the subject of a growing literature into resilience in families (Dolan 2008; Hill *et al.* 2007; Lietz 2006). Lietz's (2006, p.580) study of families facing significant adversities found that although 'focusing on reducing risk is important, strength building is another important way in which we can intervene with high risk families'. Lietz adopted a systemic approach which could be relevant when working with foster carers, that is, looking at the level of support and protective factors available to the carers. Indeed, in Chapters 3 and 4 we use this very approach when we introduce the foster families and consider factors such as the availability of advice, assistance, remuneration and the use of self-help/support groups and how these may function as moderators of stress.

While the discussion so far has identified many variables to do with risk and protection that affect resilience there remains the essential nature of care itself which provides the foundation on which activities, meanings, relationships and settings are understood by the carers and child and which is likely to underpin attachment and resilience in multiple ways (see also Oosterman *et al.* 2007). We now turn to the notion of care which we view as based upon interconnectedness and interdependence in people's lives and which provides the protection and resilience we all need, but especially so for fostered children (see also Fraser *et al.* 1999).

Ethic of care

Some of the protective factors referred to earlier in this chapter that promote resilience were (i) the experience of fulfilling relationships and close attachments, (ii) indications that one is a person of value, (iii) the presence of supportive extended family members or significant others. Thus we can see that the importance of caring and being connected to a supportive network of others is part of a resilience framework (see Boddy 2013; Williams 2004). Indeed, when looked at in these terms plans for young people to 'leave care' and become somehow autonomous at an early age are probably implausible if not undesirable, as they may lose these valued connections or may not have developed them at all (Boddy 2013; Holland 2010).

Thus, as Tronto (1994, p.101) observes, 'we need to re-think our conceptions of human nature to shift from the dilemma of autonomy or dependency to a more sophisticated sense of human interdependence'. This suggests that looked after young people in leaving care do not somehow become completely autonomous; on the contrary, it should be the case that young people have the opportunity, like most of us, to remain connected, interdependent and relying on a matrix of continuing support (Roberts 2011). Happer *et al.* (2006) noted in their study that some young people continued to live with or remain strongly connected to their foster families long after they had stopped being looked after, and that some foster carers continued to be committed to children long after they had grown up (see Rees *et al.* 2014).

Foster care is not necessarily time-limited and contractually bounded but can be more encompassing, lasting and reciprocal. Hence, Tronto (1994) asserts that care is both a performance (we demonstrate care) and a disposition (we are caring). This assumes some ongoing relationship based upon attachment and commitment that cannot be understood solely at the level of a set of professional practices (see also Mehmet 2005; Smith *et al.* 2004). Thus Tronto (1994) suggests that caring cannot happen without an emotional content and offers four dimensions of caring which she terms 'phases'. These are not necessarily in sequence but are likely to occur at varying points in a caring relationship (see Table 2.2).

Table 2.2 Tronto's dimensions of caring

Phase One	Caring about – acknowledging need
Phase Two	Taking care of – assuming some responsibility for the need
Phase Three	Care giving – involves meeting needs, some physical work and direct contact
Phase Four	Care receiving – the object of care will respond to the care received

From Table 2.2, we can see that in phase four, care is responded to and may well be appreciated and reciprocated. Thus the key message here is that caring creates interdependencies and interconnections between people, often in ways that we are not always conscious about. Thus if we analyse our own lives we might notice that care often consumes much of our time, nevertheless we do not pay systematic attention to this. Nor do we always recognise when we are cared for and often take for granted the caring that has underwritten our own development and that which sustains us in the present. Indeed, care is generally underplayed and is often associated with the private, the emotional, and often the 'needy'. Furthermore, giving care and the need for care may be cast as weakness by some in our acquisitive culture that asserts competitive striving and the primacy of independence and individualism. As Tronto (1994, p.117) argues, 'Society treats accomplishment, rationality and autonomy as worthy qualities, care is devalued in so far as it embodies their opposites'.

Care can also be seen to be closely connected to women and is thereby assumed to be socially constituted within the household, so that it often becomes part of the work of the least well off (Orme 2002). For those in foster care too it is often seen as a female role as Bullock (2012, p.2) notes: 'Foster carers are often referred to in the plural yet the focus is usually on foster mothers'. Feminist theorists have long made the connection between women and caring responsibilities, most notably Finch and Groves (1983) in their classic text *A Labour of Love*. While this much-justified critique still applies there are other issues around ethnicity, class/wealth, age and disability which also complicate and challenge our understanding of care. While we cannot engage with these themes here in any detail we can perhaps agree with Held (2006) that we need a much clearer moral framework in society about the caring obligations of both male and female citizens. We might also endorse Parton's (2003, p.11) observation that 'care is central to everyone; it is not a parochial concern of women alone'. Thus it is important when exploring the 'care' in foster care that it is not devalued by assuming it somehow just 'happens' in the privacy of the family and the internal realm of emotion. Instead, we need to understand and make visible the many meanings of care within the dynamics of the physical and subjective world of the foster home itself – which is the very focus of the chapters to come.

It is the case that the value of the care provided by those who foster has been widely and positively regarded. Furthermore, some might argue that the drive to professionalise the fostering role over the last few decades has been an expression of this validation (see also Testa and Rolock 1999). However, there have long been opposing views which argue that the drive to professionalise and regulate foster care can be seen as an attempt to exercise control over foster carers and their caring work (Waerness 1996; Wilson and Evetts 2006). A long paper trail of regulation and legislative change has laid down with increasing precision the requirements for a foster care service. It has shifted 'from an ordinary activity to one which requires regulation and by extension training' (Wilson and Evetts 2006, p.40). Some argue that 'care is no longer associated with altruism or love; it is regulated' (Orme 2002, p.802). Similarly, Parton (2003) argues that the appeal of professionalism for those that commission or manage public services is that it allows for bureaucratic and hierarchical controls. It generates standards (Mehmet 2005) and performance indicators to codify and measure the achievement of targets, thereby limiting the amount of individual discretion. Such a view would evidently challenge the idea that a care ethic, rather than regulations, should or could be the dominant rationale for accountability in social work and fostering (see Beck 2012). Hence some might argue that professionalisation of fostering may devalue the importance of care rather than assert its centrality.

For our part, we would argue that care finds its authentic meaning and practice within relationships. That is, within the countless interactions between ourselves and others where the self is nurtured and strengthened socially and psychologically by positive support and human engagement. Featherstone (2009) in her analysis of the literature on the ethic of care explores how people develop and maintain a capacity to care within the dynamic and ongoing interplay between the social and the psychological. Here, the ethic of care assumes relationships which are bound by mutual interdependence, and its practice involves the values of attentiveness, responsiveness, competence and responsibility, negotiation and mutual recognition (Williams 1996). Interestingly, Williams (2004) noted that what children valued in their relationships with adults was an ethical component of care relating to 'fairness, care, respect and trust' (2004, p.51). Care, respect and trust are relational and can only be achieved through interaction and relationships (Beck 2012). Thus our moral identity as people who care and who can be cared about is developed through interactive patterns of behaviour, perception and interpretations in which our sense of emotional commitment to others comes about.

However, it is important that we understand care not only at the individual level but locate it in the broader spheres of childhood and family in order to grasp care in culture, time and place. To explore this briefly we turn to sociology to link to a wider set of ideas about children in society in order for us to better understand the role that contemporary fostering occupies.

Understanding fostering from a sociology of childhood – key ideas

It is important to consider foster families in relation to developments in the sociology of childhood as this offers an important context within which to frame how we engage with children (Holland and Crowley 2013). Traditionally, children were seen as in a process of 'becoming'; that process being maturation into adulthood. However James and James (2004, p.13) assert that:

> Childhood cannot be regarded as an unproblematic descriptor of a natural biological phase. Rather the idea of childhood must be seen as a particular cultural phrasing of the early part of the life course, historically and politically contingent and subject to change.

Since the mid 1980s a number of academic observers have identified factors that led them to claim contemporary childhood is a matter of new and pressing interest (Mayall 2002). One theme is that the boundaries between childhood and adulthood in some areas are drawn ever more distinctly and thus the gulf between the two grows. For example, the beginning of compulsory schooling in Europe led to the emergence of childhood as a separate state and the start of an attempt to better produce rational, stable adults through education, so that they could in time take part in society as full democratic citizens (Walkerdine 2004). This profound shift in generational boundaries led to children being increasingly removed from the shared world of family and communal labour and restricted to subordinate and supervised social roles in school and community. This new divide led to the emergence of childhood as some special time of innocence and protection from the rigours of the adult world. Such ideas, as they came to prominence in the early nineteenth century, took hold of the public and political imagination and, despite their distance from the real world of many children, have become a lasting cultural belief.

While we might agree that childhood is now long embedded as something of a sacred ideal, we have also long had the alternative and to some extent media-demonised view of particular children and young people (their parents and communities too) as dangerous and feral, and a threat to society (see James and Jenks 1996). Bullying in school, cyber intimidation, gang culture, violence and communal misbehaviour, drug misuse and so forth are the familiar flip-side of the idealised childhood coin. There is also the view of childhood as now either too protected by risk-averse anxious parents (Furedi 2008) or childhood innocence undermined by a commercialising and sexualising society that exploits children and exposes them to adult tastes and interests (Hallett 2013). Similarly, Prout (2005) notes that towards the end of the twentieth century there developed a sense that the boundaries of adults' and children's worlds were fragmenting or blurring due to rapid economic, social and technological change.

New ways of understanding childhood in contemporary western societies have cast children as very different from the innocent and dependent creatures within early and mid twentieth century cultural and policy assumptions. Current social science now reveals children as more active, knowing, knowledgeable and socially participative than earlier theories or beliefs allowed. As a result children are, potentially, more difficult to manage, more troublesome and troubling, not least because they have been positioned by policy and professionals as social actors with rights and an active role in the construction and determination of their own social lives (see also James and Prout 1997; Prout 2000). It is perhaps unsurprising that, for some, the notion of dependency in childhood and the idea of 'becoming' or maturing slowly into adults needs revision and that we should consider children as perhaps less reliant than before on adults, and able to take more responsibility for their own affairs (Mayall 2002; OFSTED 2012).

The idea that children are now to be seen as integral social actors, coming from diverse social and cultural backgrounds, and with competence to voice their needs and interests has led to their being better empowered with participatory rights (Kellett and Ding 2004; OFSTED 2012; Wyness 2011). Thus we have seen the emergence in policy and in sociology of the 'new' child who is self-regulating, active and socially participative, having more of a life of his/her own. Children have also come to have specific rights as outlined in the UN Convention of the Rights of the Child (1989); this places emphasis on the duties of adults towards children which has profoundly influenced the way policies affecting children are developed and applied (see Welsh Government 2013). Children's participation has also become a goal of this convention, alongside protection and the provision of services for children, rendering them a decisive shift in status as key stakeholders to be engaged.

Thus we can see numerous changes in our conceptualisation of childhood over the last century that have left us with new ideas about what it is to be a child. These ideas have not been without ambiguity or anomaly in the way we engage with children as dependent or not, as competent or not, as participating meaningfully or not (see Shanahan 2007); indeed, for some, as non-compliant, defiant and difficult (see Greishaber 2004). Yet ultimately we can chart a movement towards seeing children more as active citizens, albeit without the political rights of an adult. We now move on to look at young people in adolescence. This is an opaque realm of transition between the divides of childhood and adulthood and it is important we explore this territory if only briefly. This is because the children we introduce in the chapters that follow are mainly adolescents with diverse problems and childhoods and we require some brief conceptual backdrop for that discussion.

Adolescence

Much research into the lives and behaviour of children and adolescents in the twentieth century has been undertaken within the discipline of psychology (Greig *et al.* 2007). Traditional developmental psychologists have viewed adolescence as a passage to adulthood which is rooted in biological factors and characterised by tasks of individual development (Brannen *et al.* 1994). Adolescence is supposedly characterised by a period of emotional turmoil and identity formation (Erikson 1968). Adolescence has been seen as a period marked by conflict with parents and adults; this has also been seen as a requisite for disengagement from parents and transition into adulthood. Young people have long been viewed as experiencing difficulty in coping with the demands of the modern world with pressures to do with education, appearance and social acceptability (Compas *et al.* 1995). Early adolescence has been characterised as a potentially chronic and stressful experience, owing to the largely uncontrollable changes in individual physical and emotional development (Smith and Carlson 1997). The notion of adolescence itself has developed because of young people's extended period of dependence through education and limited access to employment opportunities. Yet we should not overgeneralise for, as Lee (2001, p.142) suggests, 'growing up is as diverse in its major and minor currents, its eddies and whirlpools as is the range of human existence'. That said, for some young people in care this transition to adult independence has been described as 'harsh, shocking and characterised by insecurity' (Rees *et al.* 2014, p.11).

We can no longer see the child as some pre-cast being with a relatively determined trajectory from birth to young adulthood (James and Prout 1997; Jenks 2004); there are inevitably numerous routes and detours towards maturity. Yet, Gillies, Ribbens McCarthy and Holland (2001) note that young people have long been positioned as problems when they fail to follow this pre-determined course. Additionally, childhood has become problematic insofar as our inability to protect children effectively from predatory adults, often known to the child.

Western societies have seen a growing realisation of the incidence of child abuse, sexual abuse and child sexual exploitation which has undermined traditional assumptions about childhood as safe, sacred and innocent (Hallett 2013). The media coverage has made public the scandal of the private lives of those children and young people who have no access to what for them must seem some mythical walled garden of a happy protected childhood (Walkerdine 2004). Looked after children are amongst those whose lives have typically not been safe or protected, and whose private family life has been subject to public scrutiny. Thus the ideal and the actual are often far apart.

While childhood varies widely across countries and cultures so too does gender and sexuality. Childhood is not androgynous (Shanahan 2007; Walkerdine 2004) and the time of developing feelings and understanding sexuality for young people will be when they want to share questions and discuss matters of intimacy with significant others in their lives. This may be the carer, and their attitudes to sexual matters which may be informed by cultural or religious beliefs, will be pivotal in whether children choose to disclose some aspect of their sexuality. Thus we know that young lesbian and gay people may face more difficulties with how others perceive their sexual orientation and this may affect their mental health and self-esteem (Cosis Brown 2014; Hind 2010). Attracting and supporting carers who can meet the range of needs of lesbian and gay young people is essential and guidance exists to support such recruitment (see Cocker and Brown 2010). Training professionals and carers in sex and relationship education for looked after children has been on the fostering agenda for some years (Bywaters and Jones 2007). Its importance is not to be underestimated given the emotional and psychological vulnerability of children coming into care, some of whom will have been sexually active at an earlier age and may have been involved in sexually harmful behaviours (see Biehal 2005). Others, because of their fractured schooling, may have missed out on this aspect of the curriculum.

Thus we can note that childhood and adolescence is not easily defined as some process of shared unproblematic socialisation but is as much about the contradictions, challenges and change that children face in growing up at a particular time, place and culture. We now turn to the place and the people that do the work of bringing up the child – the family. This is a subject of considerable complexity and we offer only a fraction of a very large sociological literature to explore its relevance for our discussion in later chapters about children's upbringing in the foster home.

Sociology of the family

The term 'family' is itself a contested term in sociology. Williams (2004) prefers to refer to 'families' as a way of acknowledging the diversity of current living arrangements and how these work. Morgan (1996, 2011) suggests we use the term 'family practices' as he sees families as a series of changing interactions rather than a static entity. Smart (2007, p.3) goes further, arguing for a new conceptual field of 'personal life' rather than a sociology of the family or sociology of kinship, 'in order to incorporate the kinds of emotional and relational dimensions that are meaningful in everyday life'. Smart (2007, p.7) argues that the term family does not (if it ever did) capture the full range of meaningful connections as:

> We know that people relate meaningfully and significantly to one another across distances, in different places and also when there is no pre-given or genetic or even legal bond.

That said, families remain a durable and basic social unit across societies and it remains pertinent to address the sociological question of who falls within the family boundary and who does not. Cheal (2002) argues that the inclusion of some people in family events and the exclusion of others demonstrate the concept of family boundaries and barriers. This is of particular interest to our discussion of foster care families where family boundaries are regularly breached by 'outsiders' (Thomson and McArthur 2009). Thus we are likely to become more keenly aware of the significance of family boundaries when a foster child enters the primary group of parent(s) and children.

Greater family complexity, and broader definitions of what a family is, have helped to focus more attention on what families actually do (Silva and Smart 1999). In a contemporary world of fluid and changing definitions of families, a basic core remains which refers to the sharing of resources, caring, responsibilities and obligations. What a family is appears to be directly related to what it does. Thus functions for Cheal (2002) have become more important than family structures. Family functions are activities that fulfil certain of the members' needs. Functional definitions of families define a family as a group of people who assume responsibility for some of the following:

- physical maintenance and care of group members
- addition of new members through procreation/adoption
- socialisation of children
- social control over members
- production, distribution and consumption of goods and services
- maintenance of motivation and morale through love.

(Cheal 2002)

In the foster family there are continuing adjustments to membership, functions and boundaries through the presence of foster children, and some have argued that this makes it a unique type of family (Erera 2002). That said, the production of fostering services may become indistinct and diffuse given that care and nurturing of children is part of what families typically seek to do; of course love is not necessarily inevitable or appropriate within the fostering relationship (Roberts 2011; Thomson and McArthur 2009). Sociology's more traditional emphasis upon functions (functionalism) is an approach which stresses the adaptive aspect of family life which responds creatively to difficulties and unmet needs (Cheal 2002). The foster child according to a functionalist view therefore enters the family unit and places stressors on the unit, which in turn has to adapt.

Traditional sociological theory has often emphasised the adaptive and positive side of families rather than the dysfunctional aspects of violence and abuse, as experienced by many foster children in their families of origin (Sinclair 2010). In recognition of the fact that families can become dysfunctional, the focus in sociology in recent decades has tended to move away from functions towards the study of interactions and transactions, often known as 'family practices' (Morgan 1996, 2011). Family practices is an approach which addresses the details of what a family does, how it interacts and the identities, relationships and meanings that are created thereby. This approach is very much the focus of later chapters.

One of the main things families 'do' is talk. By communicating the meanings that they give to their experiences, family members construct a shared knowledge of each others' needs and desires which is the basis for everyday engagements within and between families. Families are typically connected to multiple external social and economic groups because they depend on these for their survival; they cannot meet all of their own needs unaided and must look outside for support and resources (see Farmer 2010). Almost all of us have a strong need for intimate human contact and most of us have a personal network that is made up of a mixture of family members, friends and acquaintances (Smart 2007). Nevertheless, family members often lie at or near the centre of our personal networks and in some families there will be a clear ethos that 'family comes first' (see Finch 1989; Morgan 2011). Thus we can see within most definitions of family there is a strong moral dimension that goes to the very root of who we are – our identity and sense of social worth is first constructed and built upon within the intimacies and practices of the family. This briefest of outlines serves simply to highlight the importance of the family and its functions, practices and settings for our later discussion of foster families and their special characteristics and qualities. It is to the contrasting and opposing notion of 'individualisation' that we move next in order to understand some of the limits of the family when it comes to being the locus of our most significant relationships, identities and place of dwelling.

Individualisation

The theme of individualisation is now a common feature of much sociological theory which seeks to capture what is unique about close personal relationships in our western post-industrial societies (see Beck-Gernsheim 2002). What then is the relevance of this for fostering? The answer in brief is that our social world now allows much more choice over relationships and our commitment to others – including but going beyond the family and kin. Choice has transformed the nature of our relationships; who we connect with in our lives and with what emotional intensity and duration is now profoundly different to that of a few generations ago (see Smart and Shipman 2004; Smart 2007).

Bauman (2003) sees the availability of choice as the undoing of fixed relationships, particularly the family which he views as ever dissolving as our prime source of individual and social stability. Choice according to Bauman is not to be confused with something positive; rather it is the undoing of commitment and the privileging of the self as *the* key project for our personal attention and satisfaction. Bauman (2003, 2007) predicts a situation where there is almost frenetic emotional mobility and only fleeting serial relationships. In this fractured scenario there will be winners and losers, particularly women and children (McVeigh 2012; Smart 2007); some children will become looked after because of their parents' choices, commitments and impermanent relationships. Yet, by contrast, the carers that take them in also exercise free choice and choose to offer a commitment of ongoing care to the children they foster.

Clearly, then, for some there remain attachments, commitment and lasting relationships – in this simple sense the world is unlikely to be as all-encompassingly negative as some theorists such as Bauman imply. Nonetheless, as a vision of social change such ideas contain much which is compelling and at the very least Bauman challenges us to re-think and question our more conventional notions of families and relationships (see also Erera 2002; Morgan 2011; Williams 2004). Indeed, it is this idea of a new social diversity and a re-formulation of family structures that emerges from a more individualised world of personal choice that will inform our exploration of foster family practices in the chapters that follow. For example, we will want to consider the complexity of some family forms and practices in order to recognise important differences in the way boundaries, relationships and interactions are constructed (Thomson and McArthur 2009).

Today, children's contribution to a family is economically minimal but emotionally priceless whereby reciprocity is thought to exist in children's capacity to give meaning and fulfilment to their parents' lives (Kehily 2004; Zelizer 2002). Yet it is also argued that children in western societies are now trained at home and school for independence, with privacy and self-expression being encouraged (Jensen and McKee 2003). In short, tensions and contradictions in the way individuals, parents and families engage together (or not) seems unavoidable. Think for a moment of the foster family which in many ways has to broach these sorts of challenges – it seeks to offer care, commitment and membership to a 'stranger' for a fixed period. The family practices of foster carers and their own children (also carers too) are likely to become much more self-conscious and interdependent in managing family boundaries, privacies and emotions when a foster child enters the setting. In that sense the family is likely to becomes a much more collective entity. Indeed it could be termed a 'family care business' in that the birth children of foster carers are explicitly involved in fostering and help to produce the care that lies behind the deceptively simple term 'placement' (Kjeldsen and Kjeldsen 2010; see also Twigg and Swan 2007).

Child care and care giving

The care that family members provide for one another is one of the most important activities carried out within families. Care giving consists of a whole set of tasks that involve one person helping another person to meet their needs for daily living. People may give care unequally depending on the distribution of tasks allotted within the family. Men generally are thought to spend more time on paid work. Attitudes to housework are developed early in life and are later reinforced by adult experiences. Employers expect men and women to devote themselves to their paid work and, because of the stereotypes about caring, men typically expect that women will take the primary responsibility for housework when difficult choices have to be made (Bullock 2012; Cheal 2002). While Young and Wilmott (1973) predicted some four decades back that there would be a trend towards more symmetrical families with less role segregation, women who today work outside the home are also expected to be the main care givers and still responsible for much housework (McVeigh 2012).

The biggest factor in 'time stress' for many mothers is caring for children, yet there are significant variations in this between different types of families, the attitudes of partners and the resources available to them. Thus one could hypothesise that making a decision to devote oneself solely to being a care giver to one's own children, and then to foster other children, might for some mothers alleviate this type of divided activity and related stress. Although it would be unwise to imagine that stress per se is somehow dissipated if one is 'only' a busy carer.

For many carers, many of whom are female, a decision has been made to undertake foster care work, as well as caring for their own children. This can lead to a broadening and a blurring of the caring role of the mother. Mothering is a gendered identity; it is a social identity which incorporates far more than bearing and raising a child (Blythe *et al.* 2012). Mothering is a benign relationship of nurturing and caring for a child so that it will flourish and grow. Foster carers (in most foster families caring is a female-led practice, see Bullock 2012) offer their private lives, their homes and their close kin as a largely unpaid public service for the care of children who are not usually their blood relations (Nutt 2006). Fostering is thus often considered an extension of the mothering role, requiring those 'natural' female virtues; in that sense fostering can be seen as a domestic vocation. Yet there is some incongruity between the role of foster carer based on natural motherhood and the notion of the professionalised carer (Blythe *et al.* 2012). As Nutt (2006, p.22) observes:

> Foster care can be seen to be a contradictory activity in which separation of motherhood from mothering and being motherly inevitably gives rise to emotional and practical problems.

Mothering typically involves the use of emotion; it includes intimacy in the detail of caring. Of course, the extent to which mothering for the fostered child is bounded or conditional and thereby 'different' to the intimacy provided to birth children must depend on a number of factors as we shall see in later chapters. Fundamentally, however, effective fostering is predicated on positive attachment and regard that develops within the everyday rhythms of family life (Biehal *et al.* 2010). Family life is ideologically constructed as the primary site for emotion; this emotional investment can cause difficulties and pain for carers when placements end and children move on (Riggs and Willsmore 2012; Roberts 2011).

The gift relationship

Finally, we turn briefly to why people foster in the first place and we try to provide some conceptual context for why people choose to become care givers, for why they are willing to offer foster children, strangers to them and their family, the 'gift' of care. The term 'gift relationship' has often been used to explain foster care as an altruistic act, for which there is usually no material reward, other than expenses (Nutt 2006). The notion of the gift relationship espoused by the classic work of Titmuss (1970) was deployed to demonstrate the pivotal role of altruism in human affairs. However, the moral value of altruism would seem to fit uneasily in today's advanced economies where personal services of all manner are subject to marketisation. The central thesis of Titmuss is that altruism, of giving without expecting some material reward, is both morally sound and economically efficient (see also Oakley and Ashton 1997). Titmuss felt that profit contaminated essentially altruistic services such as volunteering, and he argued against paying for altruistic deeds as this would undermine the fabric of a human caring essence which he believed was imperative to our shared wellbeing. In a world of fast-changing and disappearing values, the principle of altruistic giving and a commitment to a service based on reciprocity and social solidarity are for some an absolute necessity to retain a civilised community (Oakley and Ashton 1997).

Self-evidently, an altruistic ethic of care and payment in foster care could be seen to be somewhat contradictory themes (Nutt 1998, 2006). That said, a realistic fee for round-the-clock foster care has hitherto been deemed unaffordable to our public services. In consequence might we suppose that carers prefer to see themselves as altruistic valued volunteers as opposed to underpaid and thereby undervalued workers? We return to this question and to altruism more generally in Chapter 4 where we explore what motivates the foster carers, what they get from fostering and why they continue to offer this most important of services to the serial child 'strangers' that enter their family home.

Conclusion

This chapter has drawn upon a number of perspectives from psychology and sociology to develop a theoretical context regarding children, families and caring (Holland and Crowley 2013). We have sought to reveal something of the multiple ways that a child who is fostered may be exposed to interwoven aspects of attachment, resilience, mothering, care and its motivations, family networks and wider social forces. The key messages that we have drawn from our exploration include the insights of Ungar (2008) and Oosterman *et al.* (2007) who urge attention to the day-to-day contexts and relationships in which children acquire protection and resilience from those who care *about* them, not just *for* them. Thus we shall examine how good foster care nurtures often fragile children and provides the safety, strengths and support they need to grow and achieve.

We shall also draw throughout the book upon Morgan's (1996, 2011) notion of *family practices* by focusing upon what families 'do', that is, the everyday activities, meanings, relationships and settings in which family members gather and engage and through which positive identities and capacities for the foster child are engendered. A thread running through the book is the ethic of care (Holland 2010), and we shall illustrate the meaning of this ethic informed by the insights provided by Titmuss (1970) about altruism. However, our approach will not be about the ethic of care as theory but about its practical expression in the countless day-to-day acts of emotional and material giving and receiving that provide the glue of attachment and family living.

ATTACHMENT AND RESILIENCE: KEY MESSAGES

- Much positive work can be done with regard to nurturing attachment and there are many practical examples (see for example BAAF's guidance by Schofield and Beek 2008 and Fostering Adventures by Fostering Network (2014)).

- It is important to consider a child's behaviour in relation to any previous maltreatment and to view behaviour as in part a likely response to previous unhappiness rather than a personal response to the foster carer or worker.

- It is important to be able to empathise and put yourself in the position of the child in order to understand the fostering situation from their perspective.

- Resilience is a key concept in fostering and carers need training to understand and promote resilience in order to bolster the confidence and capacities of the child. Much of this will be about doing activities with the child and helping or arranging for them to access resources. Gilligan (2009) offers carers user-friendly guidance on building resilience.

- Foster carers might also benefit from using ideas about resilience to enhance capacities and fortitude in their own family.

- Health, education and social care do not always liaise effectively and multi-agency meetings may not be as frequent as needed. It is important therefore that the different professionals involved with a child understand resilience and are able to promote it in regular meetings to progress a child's care plan.

- Education and health are key elements in building resilience and liaising with schools, educational welfare and health services is a critical part of the carer role. Children who have a number of moves are unlikely to have seamless health care and schooling and carers may need to advocate firmly on their behalf.

- Undertaking individual reading with a child to enhance literacy and communication skills is very important and not always considered. Groups which help young people develop and practise their communication and relationship-building skills can be highly effective in helping young people build resilience. This too should be approached through a team or partnership approach (see Cameron and Petrie 2011; Ryan 2012).

- Attachment is a two-way process and foster families do become close emotionally to foster children. Letting go and dealing with their own loss when a child leaves the family may be difficult to cope with. This type of loss can be anticipated by professionals and individual time and support should be made available to carers and their children for this.

CHAPTER 3

Meet the Families

Introduction

Our aim in this chapter is to introduce the ten families in the study and to consider their key characteristics in relation to relevant research in order to establish their similarity and differences to other UK foster carers. As we shall see, the families are varied in their make up and individual in their parenting practices, yet there are notable commonalities in the way that these very remarkable, nurturing and flexible families function. We start by outlining basic family composition (see Table 3.1). A brief pen picture then follows with biographical background about each family. We also utilised the familiar diagrammatic social work tool of the genogram (Department of Health 1988; Parker and Bradley 2010) to aid our visualisation of the participants. The chapter then moves on to discuss the roles of females and males and the division of labour within fostering households. The chapter concludes with some preliminary reflection about how these families display and enact family life.

Hereafter, we will refer to each family by their number as documented in Table 3.1. When referring to adults and children, pseudonyms will be used to preserve anonymity. Some minor adjustments have also been made to the personal details of the families for the same purpose; for example, the ages of foster carers and also adult birth children not in the home have been placed in age-bands in order to avoid a level of detail likely to assist identification. However the specific ages of the children are a key factor in the analysis and are 'actual' at the time of their participation.

Table 3.1 Family composition

	Male carer age band	Female carer age band	Birth children at home, M and F, age actual	Foster children M and F, age actual	Birth children not at home, M and F, age band
Family 1 **Agency 1**	55–60	50–55	F13 (+ F9 adopted)	F13	F20–25
Family 2 **Agency 1**	40–45	35–40	0	F15, M14, F12	0
Family 3 **Agency 1**	50–55	45–50	F16, M17	M11, F10, F9	2 × M20–25
Family 4 **Agency 2**	45–50	50–55	M21 (stepchild)	M18	M20–25, M30–35 (stepchildren)
Family 5 **Agency 2**	45–50	45–50	F20	M13	F20–25
Family 6 **Agency 2**	45–50	45–50	F16, M15, M13	M11, M9	0
Family 7 **Agency 2**	0	50–55	M30	F14	F30–35
Family 8 **Agency 2**	60–65	55–60	0	M16, M15	F25–30, 2 × F30–35, M30–35
Family 9 **Agency 3**	50–55	50–55	M18, M23	0	M20–25
Family 10 **Agency 3**	0	55–60	F20	F16, F12	2 × F20–25

The ten families were involved with three different fostering agencies, as follows:

- Agency 1 = (local authority, urban), Families 1–3.
- Agency 2 = (independent fostering organisation), Families 4–8.
- Agency 3 = (local authority, semi-rural), Families 9–10.

Snapshots of the families

Family 1: Liz and Greg have two birth children, Helen and Fiona, and an adopted child, Carla. They have one foster child placed with them, Melonie. They have been carers for 11 years. Liz used to be a nursing assistant but looked for work which would fit around child care. Greg used to work in a sports centre but is unable to work for health reasons. They both felt that they wanted more children, but were unable to and fostering and adoption was their solution. They are a relaxed yet organised family. Both parents work as a team, sharing equally the household chores. They live on a wide street in an ex-local authority house adjacent to parkland. Many children play in the street and in their large garden. There is a friendly dog in the home which is referred to in most of the interviews and diary material and the overall impression is of a sunny and welcoming household.

Family 2: Dawn and Ian are fostering three children (Nadia, Libby and Jake). They have chosen not to have children of their own as they wished to dedicate themselves to fostering and working with disadvantaged children. They live in a large private detached house, backing on to countryside. Dawn is a white-collar professional and Ian, who used to work in catering, gave this up to dedicate himself to fostering full time. They have been carers for seven years. The house is largely given over to children, with books, games and sports equipment being situated in the lounge and kitchen. Both are active people and have lots of hobbies and relish taking on new challenges, particularly the interests brought by the foster children. The household appears organised, without being regimented. The couple have dogs, cats and reptiles, all of which are very much part of the family.

Family 3: Sally and Chris have been full-time foster carers for six years. They also offer day care to children excluded from school. The couple have four children of their own, two of whom have left home. They are also grandparents of their son's three children. They are fostering three children (Jade, Candice and Peter). Chris is unable to work for health reasons, but had worked in adult social care. Sally too previously worked in other areas of social care. They live in a local authority house on a large public housing estate. The family are well integrated into the local community. They have a dog and a cat. It appears to be an open home with frequent young callers to the front door asking if the children can come out and play.

Family 4: Josie and Philip live in a private dwelling in a rural area. They became a couple later in life. Josie has one son who lives some distance away. Philip works for environmental services and looks after local waterways. Philip has two sons, one of whom still lives at home. They foster one child, Stuart. They have been fostering for two years. Josie used to work as an administrator but has also worked in a children's residential unit in the past. They felt that fostering would allow Josie more time at home to look after the family, whilst doing something for other people as well. The house is homely, with the kitchen at the centre of events. There are various animals in the household – cats, dogs, rabbits and ferrets. The family also own a horse which is entered into riding competitions and the children go to these events too.

Family 5: Rachael and Mark live in a private house in a small rural hamlet. They have been fostering for six years. They have two children. Rachael, a former countryside warden, now dedicates herself full time to fostering and child care. Mark works as a senior technician for a light manufacturing company in a nearby small town. They have regular contact with Mark's siblings and Rachael's mother. They have one child placed with them, Christopher. Both are interested in the countryside and in outdoors activities. One birth child lives with them and is training to become a social care professional; the other is training to become a teacher.

Family 6: Steve and Sue have been fostering for 19 years. They initially thought they could not have children of their own and started fostering because they very much wanted to be parents. They now have three birth children and two foster children placed with them, Carl and Craig. They fostered throughout the time that their birth children were babies. They live in a semi-detached home on the edge of a village. Sue works locally as a teaching assistant; Steve was a skilled artisan but now dedicates himself fully to fostering. Some of Steve's family live locally and a sister plays a large supporting role. Sport features widely as an interest for the family and all of the children pursue sporting interests.

Family 7: Judith is a single foster carer. She has been a carer for some 16 years. She initially started caring jointly with her daughter. Judith lives in local authority housing on a large urban estate. The house is well maintained and ordered. Her daughter works in social care. Judith's son lives at home for part of the week and supports his mother with fostering. Judith is a strong advocate for the children in her care. She has one foster child placed with her, Suzanne. The local children all play out in the street and the foster child is well integrated into the community. Judith presents as a strong character with a warm sense of humour. They have a large cat and a small dog.

Family 8: Hazel and Josh live in a terraced house which they have occupied for 30 years and are well integrated into their local mainly rural community. They have fostered for four years. Josh works in light engineering and Hazel used to work in a nursery. She found the hours too long and so fostered in order to offer a caring home and to better meet the needs of her own family. They have four birth children, all of whom have left home. Hazel is a childminder for local children. She has two foster children placed with her (Callum and Alan). They have regular contact with all of their birth children. They are about to become grandparents and are excited at the prospect. Hazel sees education as important and has strongly encouraged foster children to pursue their studies. Family life is very important for Josh and Hazel. Sport is a major interest for all the males in the family and both male foster children share in these interests.

Family 9: Kerry and Mervyn have fostered for four years. They live in a local authority home on a large housing estate in an urban area. Kerry also works part-time in a care home for the elderly. Mervyn, a former bus driver, is unable to work after an accident. The couple have three sons, two of whom are living at home. The couple also do much of the child care for their grandchildren. Two foster children had recently moved out of the placement so they had no children placed with them at the point of interview. Mervyn is very interested in DIY and gardening. The couple have a small excitable dog. Many of the foster children that they have looked after return to visit on a regular, sometimes daily basis, and they seem to offer an 'open door' approach to fostering.

Family 10: Julie is a single carer. She has been fostering for 17 years and she was fostering when her own children were young. She lives in local authority housing on the outskirts of a small town. Julie has three birth children, one of whom still lives at home. Julie also works in a local play group. Julie has two foster children placed with her, Lilly and Jade. Julie is well integrated in to the local community and has lived in the same house for 20 years. She has two cats. Julie looks after her grandchildren regularly. A friend had suggested to Julie that she take up fostering. Julie cannot afford to go on holiday or undertake many social pursuits and trips. Walking to the nearby town to shop is one of the main activities for the family.

Family characteristics
Age of carers

The average age of the female and male carers in our study was 50. Given that they were deemed by their respective agencies to be making a success of fostering, what significance if any can we attach to their age? Past research by Berridge and Cleaver (1987) and Kelly (1995) found that female carers of failed placements tended to be younger (mostly under 40 years of age). By contrast, Sinclair et al. (2005a) found that the older the carer, the more likely the placement was to disrupt. However, this was likely to be because older carers tended to have older often challenging young people placed with them and when age of children was taken into account, the association disappeared. Sinclair et al. also found that 'lone carers were somewhat more likely to experience a disruption but not significantly so' (2005a, p.182).

Age of children/presence of birth children

The youngest birth child in the families was aged 13, although Family 1 had an adopted child of nine years of age, who came to them via fostering. The birth children in this study were generally all older than the fostered children by between two and five years, with the exception of Family 1 where the birth and the foster child were the same age and the adopted child was younger than the foster child by four years. The presence of birth children near to the age of the foster children has been cited as a potential factor affecting the likelihood of placement breakdown (Berridge and Cleaver 1987; Quinton et al. 1998). It may well be that it is easier for birth children to adapt to a younger foster child than an older child whose behaviour the families have not had experience of dealing with (Sinclair et al. 2005a). It is possible that foster carers feel that there is less likelihood of foster children having a detrimental influence on an older birth child, although this was not explicitly said by the carers or birth children in this study. Interestingly, in Sinclair et al. (2005a) the more children living in a family, the less likely a placement was to break down, suggesting that children could be mutually supportive and beneficial to each other. In our study, foster children who were living with other foster children were generally close in age. It has been argued that this promotes resilience in that their capacity to build and sustain relationships with their peers is a useful barometer of emotional health (Schaffer 2008). While the average age of the young people in placement was 13 years; there was an 18-year-old, two 16-year-olds and two 15-year-olds. It has been found that the older the children are at placement, the more likely it is to fail (Berridge and Cleaver 1987; Biehal et al. 2010; Sinclair et al. 2005a) possibly because the children may have experienced more disruption and numerous separations and failed 'reunions' with their birth families. By contrast, in this study it was the longevity and 'indefinite' nature of most of the placements that suggested their success; the reasons for this will be explored in later chapters.

Ethnicity

It is of note that whilst all of the adult carers and their own children were English-speaking White British, six of the foster children were

Black British. While it is acknowledged that minority ethnic children are over-represented in the care system (Owen and Statham 2009) it was interesting that ethnicity was never commented upon by any of the foster carers, birth children or foster children in the course of our research. A similar finding can be noted in a study by Spears and Cross (2003) where ethnicity was rarely mentioned by respondents, despite it being an aspect of placement arrangements. We return to this issue later but observe here that there has long been an assumption that children should be placed with foster families of similar ethnic and cultural origin (see Perez del Aguila *et al.* 2003; Small 1991). Thoburn *et al.* (2000) found that disruption rates did not differ for non-white children placed with white carers, but nevertheless concluded that children should be placed with carers who can meet their needs and who are of a similar cultural and ethnic background. Ethnicity however is not always clear cut and the broad categories utilised to locate ethnicity have in reality limited ability to 'capture the complexity of mixed racial and ethnic people and their families (and) can obscure more multi-dimensional patterns and experiences' (Caballero *et al.* 2012, p.10). That said, there does appear to be insufficient numbers of black foster families (Selwyn *et al.* 2010b) and in consequence we are likely to see more children with minority ethnic heritage being placed with white families (Wainwright and Ridley 2012). In a diverse society it is in any event important that social workers and foster care families receive support and training to ensure full attention is paid to a looked after child's gender, faith, ethnic origin, cultural and linguistic background, sexual orientation and disability (Cosis Brown 2014). This is clearly embedded in policy (see DfE 2011; DfES 2007; Welsh Government 2011), and similarly it is important that carers and fostering services can recognise discrimination and help children to understand and cope with it (see Caballero *et al.* 2012; De Sousa *et al.* 2011).

Class and culture

The dynamics and features of social class have long been a sociological preoccupation but less so in social work and fostering research. Whilst we accept the importance of class we do not divert our attention too far in this direction and would only observe that three of the ten families had an adult carer in white-collar skilled employment outside the home. Two carers had professional/university-based qualifications, the highest qualification thereafter were GCSE/O-levels followed by an NVQ. Research in Wales by Collis and Butler (2003) found that 34 per cent of foster carers had no qualifications, 30 per cent had GCSEs, those with A-levels 21 per cent and degrees 9 per cent. They concluded that the educational profile of newly qualified foster carers had not changed significantly over the past 20 years. More recent research by McDermid et al. (2012) suggests that foster carers are somewhat less likely than the wider population to hold average qualifications.

It is likely that matching with regard to culture and class may add another layer of 'glue' to the harmonisation and success of a foster placement (Reiner 2010; Thoburn et al. 2000). Contact with the birth parents may be easier and less threatening for both parties if they have broadly similar cultural backgrounds. For example, one carer in this study when discussing relationships with a foster child's birth parents stated that she did not feel uncomfortable or intimidated by their behaviour because she came from a similar background and locality:

> We always manage to do that [get on with birth parents], but there was one [birth parent] who threatened me in a school playground, a real nice boy [foster child], and they, the terminology is she 'kicked off' and I 'kicked off', she wasn't nice... You know I've been brought up here on this [council] estate... I've always been able to fend for myself and so can the children, so when she faced me up and I faced her, I had no qualms at all and I said to her there and then, because she raised her hand to me, you lay one finger on me, I said to her, if that hand lands, you forget about that [this placement] and she didn't and there was never a problem after that.
>
> (Sally, foster carer, Family 3)

Class and culture will of course leave its indelible mark on childhood (Gillies 2007) and can impact upon stability in foster placements (Caballero et al. 2012). However, it was not possible to assess whether there had been any such matching as interviewing professionals was not part of our study design. Given the much over-stretched resource that is UK fostering (Fostering Network 2013; Tapsfield 2012), it is perhaps unlikely that class and cultural matching was a defining criteria on the placement planning agenda for the children in this study.

Length of time as foster carers

All of the carers had been foster carers for at least one year and had at least one successful foster placement (i.e. a placement that did not disrupt or break down). The social workers, carers, birth children and the young people in placement all described the current arrangements as successful (this is not dissimilar to the criteria used by Sinclair 2005). Their average length of time as a foster carer was nine and a half years. This was less than the national average of around 20 years (Wilson *et al.* 2007). This may perhaps have been influenced by the fact that foster carers from the independent fostering agency made up five of the ten families. Independent agencies have in the past been cast as energetic and successful recruiters of new foster carers, able to offer a range of supports. Thereby they may have a higher proportion of younger carers on their 'books' than some local authorities (see Sellick 2002, 2011, 2013).

Family diversity

There are many new domestic arrangements within contemporary UK households but a vocabulary has yet to emerge to capture these shifting relationships and the term 'family' is still being used to cover most groupings (Chambers 2001; Morgan 2011; Williams 2004). Some have suggested that foster families are more 'conventional' than other families in the general population in that they are more likely to feature two parents who have been in a long-term relationship and have brought up two to three birth children (see Wilson *et al.* 2007). While we did not seek to classify the ten families as variants of contemporary family life we did note that they were configured in diverse ways. For example, Family 2 had no biological birth children, whilst Family 7 and Family 10 were single-parent families. There were reconstituted families such as Family 1 with an adopted child and Family 4 with stepchildren. Indeed, in Family 4, the female carer stated how coming into a reconstituted family, where her partner and his two sons already resided, allowed her to better understand the fostering process of first being an 'outsider' and becoming slowly assimilated into the family over time. As with Erera (2002, p.17), we approached these diverse families from a strengths perspective, 'acknowledging their capacities, competence and resilience'. For example, most were living in close proximity with extended kin who provided additional support for the fostered child.

It is the everyday home setting that is one of the major influences upon the developing child (albeit given the time-limited nature of much fostering its impact on the looked after child may vary; see Sinclair *et al.* (2005a)). The point however is well made by Fisher and DeBell (2007, p.59):

> The most important and probably the most influential setting for childhood during school age years is the home environment, whether that child is with the child's natural or adoptive parent(s), reconstituted families, carers, extended family members, foster parents, or within the supervision of the state.

Thus the site of 'a secure, stable and loving family' continues to be promoted in policy and practice as the optimal environment in which a child can grow and mature (DfE 2010, p.12). But what is it about 'families' that promotes and facilitates the development of children placed with them? In addressing this question we will draw on Morgan (1996, 2011) who observes that family (however constituted) can be understood as something people 'do', rather than something people 'are'. Similarly Smart (1999) argues that what a family 'is' appears to be intrinsically related to what a family 'does'. Thus in the chapters that follow we examine what it is that these foster families *do* that makes them function to benefit the looked after child. First, however, we continue with our presentation of key features of the families in order to grasp more of their unique character and we turn next to gender and employment.

Gender and employment

Typically, men and women experience family differently (Erera 2002). For example, Chapman (2004), in focusing on what families 'do', presents a delineation of domestic tasks (such as laundry, cooking, gardening) and exposes our gendered assumptions about who usually adopts responsibility for these. Chapman links our perceptions of femininity and masculinity within families to particular activities and how over time these become subject to re-negotiation and change as men and women make new demands upon one another, as does society upon them and vice versa (2004). The home then is a key social institution which both responds to and produces social change. The foster families within this study reflect these recent social changes insofar as traditional models of males as the major 'breadwinner' working outside the home no longer apply. Consider Table 3.2.

Table 3.2 Employment status of carers

	Male working outside the home	Female working outside the home	All available carers at home
Family 1			X
Family 2		X	
Family 3			X
Family 4	X		
Family 5	X		
Family 6		X	
Family 7*			X
Family 8	X		
Family 9		X	
Family 10*		X	

* Single carer – female.

We can see above that there are five families where the male carer does not have paid work outside of the home. There are four families where the female carer does work outside the home and in three of these the male carer takes primary responsibility for fostering. Such arrangements evidently challenge dated ideas about 'male breadwinners' and 'female homemakers'. This is interesting given that the image of foster care is often one of a more 'traditional' family where the female stays at home enacting the caring role and the male goes out to work. Additionally, research by Wilson *et al.* (2007) has suggested that contact with officialdom has tended to be the preserve of female partners who often assume responsibility for contact with the child's social worker. This however was not evident in our study where there was a marked mix of males and females negotiating with agencies and their staff.

In relation to household chores and foster families, Wilson *et al.* (2007) describe a fairly traditional gendered division of domestic work. In terms of direct involvement with children, however, a clear majority of tasks were judged as equally shared but the men did much more outdoor and sports activities. In our study, where there were male and female carers and neither worked outside the home then the fostering/parenting tasks appeared to be shared equally. Many of the respondents talked about the male carers doing the cooking and cleaning. The male carer in Family 1 appeared to do most of the cooking, for example. However, where one of the carers was working outside of the home, the other carer took on the responsibility for the majority of the caring/parenting, and this was the case regardless of gender. When the carers working outside of the home returned, they helped out with caring and household tasks in order to assist and reduce the demands on their partners. The following brief extract from an interview with Kerry and Mervyn exemplifies this point. Kerry works away from home and occasionally stays away overnight for two days a week:

> When I'm in work Mervyn will cook for the boys, he'll wash up the dishes, he'll peg washing out on the line and bring them in and he'll fold them and put them in the washing basket and he takes the boys where they got to go.
>
> (Kerry, foster carer, Family 9)

Contact and activity with the foster children was undertaken by both partners in all of the families. In Families 4, 5 and 8, where the male partners were working outside the home, when they returned they typically undertook an activity with the foster children in the evening. Each of these families remarked upon this without being prompted, referring to dog walking, horse riding and sports as examples of shared activities between the male foster carers and the foster children. Notably, this was predominantly where there were only male young people in placement. In Family 7, Kevin the birth child, who only lived at the home part of the week, describes himself as having more of a role with male foster children than female:

> I try and step back a bit now more than anything because I'm not there [all week]. 'Cos I found when I'm there with the boys they'll want me to go here there and everywhere, I did at the beginning, not so much playing football, having a chat with them, now my mother always has girls, I don't know why.
>
> (Kevin, birth child, Family 7)

Kevin sees his current role as more of a 'big brother, fixing the play station and that'. The importance of the male taking a role in the fostering process, even while working externally full time, has been noted (see Gilligan 2009; Newstone 1999; Wilson *et al.* 2007) as is the helping role of older birth children even when no longer living at home (Farmer 2010). The role of males in fostering may not always be fully recognised and their need for support is acknowledged by Fostering Network (2011).

Displaying 'family'

In our approach to describing what foster families 'do' in later chapters we very much draw upon the ideas of Finch (2007, 2011) who argues that families display meanings through their actions. Display is the process by which individuals convey to each other and to a range of audiences that certain of their activities constitute 'doing family'. The fluidity of family life means that what we consider to be our family will usually change in the course of our life time (Williams 2004). Thus there is always a sense in which we display what the family is 'now', that is, at a particular point in time. Also, for many of us, who is in our 'household' cannot adequately define our 'family' (Smart 2007). This is certainly true for foster families which are constantly mutating and are essentially temporary if often durable arrangements (Thomson and McArthur 2009). This much was also evident from the foster children in that their drawings of their eco-maps (Department of Health 1988; Parker and Bradley 2010) depicted practices, identities and relationships denoting the continually evolving character of foster family relationships (Roberts 2014). These included people from birth and foster families and networks beyond.

Accordingly, our study can only ever reflect a snap-shot in time. Our approach therefore was not to try and identify the specific membership of some family or other; rather we sought to identify which symbols, activities and relationships had the character of a family relationship. There are various ways we both display and detect the meaning of family. For example, photographs and keepsakes may symbolise relationships (Humphries and Kertesz 2012). Likewise, family stories are told and re-told to refresh and reinforce shared understanding about relationships (Shotton 2010). This often occurred in the process of our interviews and observation of the families. For example, in interviewing carers and birth children in Family 5, there was much shared recollection of a child that had been fostered and moved on but had become part of the family narrative:

> He just made you laugh. He was such a ray of sunshine although very violent. We still miss him…
>
> (Sara, birth child, Family 5)

In this family, the young man in question had taken on an almost mythical status in the family history, demonstrating to the outsider the trials and tribulations of the fostering experience but also the warmth and affection received in return. In the course of interviews and observation many of the carers showed photographs of children who had previously been placed with them, pointing out all manner of attributes, attractive and otherwise. Displaying refers not only to verbal or visual phenomena (such as stories and photos) but shared activities such as the preparation and communal partaking of food, as we discuss in some detail in Chapter 5. Family meals and especially eating out allow a family to display itself to a public audience. Of course not everything is up for display; much takes place behind closed doors, for example, bathroom activities or going to bed. As Chapters 6 and 7 will reveal, it is these often hidden aspects of the family, that is, the 'rules' relating to space, intimacy, privacy, touch – the very basics of cohabitation – that the foster child must learn in order to become an accepted part of the family.

Thus, displaying 'family' confirms much of the unique character of a given relationship (Finch 2007, 2011) and, conceptually, this is an approach we shall use throughout to illuminate the ways in which adults and children in the foster families provide and reciprocate care. By way of conclusion to this chapter we offer a brief example of one such display. It concerns how children's clothing and presentation symbolise a vital aspect of 'who we are' as a family, of membership – of belonging. One carer in particular believed that outside of her family nobody could identify which were the foster children as they were actively displayed as her own in public contexts. In her view their clothing had to be as good as that worn by her birth children, as this would demonstrate to the foster children their worth and acceptance in the family group:

> People outside, right, who know that we foster but don't know how many I got, or who I got…they say…'Oh how many have you got', 'well we got three', 'Oh any of them with you' and we say, 'yeah'…those who don't know, lots of them think it's Mike [birth child] who's seventeen and do you know what, that's Mike, he wears a hoody up over his head with a baseball cap on and walks like this, and people think it's him [fostered child] and they think it's Serena [grand-daughter] quite often, or think it's the two boys [birth children]…they never ever get it right! People who don't know us very well but know we foster, never ever once have got it right.

> (Sally, foster carer, Family 3)

The foster children here were well assimilated as were the household as a family; in this sense they sought to enact and display 'family' rather than 'foster family'. For example, Sally went on to say that she did not readily encourage the foster children to disclose that they were fostered; she believed this to be personal information not to be divulged unless they knew and trusted people well. She talked about one of the current foster children using, inappropriately in her view, her status as fostered to elicit sympathy and interest:

> On Friday when I went to the dance [to collect foster child] a mother was there…so she came up to me, she said, 'Oh I didn't realise you fostered'. Right, now I try to encourage the children not to discuss outside the house…that they're fostered and [about] their private life, because it's not for everyone else to

[know]; that's private, you know, that's for them. If they choose to get the reaction, Candice at times can use the fostering, her being fostered as a sort of her thing, because she would quite like, enjoys somebody to feel sorry for her, she loves to be the centre of attention.

(Sally, foster carer, Family 3)

Sally's comments reveal a conscious attempt to control the family's external image to a wider public. Such an approach was by no means uniform across our small sample. Sally's example is noted here simply to reinforce the point that behind the policies and procedures exists the 'real' world in which adults and children make sense, in their own way, of fostering. In doing this, the foster family is not somehow innately 'different' to other families, yet at the same time nor is it quite like most families. It looks after children as serial 'strangers' who over time become known and accepted albeit on a temporary basis. It seeks to 'normalise' the new child as a member and it is often the case that fostered children too wish to be seen as the 'same' as other children and not marked out as 'different' because of their fostered status (Madigan et al. 2013). It is in this daily display of 'family', of 'we', enacted through countless symbolic and practical activities in and out of the home that relationships of care are built and which is the subject of the chapters that follow.

Conclusion

The foster family has to incorporate newcomers, demonstrate unity and absorb difference. This calls forth styles of caring and parenting that enact a meaningful sense of family group, while recognising the partial and often needful membership of the foster child whose status and tenure are typically time-limited and contingent on a care plan and other key supports that sustain a stable placement. Yet it is the family itself that is the key resource and the capacities of the carers that are paramount in this venture. It is towards the motives, commitment and parenting skills of the carers that we turn next in Chapter 4.

FOSTER FAMILIES – DIVERSITY AND CHANGE: KEY MESSAGES

- Foster families are diverse as are all families and the traditional nuclear family is not necessarily the only or the most effective type of family at providing the resources needed for looked after children.

- The main carer can be male or female; both can provide important role modelling and both can provide meaningful care to young people.

- It is essential for carers to think about and utilise the web of support and resources around their families and help children access these.

- Attracting foster carers with higher academic and professional achievements would seem to be a challenge. This may be important in exposing looked after children to a more representative range of family contexts.

- Foster families need to be flexible and responsive to the changing domestic circumstances of all its members.

- The 'doing' of family is vital, so the more involved that foster children can be in family activities, the more they will feel (and become) accepted.

- Doing activities outside the home allows children to be seen and display to others that they are part of the family.

- Activity-based contact with foster carers facilitates the relaxed flow of communication between carer and foster child.

CHAPTER 4

Tough Job Fostering

Why Do It?

I have always had kids around me, I love kids. I felt I had something to offer children that had missed out... If I can help someone I will. I haven't got two pennies to rub together...

Introduction

We now consider the ten families in regard to their motivation to foster, their values that inform fostering, their cultural and biographical histories and we look in more depth at the typical roles of females and males in creating care. First, however, we provide some conceptual context by briefly outlining something of the expectations we have of fostering in providing good parenting for children whose adverse circumstances have precipitated removal from home. We conclude the chapter by considering the implications of our findings for placement stability for a child and how achievable this is in a fostering system designed, typically, to offer short-term solutions.

Effective parenting – high expectations in foster care

We know from studies into parenting (Biehal *et al.* 2010; Erera 2002; Fisher and DeBell 2007; Flynn *et al.* 2004) that much depends upon parenting style in regard to the way children respond and grow. Thus some notion of the ideal parent might be conceived as one who is neither permissive nor authoritarian but authoritative and consistent in (i) their expectations of a child, (ii) the 'rules' they set, (iii) the way they communicate with the child and (iv) the warmth and responsiveness they display, often reflected in the emotional tone of the family. Such a model of parenting may be hard for most of us to achieve yet these capacities have been evidenced as most likely to respond to children who have experienced trauma and need high levels of nurturance and understanding.

Likewise, Hill *et al.* (2007), in their overview of research in parenting, note that warmth and responsiveness, providing adequate and consistent role models, harmony between parents, spending time with children, promoting constructive use of leisure, offering consistent guidance, structure and rules during adolescence, were parental strategies that helped promote resilience in children. Sinclair (2010) too observes that carers needed to be child-centred, caring, accepting and to see things from the child's perspective. While foster carers need to be able to facilitate the development of resilience within the children placed with them, they also need to be resilient themselves. For example, carers sometimes have allegations made about them by children in placement that prove to be groundless. Carers need to be able to cope with such complaints and investigations and not let these inhibit their parenting and caring in the future (Sinclair *et al.* 2004).

In short, successful foster carers need to have effective parenting skills and in this and later chapters we will look at aspects of motivation, care, warmth and responsiveness, rules, consistency and styles of communication. In doing so we will not underplay the challenges fostering can present to the best of carers. For example O'Connor and Scott (2007, p.25) in their analysis of parenting styles in fostering noted that:

> Empirical data suggest that foster families...do experience significant parent-child relationship difficulties. Research groups in the UK have found that foster parent-child relationships are at risk in terms of increased conflict and lower levels of positive engagement.

Thus Cameron and Maginn (2008) argue that carers need to include both warmth and control strategies. They observe that children in the care system have often experienced rejection and argue that foster children need a specific form of positive response, of 'acceptance', which involves the warmth, affection, care and comfort that any child might expect of its parents. It is this aspect of warmth and acceptance that seems to be one of the pivotal factors in fostering and was often remarked upon in interviews with carers. It can be linked to the notion of the authoritative parent who can manage the balance between appropriate control, responsiveness and care. While socially responsive and mature behaviour is expected and encouraged, authoritative parents are also warm and supportive in the face of negative engagement. It is perhaps not surprising that Cameron and Maginn (2008) suggest that foster carers are likely to require above-average parenting capacities and skills.

Emotional work

Children in the care system will have experienced many losses – temporary and permanent. These may well include the loss of their birth parents, the loss of their extended family, the loss of siblings, the repeated loss of foster carers, the loss of a happy childhood and the loss of an unbroken education. Cameron and Maginn (2008) outline a phased recovery model for those experiencing major disrupted life transitions and the post-traumatic stress that may accompany this. The model encompasses an arc of emotions related to loss: shock and numbness, guilt, anger, resentment and fear, disengagement, apathy, the beginning of hope and a gradual move towards new directions. This framework is similar to traditional bereavement models which foster families can use to assist children move through a sense of loss that often accompanies going into care. Carers can support this grieving process by providing experiences which rebuild a child's coping strategies, and by highlighting any successes that help enhance the child's sense of self-worth. Consider here the view of foster carer, Josie, who in discussing the deep unhappiness that can accompany coming into care raised this very point about positive self-regard as part of recovery from loss:

> I found whatever teenager I had, doesn't matter what their home problem was, whatever their problem...every single teenager had something, a brilliant artist, a brilliant dancer or maybe a fantastic

cook. Or they were fantastic doing their make up or whatever... Everybody had something good and I found that within them. It doesn't matter how rotten all the rest of it was, they always had something and it was magical to me and I tried to find it in all of them and once I found what it was, we worked on it...

(Josie, foster carer, Family 4)

It is vital that foster carers are able to view disruptive and problematic behaviour within a bigger picture of the child responding to loss and the difficult situations they previously experienced (Holmes and Silver 2010; Ironside 2012). Cairn's model (2002) of trauma, bereavement and loss is also helpful in grasping the emotional context in fostering. She suggests that after major life disruptions, young people tend to follow a three-stage process of stabilisation–integration–adaptation. Thus helping the child to settle in a regular routine, and helping a child to understand and accept the past should in turn allow the child to establish a connectedness with the current family and support the child's attempts to adapt to their new environment. This can assist the child to begin attaching themselves to the foster family; this process was recognised by several carers including Rachael who makes the point thus:

He'll sit and stare at you and he'll come and he'll want a cuddle but it's a normal sort of cuddle...because he's not, never been used to having any but he is starting to attach but we've had him for a year now.

(Rachael, foster carer, Family 5)

This context of prior trauma and subsequent stress can be a prominent part of fostering and understanding this is essential for carers and their birth children who may be faced with a variety of potentially hurtful rebuffs to their well-intentioned motives. Facing difficult or emotionally withdrawn children in personal turmoil and helping them, over time, through their loss towards a more stabilised sense of belonging was noted by Sally, a carer in Family 3:

She would scream, high pitch scream or run up and down the stairs...because that's all she would do and she would do really silly, daft things, like punch the boys and they weren't used to it and I said she'll have some reactions and people were shocked. I said to the children carry on with what we're doing, don't give her a reaction and like I said, it was six weeks on a trot this went on [before the child became more settled].

(Sally, foster carer, Family 3)

Sally went on to describe an embarrassing event in a shop where other members of the public were watching the child's behaviour and possibly making judgements about them both. She described how in handling such scenarios carers and their families need to draw upon their training and be patient, informed and adept in their reactions to difficult behaviour (see Holmes and Silver 2010). Through such training (see for example Cairns and Fursland 2007) carers can acquire an understanding of the often traumatic experiences leading to foster care and can grasp difficult behaviour as an expression of the child's history rather than interpreting this as some personal rejection.

Nonetheless, there is an emotional impact to fostering on all participants which can be significant. Ironside (2004, 2012), a child psychotherapist, describes the discomfort associated with an unhealthy and upsetting relationship between carers and child, particularly where a child projects their feelings of anger and hurt on to the foster family. She notes that the caring task is a complex one: carers need to be close enough to the child to feel emotionally involved, offering consistent ongoing warmth, and yet distant enough not to be overwhelmed by the child's behaviour. Foster families need space for reflection and support to understand a child's sense of loss and consequent projection of hostility and rejection towards others.

It is difficult not to see effective foster families as impressive, able to repeatedly offer authentic warmth, communicate acceptance, and be authoritative but also flexible in response to the needs of the child. Female and male carers but also birth children need to be able to function in this way in order to facilitate the child's stabilisation, integration and adaptation (Cairns 2006). In essence 'care is about creating and maintaining committed and co-operative relations with others' (Brannen and Moss 2003, p.207). But giving care is not a one-way street and, as we shall see shortly, it is the case that caring yields various benefits for the foster family too (see Lipscombe et al. 2004). Thus we now ask, given the high expectations set for carers over their style of parenting and their resilience in the face of emotional challenges brought by unsettled and often unhappy children, who would really want to do this job and why? In addressing this question from the perspectives of our small sample we first set out some general ideas about motivation to foster that are likely to underpin success in doing this extraordinary job.

Motivation to foster

Drawing on the concept of the gift relationship introduced in Chapter 2, we now consider the families in respect of why they chose to foster, their values that inform fostering and their cultural and biographical histories that contributed to this decision. The 'gift relationship' is about giving without expectation of reward, an act of altruism whereby a moral choice is made to benefit another to whom there is no direct obligation to assist. This notion of the 'gift' has often been used to explain foster care whereby the impulse to help another is made in the knowledge of no material reward, other than expenses (see Holland 2010; Nutt 2006; Titmuss 1970). The notion of a 'gift' is useful in sensitising us to the fostering role but we do not suggest that carers necessarily see fostering in this way. Indeed, we shall see if the salience of the concept applies in regard to the carers in this study and whether other sentiments held by them will better typify the essential character of foster family care.

We shall see below that across our sample the sole motivation to foster was never financial (albeit this was an additional consideration for some) but like other carers was informed by the desire to do something meaningful and 'put something back in to society' (Rock et al. 2013; Sebba 2012). Many of the carers referred to their family unit (rather than themselves) as the primary means by which to assist others. All viewed childhood as something worthy of being treasured and children being of value in their own right. Carers and/or family members had often been working in a care or public service occupation and through this or other connections with social care had some prior understanding of the caring ethos underpinning the fostering role (as also found by Triseliotis et al. 2000).

As we discussed in Chapter 2, the sociological notion of 'individualisation' describes changes in advanced societies that see the undoing of traditional relationships and the arrival of new personal freedoms. It is suggested that everyday family relationships today are characterised more by selective arrangements which are founded less on notions of absolute commitment and more on their continuing for as long as they give partners satisfaction (Bauman 2003). Against this trend towards impermanence in our more intimate relationships, Ribbens McCarthy *et al.* (2003, p.7) note that 'putting family first and foregoing individual self interest still has a strong hold' in our contemporary world. Indeed, it will become clear that carers in this study held very different values to those contained within the above individualisation thesis. For they enjoy lives that are not prompted by restless self-interest but enmeshed with others, including the foster children, in ways that are enduring and reciprocal. Their various reasons for fostering now come to the fore and we start by looking at aspects of financial reward and the salience of this for carers.

Financial motivation

The difficult and much-debated question in fostering is whether carers are paid for their labour, or merely reimbursed in order to cover their costs. This ongoing debate is elucidated by Tapsfield (2007, p.1):

> Foster carers are increasingly required to work full time and take on complex duties and responsibilities but often they are treated as volunteers when it comes to pay. Foster carers do not and should not foster because of the money but neither should society expect them to do it for love alone.

Within our ten families five were linked to an independent agency and the others to two local authorities. This had consequences from a monetary and resource persepective. Thus the carers working for an independent agency could be seen to draw a wage of sorts, as they received an income on average three to four times that of their local authority counterparts who by contrast were simply reimbursed for their basic costs of looking after a young person. For example, Families 4, 5 and 6 working for the independent agency tended to discuss fostering by talking about it more as an occupational role in which monetary reward held some importance:

> When they [local authority] said how much money they were
> paying, I said there's no way I would be available twenty four
> hours a day for ninety pounds a week, you know. They were
> asking an awful lot for what they were paying.
>
> (Mark, foster carer, Family 5)

Certainly some of the motivation to foster came from the financial
circumstances of these families. In recent decades there has been
pressure on parent couples to be dual earners to meet the costs of
family life in the UK. While such dual earning families might be
work-rich they may well be time-poor; also many have to work
longer and harder to maintain often quite modest if not marginal
lifestyles (Chapman 2004; Lawton and Thompson 2013). Notably,
some carers felt that it was financial considerations that stopped them
from offering the children in their care a permanent home outside of
fostering (e.g. adoption) as they would no longer be remunerated:

> If we could afford it, we're not in that situation, but if we could
> afford it we would have...all three of them [i.e. offer a permanent
> home]...we couldn't afford to do it because we couldn't afford
> to bring three more up...and we just couldn't afford to do it and
> that is the only thing stops us from doing it.
>
> (Sally, foster carer, Family 3)

Several carers spoke of deciding that one of the partners (typically
the female) needed to work within the home to allow more time to
manage the needs of their own family, and fostering seemed to fit
with their domestic arrangements providing it also enhanced family
income:

> So we were looking for a job with transferable skills. ...and we
> were just trying to find something to fill the financial slot in
> other words because...we had to have two incomes coming in...
> we heard about fostering...so I just thought, well no if I'm going
> to be looking after children with problems, then I want to,
> want to be paid for it.
>
> (Mark, foster carer, Family 5)

Liz, a foster carer in Family 1, talked about her own child, Helen, needing to acknowledge that there was a financial benefit from fostering which paid for some of the family comforts:

> Well for us now, Helen [birth child] is growing up and when she hasn't got on with Melonie [foster child], the financial advantage, because we are a low income family. And I mean you do get paid, it's a financial reward at the end of it, and although I've never mentioned it to Helen before, I do try to get her to understand that we, besides what we do for the children who live with us, she [Helen] has benefits you know. We wouldn't have been able to afford what we do without fostering. I think Helen is at an age to understand that she does get a benefit from it, even when it's not going all her way.
>
> (Liz, foster carer, Family 1)

It is hardly unreasonable for carers to expect some adequate financial support for the difficult tasks they do. Whether this is a fee, a wage or only basic expenses will of course reflect different arrangements and market effects but across our small sample financial gain was never the dominant impulse. An altruistic instinct of wanting to help, as we discuss next, remained central to much of their motivation to become involved in fostering.

Foster care – the roots of altruism and 'giving'

In interviews, carers conveyed that they wanted to offer care in order to contribute and 'put something back into society'. They talked about their decisions to foster in the following ways:

> I just thought, one of the reasons was, I thought in society it was good to give, you know I think in society so many people want to, they want to take and people don't care and I could see that this was a good way of contributing.
>
> (Liz, foster carer, Family 1)

It was, it was something that I'd been mulling over in my mind. We both had previous relationships, unfortunately both fell by the wayside and we both met each other. I think life has turned out quite nicely for us both and so I just thought well, seeing what life has done for us, wouldn't it be nice to perhaps try to put something back into life, society and help somebody else if we can.

(Philip, foster carer, Family 4)

We've brought up one family and now we're bringing up another, we will hopefully bring up seven children who all go on to do something, whatever, how little or how much you might be, it doesn't matter as long as they go out and live independently and get on as best they can.

(Sally, foster carer, Family 3)

All the families invoked similar sentiments as underpinning their decision to enter fostering. Often it was a feeling that their families had something to offer children who were less fortunate, or in some cases as unfortunate as they themselves had once been. For example, two male (primary) carers drew on their own difficult family histories which led to their admission to care which they recalled as an unhappy time. Both felt keenly that they wanted to ameliorate any similar negative experiences that the fostered young people had been exposed to. As a consequence, both were uniquely positioned to understand and guide children in ways not immediately available to other carers. For example, Ian (foster carer, Family 2) recalled how his own loss of parents at an early age made him sensitive to any thoughtless use of simple words such as 'mother' and 'father' by those who looked after him. This early experience of foster care had made him more reflective about the language he used when getting to know the children placed with him and his partner Dawn:

But like I remember one foster carer saying like er 'my mother' this or 'my father' that, which made you feel very different. Not big things but certain things that some people might not even see.

(Ian, foster carer, Family 2)

Ian's partner Dawn continues:

> I try to stop them [foster children] feeling grateful because it is
> what they deserve; these children are at the other end of the
> spectrum, they are not used to having things, or time spent
> with them.
>
> (Dawn, foster carer, Family 2)

While two of the 18 cares had been in care themselves, the remainder,
apart from one couple, had family or working experiences of caring
prior to being a foster carer themselves. Thus caring was seen (and
known) as a valuable and important aspect of life as we discuss next.

Caring and the family history

Nine of the ten families had a previous connection with other types
of caring roles. Similarly, Triseliotis *et al.* (2000) found in their study
that two-fifths of female carers were recruited mainly from the caring
professions. The following describes some of the ways that the families
in our study entered fostering. The carer in Family 8, Hazel, had been
a birth child in a foster family and as a result of this has an adopted
sister. Her birth sister had also been a foster carer for 20 years. Hazel
had worked for many years in a nursery and it had seemed to her a
natural transition to take on the foster care role herself. She was also
involved in paid child care and very much enjoyed taking care of other
children including her own grandchildren:

> I have always had kids around me, I love kids. I felt I had
> something to offer children that had missed out... If I can help
> someone I will. I haven't got two pennies to rub together...
>
> (Hazel, foster carer, Family 8)

In Family 3, both carers offered day care and holidays to children who
had been excluded from school. The female carer had also worked in
a care setting. They saw it as an obvious extension to move into foster
care. In Family 2, both carers had decided they would prefer not to
have children of their own but would foster instead:

I'd always said I wanted to foster. I used to say to my mum I'm not having my own kids I'm going to look after all the little poor kids, [I was sat] in front of the telly crying – I'm going to look after them. She said you'll change your mind, there is nothing like having your own kids. I don't need to bear my own... Well we'd always been very children orientated. Ian had worked with young people and adults before. As a support worker. I suppose I had always had an interest with Ian's work as well... We were always that way inclined. And then there was this ad in the newspaper 'if you have a spare room' and we thought we'll have a go. It was a pilot scheme which they now run properly. At 16 [years of age] we were thinking we wish we had them [foster children] earlier... perhaps in an idealistic way, but maybe having the opportunity to help them more. I've always wanted to do this...

(Dawn, foster carer, Family 2)

Both carers in Family 6 talked similarly about their early decision to foster:

It was my decision really, well it was a joint decision but it was my idea, but I've always wanted to, always... Because I come from a broken home and I love children and Sue and I were together for 13 years, engaged for 13 years and we never had any children basically... Well it's like I said all those years ago, we wanted children, so we could eat jelly and ice cream and go to the park. We like learning from children, taking up new interests because of the children. Plus when we met, the first couple of weeks of meeting, we said we always wanted to foster, the both of us, separate like...

(Steve, foster carer, Family 6)

This couple started fostering before having children of their own and continued fostering whilst bringing up their three birth children.

An adult birth child in Family 7 spoke of her desire as a child to foster children when she was grown up. She recalled a childhood friend who was fostered and she was much impressed with the impact of the care provided by the foster family. She persuaded her mother to start fostering:

But I always wanted to help people, but my father didn't want us to do it. Then my father passed away. Jenny (fostered friend) moved on. She set up home and had children young. We lost contact but I kept in contact with her foster family. I was really close to them. I had a big bond and I'm really close to them today.

(Katie, adult birth child, Family 7)

One set of carers stood apart in that they stated they were prompted to foster by religious conviction which they described as motivating them rather than any prior family affiliation with care work. What was notable in their accounts was more a religious calling to care as a social duty in which the emotional aspect of caring seemed less prominent and more a matter of task-based support:

I firmly believe...that if you tackle it as a job and isolate some emotions, I think you can do your job better but...you cannot isolate your emotions because crumbs you know you'd be totally heartless. You wouldn't feel anything... There's got to be some sort of emotion there, some sort of, something inside of you that wants to help this child.

(Mark, foster carer, Family 5)

Mark's comments are illuminating and he went on to argue that it was not necessary to 'like' or have some deep emotional affinity in order to help and that some detachment was appropriate and unavoidable. We do not question his commitment or authenticity in the realm of care nor the need for some emotional control in a complex relationship. The issue is rather one of degree and returns us to the point about whether we expect foster carers to care *for* or care *about* a foster child – the former assumes some detachment and the latter a deeper emotional connection. This distinction goes to the heart of the fostering relationship but allows no easy measurement of motive or outcome. Thus, while Mark spoke openly of not liking a particular child and not needing to do so to help, he still cared for the child and provided a high level of physical and professional care.

What then distinguishes foster care – are the motives to foster to be best conceptualised within an ethic of care which extols the empathic gift of attachment and acceptance, of caring *about* someone? Or, should it be understood more instrumentally within an ethic of justice (see Held 2006), of caring *for* someone based upon their rights, and where care has become a collection of monitored tasks and remunerated roles that have become increasingly rule-based and professionalised? Such a divide is perhaps artificial and in the 'real' world these different spheres often overlap. However, in exploring this we shall consider how our sample understood their own unique relationships and obligations towards the fostered child.

Positioning the children: a priority

All of the families described how they placed the child and the child's needs as central to the foster family endeavour. Their sense of commitment and empathy was often fervently expressed as can be seen in the claims made by one of the carers in Family 2 when asked to indicate how they engage with the emotional and practical needs of fostered children:

> Our whole life really. We always said when we went into fostering unless we could give them everything and be prepared to sacrifice everything, which you need to do, then there was no point going into it. We have had kids where I have had to be able to offer that. We have always said that whatever child comes along our focus is around finding out what makes them tick. And you do. You will find something. There will be something. So we throw ourselves into different activities all of the time. Something clicks. Which is rather wonderful for us. It has its stresses and its emotional times but we move on.
>
> (Ian, foster carer, Family 2)

Unprompted and at a later time the foster child in the same family corroborated this claim. As can be seen, she is quite clear that she is the carers' priority and that the carers have made this abundantly clear to her too:

> Like I'm always worried about finances and I don't like asking for things but they have taught me to be able to ask for anything. I come first with them... Yeah, they give us a chance to do anything we are interested in and they say they want us to

have good childhood memories. This house has been changed a lot and extended. They are going to get a shed for me to do drumming and that is going to cost two grand... They don't worry about the furniture. But you don't remember a sofa when you are grown up do you? You remember a holiday [a foreign holiday was being planned].

(Nadia, foster child, Family 2)

Another carer talked in similar terms about sacrifices willingly made to give the fostered child the opportunities and experiences they would not otherwise have. She summarised the values that underpinned this commitment as:

Plenty of love, being a normal person and putting those children's needs before anybody else's.

(Judith, foster carer, Family 7)

This respondent and others readily gave examples of prioritising the child above their own interests as an everyday feature of family care. Thus it seemed that all manner of changes were routinely made to family practices so as to accommodate the child's interests and put their needs first. Of families generally, Ribbens McCarthy, Edwards and Gilles (2000, p.271) argue strongly 'that there is a non-negotiable moral obligation within families to put children's needs first'. It was notable that this appeared to be as pronounced for foster children in these families as it was for the birth children. One fostered young person reflected on this in relation to the adult birth children in the family:

I am still a foster child and they are their biological children and I would never, ever try and come between them and I don't feel I have to compete with them anyway, because I get so much attention. They sometimes say to me, 'when we were at home living with Mum, we never got half the things you get'. So I'm treated very, very good.

(Callum, foster child, Family 8)

This sense of both equity and difference between the fostered and the birth child in relation to care and consideration was often a conscious act of balancing by carers and the children themselves. An interesting example of this was where a carer spoke about her daughter being bruised by a foster child. She described how she needed to demonstrate to her child that she would be protected and treated with the same priority as the foster child, were that child hurt by someone:

> Colin who was here was violent, and I mean, violent. He really bruised Helen badly… Over Christmas it was, so no support. I didn't have that support anyway but we, I mean by the time they bruised your child the damage is done, isn't it? So when they [local authority] started back to work I asked, and then insisted on a proper meeting, where my child could go and be supported by whoever was around…and wanted them there for Helen, for Helen to see that she is important as him, and it did happen.

> (Liz, foster carer, Family 3)

While the foster children in the families were prioritised and cherished as part of the family, they were not seen as 'sons' and 'daughters', nor did most of the carers see themselves as their 'parents' as such. The normative relationship between children and their parents includes an expectation of love, a duty of care and a long-term relationship (see Finch and Mason 1993). By contrast the term 'foster mother/father' has long been superseded within the UK by the term 'foster carer' which denotes that carers cannot (and are not intending to) take over the long-term role of motherhood and fatherhood. Nevertheless some of the young people in this study did refer to their foster carers as 'Mum' and 'Dad'. And some of the carers referred to each other as 'Mum' and 'Dad' in everyday talk with the foster children (see Blythe et al. 2012; Finch 2008).

> You know there are lots of reasons why someone [can't look after their children] but they've tried their best and they just couldn't cope, so there's people like me and Dad around, because they call us Mum and Dad, who can help them and looking after their children but making sure you never forget who your mum is, who your dad is…

> (Sally, foster carer, Family 3)

Whilst the official terminology has changed, linguistic preferences and their tacit and taken-for-granted meanings are not so easily extinguished and there are inevitably aspects of mothering and fathering that enter the fostering relationship (Finch 2008), and it is towards the role of the males in our ten families that we look next.

Fatherhood: the male foster carer

While fathers are now expected to participate in their children's lives by providing more day-to-day physical and emotional care, for some this shift seems to be more rhetorical than actual. Certainly in the recent past there have been claims that fathers do relatively little child care compared to mothers and that what they do with their children is often mediated through the guidance of the mother (Eichler 1997; Smart 1999). However, a study by Brannen et al. (2011) of intergenerational fathering has suggested that this is beginning to change; fathers are more involved but still not necessarily as 'hands on' as some mothers might wish. 'Hands on' fathering may well be more a feature of working-class males rather than high-earning middle-class men; however, the varied and shifting forms of family life in multi-cultural UK make generalisation unwise (see Brannen and Nilson 2006; Brannen et al. 2011).

But what do we know about men in foster care and their contribution to domestic chores and family activities? Understanding the role that men play in fostering is vital in improving recruitment, service delivery and retention of foster carers. Rhodes et al. (2003) in their US study found that workers often underestimated the involvement of adult male carers in the lives of foster children and noted that much research has focused on female carers. Gilligan's (2000) important focus group study with male foster carers highlighted the distinctive role they play. Similarly, the adult males within this research were often pivotal to family care and were seen positively by many of the fostered young people.

There is a relative dearth of UK research on fathers, children and welfare in the social care system and there has also been a relative lack of attention paid to male foster carers by agencies and social workers (Ashley et al. 2006; Nutt 2002, 2006; Wilson et al. 2007). This gap in our knowledge has long been noted (see Gilligan 2000; Newstone 1999) whilst at the same time there have been many who have stressed the importance of the role of the male foster carer, without much of a research evidence base to explain why. Sinclair *et al.* (2004) note that because foster care research usually focuses upon the main carer which typically is a woman, so it is that male carers have remained largely invisible (see also Wilson *et al.* 2007). Morgan (1996, p.101) too notes that 'men are not absent from caring work and, indeed, their involvement in such activities may have been underestimated by some previous commentators'. Hojer's (2004) study in Sweden also suggests that male carers have featured more prominently in recent years in regard to their commitment and interest in the task. However, according to Hojer, women were likely to remain the party responsible for the fostering endeavour and to stand at the interface between the family and the outside world of professionals and agencies involved with the child.

It is evident that the contribution to fostering by males can be signficant. All of the carers in this study, male and female, felt that men had a valuable part to play. Like other male carers (see Fostering Network 2010) the men in our study were eager to embrace both the practical and emotional aspects of foster caring; they were aware that many foster children have a history of difficult relationships with men and believed they could be important role models. A positive male influence needs to be more consciously and explicitly articulated in planning placements not least because in many foster families the number of children outnumber adults; as a result this inevitably 'draws males to the centre of family life' (Hojer 2004). To get a sense of the impact of the male role and its often tacit if not explicit connections with fathering, consider the following brief excerpt from an interview with foster child Callum in Family 8. This reflects something of the sorts of close relations that evolve over time and which denote a sense of attachment that common-sensically at least may be perceived as 'father like', at least from the perspective of the child:

> He [Josh] used to take me down the pub and buy me a shandy, I used to play on the machines and it was just nice to be treated like that...and we became very close that way and me and Josh we had a real great start... Now Josh is very fatherly as well, he looks out for me. First he was a very, very good friend and then he became a father figure to me.

> (Callum, foster child, Family 8)

It was notable in this study that 'hands-on' fathering was undertaken by all the males but especially by those who were (i) the primary carer or (ii) were joint carer with female partner or (iii) not the main breadwinner or (iv) were not working. In three of the families, older male birth children were also evident in providing support and being a role model in one family where there was no male carer. There was therefore an overt male presence in all but one of the family homes. One carer outlined the types of activities that her partner undertook with the children. In some ways these are gender specific, but it does reveal a male carer engaged independently of the female carer:

> Chris [foster carer] normally does the [outdoor] things with them, he takes them down to the sea wall and they might make a camp fire, take some sausages and potatoes and they cook or he'll take them up the forest, and they might build things out of logs or you need to take them down the caravan for the day because perhaps the boat needs moving or something needs mending on the caravan and he takes them down there for the day and they help him do whatever needs to be done down there and then he brings them back and all sorts, I've never ever had a row with him, never...
>
> (Sally, foster carer, Family 3)

Predictably much of the involvement of male foster carers with children was activity based including sports, horse riding, football, tennis, dog walking and playing pool. Brannen and Nilson (2006) also observe fathering to be typically about 'doing'. Such activities were a vehicle for communication by males with young people as many talked while dog walking or playing sports. Activities also allowed young people to develop a range of interests and enjoy self-esteem through their achievements. Thus men seemed to play a key role in providing activity-based care for foster children but were not inactive in more domestic home-based events as we shall see in later chapters.

Motherhood and love

Many have observed that care is inextricably linked to femininity as women are assumed to be predisposed to nurturing others. As Ribbens

McCarthy *et al.* (2003, p.80) observe, 'discourses on femininity and motherhood are closely interlinked with definitions of selflessness, sensitivity, warmth, traits which are seen as constituting a disposition to care'. Family life is ideologically constructed as the primary site for emotion and mothering inevitably involves the use of emotion and love (see Ribbens McCarthy *et al.* 2003; Nutt 2006), but how does this play out in fostering where the female carer is clearly not the mother in any obvious sense? Glenn, Chang and Foley (1994, p.104) succinctly summarise the issue thus:

> Foster care can be seen to be a contradictory activity in which separation of motherhood from mothering and being motherly inevitably gives rise to emotional and practical problems.

It is both the time-limited nature of foster care and the existence elsewhere of birth parents that differentiates foster care from a conventional mothering or fathering context. That the female foster carer is not the mother is of course objectively true but the complex world of care and emotions both creates and re-orders the identities and relationships of the participants – whether intended or not. Consider how Nadia talks about the differences between her own mother and her foster carer and the way that time and attachment in the foster home has recast these relations:

> I love my mum to bits but I'll be honest, Dawn [the foster carer] should be my mum. I know it sounds horrible because I do love my mum so much. I love Dawn better...because I think she understands me more, and she is more of a mum... Like my [birth] mother...she's too soft. I love her but I don't like her ways...she is like a big kid. She is embarrassing, I hate going out with her! When we are on our own she's fine but when we are on the bus like...she'll say 'Oh my Nadia give me a big kiss' [funny voice]. Everyone is having a good nose and I just felt like walking off. I love her because of who she is but I'm so embarrassed about being a big family. I'm embarrassed about being well – I'm embarrassed – if she didn't look like a bag lady, she could be attractive. I've never seen her wear make up, she never had her hair done in her life or had new shoes... I always wanted a girly mum to share make up and clothes, but I can't.

Like with Dawn she really likes make-up... Yeah. I can talk to my mum for hours; she swears at me; I swear at her and I can say ef off like and she don't mind. Whereas I don't feel I could say that with Dawn. It's just not her way. Like my mum is more a friend. A friend or a sister, but Dawn is more like a mother...

(Nadia, foster child, Family 2)

Nadia invokes her own notion of what a 'normal' mother should be like and how her birth mother does not match up to this. She has clear expectations of what a mother should be, that is, someone feminine, presentable, responsible, who can share interests, has boundaries. For Nadia, the foster carer personifies something of her mothering ideal and raises questions about the way carers, intentionally or not, provide parenting role models – in this instance a 'girly mum' – and the degree to which role-modelling more specifically should become part of the matching process. There are no easy answers to this and, anecdotally, it is likely that in training foster carers we shy away from promoting traditional gendered role models yet children may have different ideas to professionals about the sort of parenting they would like.

What we glean from Nadias's comments is that fostering generates complex emotional constructions that imply strong 'parent-like' attachments, yet it remains the case that carers do not provide the ties of birth. Carers must somehow act as good fathers or mothers would but also know they are not the parents – nor intended to be. This seeming contradiction is not without its emotional strains (Riggs and Willsmore 2012). Thus while it is expected that foster carers should nurture, care about and potentially love a young person in their care, they must also be able and willing to let them go (Buehler *et al.* 2006). Most of the foster carers could recall their sense of loss when a placement ended and they had to relinquish their attachment to a child they had looked after as their own:

...when you get too attached and children have to go for adoption then that is a different aspect of the job altogether then. When you get a little bit too close...I had two placements like that which after they go, you tend to say I'm not doing this anymore and it takes a good few months down the line. It's like a bereavement you know, because I have had some darling little kids here and perhaps you have had them 12 months and then you get a phone call and they say we've got an adoptive parent for…and you can feel yourself going ugh, you know your insides flop and then you think oh it will be a few months before they introduce them and all of a sudden it's just a few weeks and bang its gone. You think to yourself you've just given this child over and it's terrible.

(Julie, foster carer, Family 10)

Social work has long drawn on theories of attachment (Bowlby 1969), yet carers are expected to offer serial intimate relationships and to then extinguish these and to thereafter be immune to the pain of detaching and letting go (Riggs and Willsmore 2012; Roberts 2011; Thomson and McArthur 2009). Indeed, many of the carers stated they had stopped offering foster care for babies on the basis that it was just too painful to give them up:

We had the babies…for about a year and a half and we had to pass them onto another foster carer because we got so attached, [we had a] huge rift between social services… Terrible it was.

(Sally, foster carer, Family 3)

In most professional relationships it is not anticipated that we have a major emotional investment in our clients. However, with fostering, dual expectations of care occur within bounded professional parameters. In order to explore this with the carers they were asked to describe how they felt about the children placed with them and whether the term 'love' was ever appropriate in this regard (see also Wilson *et al.* 2003). The definition of 'love' we used in the interviews was normative in the sense of any parent being assumed to 'love' their children (Blythe *et al.* 2012). There were a variety of responses to this topic. Some carers felt that they were attached and cared deeply but that this did not amount to 'love'. Others were clear that they loved the children in their care, as any parent would:

Sally: Slowly she [foster child] began saying 'love you' and I used to say to her 'and I love you' and 'I love you as well'.

Researcher: And do you 'love' her?

Sally: Yeah I love her.

Researcher: And you say, you were saying you love all three now, do you think it's necessary to 'love' a child in foster care?

Sally: Certainly to love I think. I don't think I could have anybody living in this house that I didn't love.

Researcher: And have you ever had that?

Sally: No.

(Sally, foster carer, Family 3)

Sally believed that she loved all of the children she fostered and was able to offer authentic emotional care and attachment which was not contrived. Another set of carers discuss their overriding concern for the children in placement but do not describe this as love. Nonetheless, they position their needs as secondary to those of the children:

Ian: For us I wouldn't say we weren't attached; I feel deeply for them but if that is what was going to happen [return to their birth mother], that is what is going to happen.

Dawn: And outside you will get on with it. You just have to get over that on the outside but inside [emotionally] they are always there.

Ian: You just want the best for them.

Researcher: It is a difficult aspect of fostering?

Ian: Of course it is. You need to give yourself time to get over it, to pick yourself up and to go marching on ready for the next.

(Dawn and Ian, foster carers, Family 2)

Thus, whilst some carers did not consider that they 'loved' the children as might a parent, their investment of concern and care was still seen as overriding. It is the expectation of love or at least a warm, nurturing affection that surfaces in these interviews and which is usually assumed to evolve in conditions of continuity, stability and security. Yet it is difficult to see how these desirable conditions can easily be achieved in the short term in which much fostering occurs. Hence we now examine briefly related issues of time and stability in the lives of children and foster families. It will be seen that part of the background to these durable placements was not only carer motivation and the primacy of the child as the object of meaningful attachment, but because time itself had played a part in making a placement successful.

Stability and time

Beck and Beck-Gernsheim (1995) point to the cultural significance of children in our everyday lives. They argue that while all manner of relationships in our contemporary world can be fleeting, interchangeable or revocable it is the case that our own child 'promises a tie which is more elemental, profound and durable than any other in society…it is the ultimate guarantee of permanence, providing an anchor for one's life'. This notion that children make such a stabilising and transformative difference to parents' lives (Boddy 2013) jars uneasily against the increasing numbers of children entering care because of damaging home circumstances and who then face further impermanence when for the best of intentions (but not always) they are moved again in a stressed and inflexible care system (see Jackson 2006; Ward *et al.* 2003). Part of the difficulty here is that for decades there has been an emphasis on short-term care in order to work towards returning children to birth families or preparing them for adoption. This overriding aim of reunification has long militated against the idea of long-term foster care as a placement of choice and instead it is seen more often a last resort when other options are no longer viable (Biehal *et al.* 2010; Schofield 2002). The predominant view that a return to birth parents should be the first choice of a care plan has led to failed attempts at reunification and delay for many children in ultimately finding a stable home (Sinclair 2010). Some years ago Ward *et al.* (2003) found that this was exacerbated by lack of concurrent planning for the child should his or her return to the birth parent prove not possible. They also found that there was some reluctance to consider foster carers as potential adopters. This was partly due to the fear of losing foster carers but also there were concerns that some foster carers would not meet the stringent requirements required of adopters, despite often having looked after the child for many months up until that point.

Thus we might impute some dual standard operating with foster carers good enough to provide short-term care but not good enough to provide long-term and particularly 'forever' care. That this may now be changing with more carers becoming adopters has been intimated by Biehal *et al.* (2010) but there are likely to remain barriers as outlined above (see Sinclair 2010).

Foster care currently offers 'a time-limited form of permanence' (Sinclair *et al.* 2005b, p.11). In that sense we may define 'successful' foster care as the provision of time-limited permanence lasting as long as was needed and which did not disrupt and terminate (Leathers 2006). All of the foster children in this study were in placements that had not disrupted and might thereby be deemed successful. Yet, most of the young people were in what might be called 'long-term' foster care sometimes seen by professionals as less desirable. It was notable that seven of the families were offering long-term foster care with the expectation that the placement would continue until the child ceased to be looked after, or until after their childhood (often termed 'objective permanence'; see Sinclair *et al.* 2005b). Foster care for these children had become less a temporary refuge and much more a family for the foreseeable future.

Thus, even though the carers, like others, had not anticipated offering a long-term home, this had nonetheless evolved and care was lasting as long as was needed (see Biehal *et al.* 2010). For example, Sally (Family 3) discussed her intention to continue offering a long-term home to the children placed with her, despite having initially gone into fostering to offer short-term care. Sally has three children who have been with her for eight, seven and five years. She states that she has given each of these children some 'good experiences of family life', and believes that at whatever point they leave, they will have acquired skills and capacities to utilise in their own adult futures.

Thus it seems that children with most of the carers in this study had assimilated well and were looking to remain long term with their foster families. It is worth pondering the fact that all children were initially short-term placements and that this might well have reduced the pressure on relationship-building and allowed these to evolve more naturally as time passed by (see Schofield *et al.* 2000). It was also evident that some carers had influenced events that led to placements becoming long term. For example, they spoke of challenging professional decisions to move the child because they believed this was not in that child's interests. For example, Julie (Family 10) disclosed how the local authority wished to retain her only as a short-term carer and wanted to free up the placement which had drifted beyond its original timeline by moving the child on:

> I was told that if I was going to take her [i.e. foster the child long term] then I wouldn't be having any other placements. I said 'fair enough, if I can get one out the system, carry on'. At least I knew she [foster child] wanted to be here and she was happy with us. She had been here two years and it is a long time in a child's life.
>
> (Julie, foster carer, Family 10)

Local authority resource constraints and the needs of other children looked after may make such decisions not uncommon, but difficult to justify when acting in the best interests of the individual child. Julie was committed to saving the child from what she perceived as the vagaries of the care 'system' and this concern trumped any financial advantages that might have been obtained by cooperating with the local authority. Hazel, carer in Family 8, also talked about influencing placement arrangements so that an adolescent could stay long term. This did not seem to present a major difficulty to the independent fostering agency responsible for placing the young person:

> At his review we asked if he could stay long term. He said 'I want to stay put!' And that is a big part. He just settled and he became human. We treat him as a member of the family... He is here for good. He will be here until at least 18...there is a home here for him – this is his home... He is just ours...
>
> (Hazel, foster carer, Family 8)

While it is vital to listen to the views of young people about where they wish to stay (Minnis and Walker 2012) it is of course the case that we must listen to the carers too. Thus what we can note from the above examples and others in our study is the obvious but critical matter of mutuality in the exercise of choice. The foster families above asserted their wish to commit long term and the children too indicated a clear enthusiasm to stay. Indeed, it might be that short-term fostering offers an opportunity to test out the 'chemistry' of the relationship and that ideally young people and carers should be allowed to jointly inform the decision about continuity from a short-term to a long-term placement. Schofield *et al.* (2000, pp.295–6) discuss the importance of long-term options thus:

> Long term foster care should not be seen as a last resort, as this could lead to children remaining with maltreating families, waiting too long for adoption, or drifting in short-term care.

Certainly within this study there were children for whom long-term care was working and working well. If placement success is deemed as lasting as long as is needed without disruption (and predicting the length of time needed is scarcely a proven technique) then there can only be a fairly arbitrary calculation of what is meant by short-term or long-term care. The artificiality of this divide was noted by Mervyn and Kerry (Family 9) who described how two boys were very settled with them but that the social worker insisted on keeping to a planned short-term six-month cut-off point:

> They both were going to go, this was what the local authority do, they say they are only here for so long…they [foster children] start to settle down here…and the social workers were saying, 'well you're only here for six months.'…so we told Adrian…he'll be going the first week in January [as the social workers had told us] and it's a time to tell him isn't it!… Then they wanted him to stay longer but it was too late! After that any settling was gone…
>
> (Kerry, foster carer, Family 9)

The carers felt that they had to be open with the children about the placement arrangements. However, when the proposed move did not materialise the carers found themselves unable to retrieve stability and the placement broke down altogether. What we can detect from such glimpses into placement uncertainty and drift is that time itself has a much under-recognised and subtle effect (as highlighted by Sinclair 2010). The placement arrangements for most of our families had de facto become long term and were then officially regularised as such. In summary, there are all manner of complex and sometimes unintended effects that underpin stable placements. For example, it is clear that carer qualities (motives, beliefs, parenting styles), and external support (material, financial and emotional) from foster agencies are essential foundations for placements lasting as long as intended to meet the child's care plan. It is also evident that time itself plays a hidden part when placements unexpectedly become long term and mutual relationships of care and attachment deepen over many months and shift profoundly the meaning and purpose of the placement.

Conclusion

This chapter has aimed to illuminate the background of these families, their motivation to foster, their underlying value systems, their cultural histories and the important roles of both female and male carers. The chapter considered the idea of the gift relationship and its relevance to fostering and noted that whilst some saw fostering as an occupational and remunerated role, all were motivated by a sense of altruism, of wanting to give something back to society, but always, and importantly, they described 'caring about children' as a commitment underwritten by heartfelt emotion rather than some more distanced contractual obligation (see also Ribbens McCarthy et al. 2003). Two of the male carers, who recalled their own childhoods in care, particularly wanted to help ameliorate some of the negative experiences that young people may have had before being looked after as well as during their time in care. There were some differences amongst the families about whether they saw their relationships with the children placed with them as best defined as 'love' or as based more upon a strong sense of positive regard. Certainly all saw children and their interests (birth and foster) as their prime focus.

The families in this study greatly valued care and care giving and most had a family history of care giving as informal or paid work. Several had worked in social care roles in the past and/or had relatives who did or who were foster carers. They were all experienced carers. The role of the male carer was seen as particularly significant. They were deemed by their partners and fostered children to be playing prominent and approved roles in providing domestic and activity-based care, and this will become more evident in the chapters that follow. Finally, the hidden histories of care and commitment in these placements were played out against an institutional backdrop of support and training, but also the unintended consequences of placements shifting across ill-defined boundaries between short and long term. The implications of time itself, of relationships deepening over months and years, while so obvious at one level, seems to have exerted its own independent and not altogether recognised effect in the evolution of attachment and identity in these placements. Thus a process was at work whereby children first placed short term were more likely to be cared *for* by the carers, but as the placements moved longer term the children became cared *about*. The children were no longer *others* but *ours*.

In the chapter that follows we turn to the question about how children learn their place in the family – that is, how they move from stranger/outsider to member/we, someone valued in their own right as part of the family. We address this question by exploring how food and its preparation reveals all manner of messages and meanings about the relationship between the fostered child and the foster family. We also look at the social organisation of mealtimes and the ways in which communal eating provides insights into parenting styles, attachment and family membership.

CHAPTER 5

Food, Fostering and Family Life

'There won't be no sprouts at Judith's this Christmas!'

Introduction

> Homo sapiens are the only species to ritually prepare and eat its
> food. All other species eat it where they find it. The community
> preparation, cooking and eating as a family or tribe is common
> for every civilisation in every country in the world, from the dawn
> of men to the present generation in the developed West. We lose
> these cooking and eating rituals at our peril. (Leith 1998, p.59)

In this chapter we explore the meanings and activities associated with
food and mealtimes in order to illuminate how the families nurture
children and signify their inclusion in the foster home. It will be seen
that the families displayed many of the principles of good parenting
through their approach to food, particularly warmth, responsiveness
and consistency. In this way they engendered a sense of membership
and belonging to the child. Food is not much discussed in fostering
or social work literature. Nor is it widely addressed in social science
given its centrality to everyday life (see Douglas 1998; Morgan
1996). More generally, there is believed to be a strong link between
child and adolescent wellbeing and families eating together which
is thought to lead to fewer behavioural problems, more trusting and
helpful relationships and higher life satisfaction (Elgar, Craig and
Trites 2013). Within fostering, however, food is seemingly so taken
for granted that it does not merit much attention, yet as Leith notes
above, we should not ignore the fundamental significance of food

preparation and consumption. It is to this under-researched domain in the foster family that we now turn.

The symbolic nature of food and 'doing' family

Food has a social and symbolic significance, particularly insofar as it involves the relationships of those who partake in the ritual of sharing meals (Douglas 1984; Emond *et al.* 2013). Anthropologists have suggested that the sharing of meals is a ritual process which sets boundaries of inclusion and exclusion, and thus expresses the identity of the group which eats together (Brannen *et al.* 1994). Mennell *et al.* (1992, p.115) note that those who eat together are also often tied to one another by friendship and mutual obligation: 'Sharing food is held to signify togetherness, an equivalence that defines and reaffirms insiders as socially similar'. Mealtimes not only allow families to enact and display family life but are an everyday event through which people recognise themselves as 'family' (Ashley *et al.* 2004; Finch 2007). It is important therefore to explore how foster families typically eat together and the significance of this for belonging and membership.

Mealtimes construct and shape key moments in daily family life. Children typically learn to structure their understanding of time through the eating of food, thus 'the cycle of breakfast, lunch and supper is the first framework into which they slot their waking experiences' (Ennew 1994, p.129). While food preparation and partaking of meals can create or reinforce unity within family groups, they may also be a site around which differences and conflict are expressed. Brannen *et al.* (1994, p.151) note that struggles over food choices and mealtimes can be a way to resist family conventions or adult influence and that conflicts about eating can be associated with 'young people's sense of powerlessness in respect of family events and situations which make them unhappy'. By contrast, catering to children's 'faddiness' can be seen as part of spoiling and being an indulgent parent. Indeed, we shall soon see that this so called 'spoiling' can be valuable in engaging with the foster child and establishing their sense of worth and inclusion.

Young people's food preferences were often seen by carers in terms of 'food personae' (Brannen *et al.* 1994), that is, those habits and preferences which are seen as an intrinsic part of a young person's identity. We all have a particular history of relationships to food that include our likes and dislikes; similarly in the foster home the food preferences of the child become part of a process of their recognition as an individual. Thus responding to the foster child's preferences can act as a source of affirmation which oils the wheels of family relations and helps embed the foster child's position in the family. Such adaptation might not be appropriate in relation to all food preferences or to all family circumstances but seemed to be functional in the way the families in our study operated. Families seemed to be able to strike a balance between indulgence and providing a tailored response to the needs and desires of the child who in turn adapted to the routines and conventions of the foster home, thereby generating harmony. As Mennell *et al.* (1992, p.107) succinctly observe, 'feeding children gets caught up in loving and pleasing them, expressed by, among other things, acquiescence to their demands for one food rather than another'.

Mealtimes also are a means whereby most children learn family and cultural norms such as table manners; meals then are a socialising process in which children become normalised into domestic and societal eating regimes. Of course attempts to regulate children at mealtimes through the conventions of table manners are not always successful. Morgan (1996, p.162) links this process of learning the rules of mealtimes to wider aspects of social control, of the 'civilising' process itself:

> Feeding the child is never a single-stranded operation but involves wider issues to do with deferred gratification, order and control, generational differences and parental rights and obligations.

Gender too is an important factor in our relationships with food. Purchase and preparation of food has traditionally fallen on the shoulders of women (Morgan 1996; Murcott 1980, 1983). That said, Brannen *et al.* (1994) note that families differ markedly over the control of the menu and the timing and regularity of meals. It was evident from our study that most families ate together with the fostered young people being both listened to and contributing to the food agenda. However, the mothers (as is more generally the case) played a leading role in relation to matters of food quality linked to their views of health and goodness concerning the meal in question

(Mennell *et al.* 1992, p.107). Food then is central in regard to domestic roles and relationships and often settles inequitably around the female carer/mother who typically is the one who prepares and serves the food (see Greishaber 2004). In short we can note that eating together is typically linked to particular roles, obligations and expected conduct. It can also be a particularly powerful way of incorporating new household members and can help develop a sense of cohesion among reconstituted families.

Food and the foster families

Food was one of the most commonly raised themes emerging often unprompted in our interviews with children and adults and also from the audio diaries they completed about their day-to-day experiences in the foster home. Children (fostered and birth) especially talked about the type and amount of food consumed. Food and mealtimes helped them understand the structure of the day and seemed to greatly enhance their enjoyment of the day too:

> I had a gorgeous dinner when I got home; I had fish and chips... After dinner we had some chocolate chip ice cream.
>
> (Audio diary, Helen, birth child, Family 1)

Another child recorded her enjoyment of food to which the foster carer had introduced her. She spoke with enthusiasm about trying new foods and developing her food palate:

> We had spaghetti and salad all mixed up. We had coleslaw in a dish and cottage cheese – that was nice 'cos Liz got me on that.
>
> (Audio diary, Melonie, foster child, Family 1)

Other young people in different families also noted this change in their food repertoire; for example, Candice, foster child in Family 3, spoke of past and new foods:

> Researcher: So you know how to make spaghetti bolognaise. Is that the kind of food you were used to eating?
>
> Candice: No.

Researcher: What were you used to eating?

Candice: Chips, food in the deep fat fryer.

Researcher: You had lots of chips?

Candice: Yeah, we used to have chicken nuggets…

(Candice, foster child, Family 3)

Candice had also become involved in food preparation and was beginning to develop an enjoyment of and interest in food. It was quickly evident how the enjoyment of food and the partaking of meals featured as key moments in their day. Of importance in all this was the matter of choice, routine and the preparation of food. First we turn to choice.

Choice

Giving children choice about food was seen as important by carers and children. It was also seen as something that facilitated the process of entry and settlement in the family. The following excerpt from an interview with a birth child talking about how she helps foster children feel at home makes the point quite simply:

[When a new child comes to stay]…I like to find out what they like doing, what they like to eat…

(Megan, birth child, Family 3)

Likewise another child talked about providing hospitality for a newly arrived foster child as a means of displaying acceptance and warmth:

I speak to them…make them drinks, biscuits and that…

(George, birth child, Family 6)

Birth children appreciated the importance of food and wanted to play their part in ensuring that a foster child was made to feel a sense of welcome and membership. Carers were deliberate in their use of choice to signal interest and care when children first arrived:

When Lilly first came, I said 'What do you like? I like pizza, but what do you like?' So it softens the blow a bit. Food is important to give them what they like. You got to take it, these kids have been uprooted into foster care, just dropping on somebody's doorstep. Imagine if it was kids of mine. You got to give them what they like...

(Julie, foster carer, Family 10)

Knowledge of the child's food preference (their food personae) was part of getting to know a child and catering for their needs. Indeed it was evident that all the carers, to varying degrees, were catering for the food preferences of the children in their care and often changing their own eating habits to accommodate them. Mennell *et al.* (1992, p.108) note that those who cook 'privilege the choice of family members over their own'. Judith (Family 7) talked about her foster child, Suzanne, who eats vegetables with much reluctance, to the extent that a forthcoming Christmas lunch was to be free of brussel sprouts as a special treat for Suzanne. Judith laughingly recounted that her friend Bessie had been astonished by what she saw as an indulgent departure from tradition: 'Bessie says there won't be no sprouts at Judith's this Christmas!'. Whilst the carer recounted this with humour, it was nonetheless the case that festive norms and expectations in this household had been adjusted to accommodate the foster child. The carer observed later in the interview and again with humour: 'sometimes I think it's her home, not mine!'

What was demonstrated above and in other interviews was the willingness of most carers to seek out and meet food choices of the young people and often to sacrifice their own preferences. These tangible demonstrations of care served a range of intended purposes around warmth and membership but stemmed primarily from the impulse of care and giving that defined the parenting approach of carers across the sample.

Routine and preparation

The significance of food routines for the child coming to a foster placement were frequently noted by children and adults. When Candice talked about her first day in the foster home she recalled being asked to take part in the preparation of food and how this had become a memorable and important ritual that continued for some years:

> I remember Grandma [foster carer's mother] here, she lived just round the corner and every Thursday she used to make pasta round here. She was doing pasta for us when [the day] I came.
>
> (Candice, foster child, Family 3)

A carer spoke of clear responsibilities with regard to mealtimes that in her view helped promote a sense of expectation and reciprocity:

> They [the foster children] take it in turns to lay the table, clear away and put things in the dishwasher.
>
> (Dawn, foster carer, Family 2)

Likewise, Nadia, the foster child in the above family, remarked upon the routines that occur with regard to the partaking of meals:

> Yeah. We've all got our own seats, mine is there, Dawn sits there, Libby there, Jake there etc. You have what you feel like. We say we don't mind; we don't all like vegetables but we do all have soya.
>
> (Nadia, foster child, Family 2)

While individual food personae were often catered for, it was also the case, as Nadia observes, that mealtimes were a time where particular conduct and contributions were established and normalised. Thus mealtimes entailed:

> Manners, respect. Everyone, every week takes turn to set the table and clear away, like say if it was my turn I'd be doing it just before dinner and someone dries and someone washes up.
>
> (Nadia, foster child, Family 2)

Thus as with Greishaber (2004), we can see the significance of clearly defined expectations around food, mealtimes, preparation and clearing up of the dishes as part of being socialised into roles, identities and membership, a 'civilising' process so to speak. For the foster child such processes are profoundly important in establishing a sense of worth, belonging and acceptance.

Regularity of food

The regularity of mealtimes was a reassuring and comforting structure for some young people which made them feel safe and cared for. Ashley *et al.* (2004, p.124) note the importance that is attached to food because it is symbolic of the significance and respect paid to the consumers of the meal: 'home cooked meals are seen as imbued with warmth, intimacy and personal touch which are seen as markers of the personal sphere'. There is an emotional 'warmth' to food that can signify responsive parenting and reinforce a sense of care and belonging. In eating the food that has been prepared for them, children implicitly display their appreciation of what has been provided. For example, Callum, foster child with Hazel, described how she catered for his food needs and how this experience denoted a significant change in his sense of wellbeing. He appreciatively observed:

> Dinner – regular 6.30. Almost like clockwork! Food is very important. I do have a very good appetite and that has only happened since I came here. I never used to be able to finish one helping of food and now I can finish about five...Hazel is a really good cook. I do have a miles better appetite here than I do anywhere. When I go out to a restaurant I can eat but when Hazel puts on Sunday lunch and if there is any left overs, I pile them on my plate.
>
> (Callum, foster child, Family 8)

Carers too expressed their feelings of affirmation when the young people enjoyed their food and perceived the child's appreciation as a form of reciprocity. Thus carers, such as Josie below, felt that they were rewarded for the effort and care that went into meal preparation:

> I like Stu's [foster child] appetite: he enjoys his food and says please and thank you whereas Thomas [stepson] tends to just pick and eat what he wants to. He doesn't seem to appreciate the work that has gone in to it, or the thought that has gone behind it. The difference in the two lads!
>
> (Josie, foster carer, Family 4)

This notion of food preparation as a demonstration of affection is one in which foster children can also participate. For example, Josie enthused about a snack made by Stu (foster child) for the family and in the extract below reveals how she too was appreciative of the unprompted effort he put into preparing the food. Thus food and its preparation can be a two-way opportunity to express intimacy and belonging between vulnerable children and their foster families:

> Stu was very thoughtful, out of the blue he made us all nice sausage sandwiches with brown sauce, oh that was delightful, and a cup of tea, and it was very, very well received that was.
>
> (Audio diary, Josie, foster carer, Family 4)

Access to food

The fostered child's access to food in the foster home on a day-to-day basis was seen as important by most carers. They described how important it was for the young people to feel free to take food items (such as biscuits, fruit, cake) themselves and not seek permission, thereby giving them some control over their own eating. It was evident from interviews that for several of the children food had been a troubling aspect of their past. This was because they simply had not had enough food, or sometimes too much access to unhealthy meals. In either event most had a history of households where they could not anticipate there would be a reliable supply of good food. Such experiences are likely to be linked to neglectful parenting (see Hamil 2007) and Callum (Family 8) described at length how his birth family contrasted with the foster home over this very basic matter of a decent meal eaten in comfort:

> I used to have to eat very quickly because if I didn't there would be hands in, nicking bits of food because there was so many of us, six of us [children] living in one house. We grew accustomed to each other and so we used to fight for food and stuff because there was never enough sausage and chips and stuff. Now I don't have to fight for the food but I still eat very, very quickly. Now I've never had it so easy, I get twice as much and I don't have to fight for it.
>
> (Callum, foster child, Family 8)

In the same way that inconsistent parenting can cause unhappiness and insecurity for a child (Bowlby 1969), so inconsistent provision of food can generate anxiety for children. In summary it is evident that foster carers can exploit the therapeutic potential that resides around the preparation and consumption of regular well-cooked and tasty food which can help a child become more trusting and receptive (see also Slater 2004).

Communication

The 'proper' meal is at a table, it is 'shared and promotes sociability and talk' (Ashley *et al.* 2004; see also Elgar *et al.* 2013). Family talk is part of a family eating together, in which mealtimes become a place and time for positive family conversation and interaction. For many of us 'memories of the kitchen are memories of gatherings around the kitchen table, of smells of cooking, and of the sound of chatter and laughter' (Craik 1989, p.48). In our study, eating together was a routine but important means of communing and interacting for all families. Eating together offers an opportunity for parents to show an interest in the child's day (Fisher and DeBell 2007) and nearly all the carers and children commented on how they looked forward to the sharing of stories and new experiences at mealtimes. In his diary, one foster child eagerly anticipates sitting down at the dinner table so that he can discuss recent events:

> And now I am waiting for tea to be ready, which is good then we can sit down and talk about what happened today...
>
> (Written diary, Stuart, foster child, Family 4)

The young people and carers frequently commented that meals were an important time when they could share news, concerns, problems and, sometimes, secrets:

> Over dinner we had a little chat because some people in my class are misbehaving.
>
> (Audio diary, Candice, foster child, Family 3)

> We have a small forum every evening after school, we all sit down with biscuits and coffee. Everyone talks about their day and the difficulties they have had…we also talk every evening over the dinner table.
>
> (Steve, foster carer, Family 6)

> We basically get together and sort it out, in the kitchen over the table while having food.
>
> (George, birth child, Family 6)

> We sit at the table and we have to spill it all out when we've got a secret.
>
> (Nadia, foster child, Family 2)

More tactically, Hazel (carer, Family 8) noted that the dining table offered an ideal opportunity to address any pressing matters as those there were a captive audience who wanted their food, and would have little choice but to stay at the table and discuss issues:

> The evening meal is the one time we are all together. The family meal on a Sunday is a good time to talk to the whole family too. They are sitting targets then once the food is on the plates, they are not going to leave!
>
> (Hazel, foster carer, Family 8)

Sunday lunch: a movable feast

The Sunday lunch became second only to the traditional family Christmas dinner as a symbol of the emergent nuclear family of the post-war era and a key aspect of its intimate domestic rituals. While this Sunday tradition is thought to be in decline in recent decades (Hill 2007) most of the participants in this study spoke of its continuing significance, and the practice of the family gathering for this event:

We always sit at the table for Sunday lunch and everyone gets together.

(Lilly, foster child, Family 10)

We have a cooked dinner every Sunday.

(Candice, foster child, Family 3)

This idea of a 'cooked dinner' is still likely to resonate with a sizeable element of the UK population that views a proper Sunday meal as containing meat, vegetables and gravy (see Ashley *et al.* 2004). While the timing of the meal and those in attendance varied across the sample, the food ritual did not. For example, Hazel comments in her audio diary about those attending Sunday lunch and she accounts for those who cannot come. The assumption is that the extended family will join for lunch, unless there is a pressing reason not to:

Sunday is a family day. The family comes and goes. Jim [one of her sons] is working, so Larry and Carmel [close family] will come up for Sunday dinner. My daughter comes for the day every Sunday. My son doesn't come this weekend because he is busy getting the nursery ready for the new baby.

(Hazel, foster carer, Family 8)

In another audio diary, Josie notes the additional significance (and the added burden) of preparing the Sunday meal. Here she notes that it remains a time-consuming task despite advancements in cooking technology:

Reflecting back on the day, I'm amazed how long it took to fill up the whole day cooking dinner for everybody. Amazing you can cook the tea on weekdays and it takes 20 minutes, an hour at most. Sunday you spend all blooming day doing it. Anyway we had a nice chicken roast dinner.

(Josie, foster carer, Family 4)

We can see how important it is for Josie to feel that the time and effort is appreciated. She went on to note that it was a peaceful day as everyone ate well. For Josie it was the preparing, the eating and the communing that contributed to the harmonious atmosphere in the house on that day. That responsibility for such events fell typically to female foster carers was notable. In summary, major events in the foster families were celebrated with food. This was noted by most respondents when discussing birthdays, Christmas and anniversaries. The coming together of the family, the 'doing' of family through such celebration was of much significance in the way foster children came to feel part of the group. The foster child has to learn the rituals and expectations of the family and while food has the potential to be a harmonising factor in the process of joining the family it can also be a site for conflict, as is explored next.

Conflict

Greishaber (2004) argues that eating regimes can be interpreted as disciplinary techniques through which families and the individuals within them are socialised. As Greishaber notes, 'the pervasiveness of normalisation processes is exemplified by the way in which these processes, once established, exert such control over the body that persons become self regulating' (2004, p.123). However, conflict can also be created or maintained around the partaking of meals. Mealtimes can provide a site for resistance and can generate frustration for all parties concerned. Thus the way in which carers chose to manage the family eating experience was important; for example, some foster children recalled unpleasant experiences in previous foster homes over the consumption of food:

> In my old house you had to eat everything, every scrap of food. Here they just say leave it...
>
> (Lilly, foster child, Family 10)

Her current carer allows her to leave food and this was seen as caring and helpful by the young person although clearly food intake will in some cases have to be regulated by carers. For example, Rachael describes trying to find a happy medium between getting the young person, Chris, to eat well but not gorge himself. His fluctuating appetite and compulsive eating, while a matter of concern and monitoring by the foster carers and social worker, had an external public dimension as both carers observed:

Dinner time he ate like a double portion of lunch which isn't something that he does very often, he tends to eat less rather than more. So on the one hand it's a good thing to see him eating well, on the other hand you wonder what is going on when he eats so much… I was really nervous that he was going to vomit on the [restaurant] table where we were because he has done that in the past…

(Rachael, foster carer, Family 5)

Here, Rachael describes finding it difficult to be out with Chris in public because of his eating habits; she is clearly pleased that he is eating well as he usually eats very little, but he vacillates between extremes and struggles to find a balance. Rachael's partner, Mark, in his audio diary, elaborates on this theme of difficulty over public displays of eating and the lack, as he sees it, of appropriate behaviour:

Yesterday was quite an important date for us and Chris because it's an anniversary. He'd been with us exactly a twelve month yesterday so what we did we went to [town] and…we used that as an excuse to go shopping and then we had a lovely meal with him but even there – his behaviour. He didn't seem to have any social skills, like he'd leave the table half way through his meal, then come back and finish off. As I say no social skills at all, so that was quite a revelation, I hadn't seen it that pronounced before. And his eating – I know they haven't been taught or they haven't been taught any social stuff at all, but it's amazing that I've noticed with these children the difference between nature and nurture. If you don't tell your child anything they don't learn and these children haven't been told and so they don't learn. A lot of the social skills we take for granted are what we glean from our parents from the people around us and if you haven't got that in your life you are losing out.

(Mark, foster carer, Family 5)

It is particularly evident from this excerpt that Mark's use of the term 'these children' seems to mark them as somehow 'other' or 'different' to most children, and contrasts notably with much of the inclusive language used by other carers in this study. Mark invokes this trip to the restaurant to share his personal views about 'nature and nurture' on behaviour, again stressing the significance of expected behaviour at meals as a measure of a socially competent young person. Whether we agree with such a view, it has long been the case that meal settings have been the site for adults transmitting their idea of appropriate conduct for children as part of a wider socialising process (see Bell and Valentine 1997; Morgan 1996). Implicitly or explicitly it is within the remit of fostering to attempt to socialise children with regard to acceptable norms of behaviour around meals and food.

Eating out in public means that the family and its fractures and differences may also be on show for others to see. The experience of not being fed regularly can create significant emotional responses in children. The warm, satiated sensation of being full and content will not be one that some fostered children associate with food. They may well draw on their negative experiences and anticipate that mealtimes will be chaotic. They may find it difficult therefore to react positively to eating and meal conventions until they can be certain that the food will keep coming, and that their needs will be met. Thus a child may seek to reject or disrupt mealtimes in order to avoid the anticipated disappointment.

The regularity and consistency of providing sufficient, good and appropriate food will therefore be of vital importance for the foster child, even if it is not well received in early weeks and months. Care and preparation of food conveys the message that a child merits special attention and that they may in fact be worthy of love (Hamil 2007). Children may have special desires with regard to food which may to some extent be indulged to reinforce the message of self-worth. All of the carers in this study appreciated this aspect and would not insist that children ate food to which they were in some way averse. This did not entail a free rein for children with regards to food choice but a certain flexibility and responsiveness.

In most of our homes, meals are usually confined to a particular area within the home, the kitchen or the dining room; snack times are more variable in their location. Children are often required to remain in one place to eat so as to enable oversight by parents. Judith comments on Suzanne and her eating habits and a tendency to snack rather than wait for a more substantial meal. She has imposed restrictions for Suzanne thus:

Today now like she came in from school, she went into the cupboard with crisps, I said 'you are not having them.' 'Why?' 'Cos you are going to have your tea.' She said 'but I'm not hungry.' I said 'that is great then you don't need crisps.' I think she used to eat a lot of rubbish, where I won't have it. She could come and eat three bags of crisps, I wouldn't mind as long as she had had her [proper] food.

(Judith, foster carer, Family 7)

Suzanne is not denied access to food and is allowed to snack once she has eaten her main meal. Eating then was a vehicle for many family-affirming events in this study. Meals provide sustenance, for demonstrating care, for bonding and allegiances, for celebrating, for communing and communicating, for expressing and for managing conflict, for socialising and, as importantly, an opportunity to display acceptance and appreciation of the providers of the meal by those who consume it. It is clear that the therapeutic function of food could be further explored in relation to family care more generally (Elgar *et al.* 2013). Food has the potential on many levels to create a warm, physical and satisfying experience. We conclude therefore with an extract from Slater's (2004) chronicles of his own childhood recalled partly through his relationships with food. It poignantly summarises a glimpse of childhood that many foster children might not ever have experienced and eloquently reinforces the message of this chapter about food, love and belonging:

My mother is scraping a piece of burned toast out of the kitchen window, a crease of annoyance across her forehead… My mother burns toast as surely as the sun rises each morning. In fact, I doubt if she has ever made toast in her life that failed to fill the kitchen with plumes of throat-catching smoke. I am nine now and have never seen butter without black bits in it. It is impossible not to love someone who makes toast for you. People's failings, even major ones, such as when they make you wear short trousers to school, fall into insignificance as your teeth break through the rough, toasted crust and sink into the doughy cushion of white bread underneath. Once the warm, salty butter has hit your tongue, you are smitten. Putty in their hands. (Slater 2004, p.1)

This notion of 'putty in their hands' made possible through food that symbolises care is highly relevant in relation to our thinking about how foster children may be helped to overcome the difficult trials and tribulations that face them.

Conclusion

In this chapter we have sought to demonstrate key family practices and parenting styles in relation to food. Caring is demonstrated through the preparation and provision of food. Food is a neglected topic in much fostering literature and merits more focus with regard to how best to help a child settle into a foster home and be incorporated within the family network. The child becomes part of the enactment of family by their very doing of a communal activity such as a shared meal. Mealtimes can both articulate social relations in a home and define the boundaries between household members and outsiders. Family meals therefore have the potential to define the foster child as an accepted insider.

While this chapter has focused upon the social and emotional significance of food it has implicitly invoked eating as a self-evidently important bodily practice (see Bell and Valentine 1997). We now turn to this notion of bodily practices and in the chapter that follows we explore aspects of the physical in the foster home. These will include matters such as hygiene, washing, touch, privacy and space and the way these areas of intimate family living shape relations in the foster home. The foster child, as a stranger, must learn the family 'rules' about these matters of the physical body in order to become and remain a welcome and cared-for member of the household.

FOOD, FOSTERING AND FAMILY LIFE: KEY MESSAGES

- Food plays a vital part in developing, cementing and sustaining foster care relationships.

- It is important for carers to learn about the food personae (choices, preferences) of each child placed with them.

- Children should be involved in all aspects of meal preparation and in cleaning up afterwards.

- The regularity and sufficiency of meals is very helpful for those who have previously experienced neglect.

- Having rules about mealtimes which apply to all are helpful and clear for a young person.

- Eating together as a family has significant benefits for young people in regard to emotional wellbeing.

- Eating together around a table aids more natural communication between young people and their carers.

- Involving foster children in family celebrations and meals is vital in helping foster children gain a sense of belonging.

- There is a foster care recipe book produced by TACT 'Care to Cook' (2013) and a Picnic Guide in Fostering Network's 'Fostering Adventures' (2014).

- Food and mealtimes can also be a site for conflict and disagreement. As ever, flexibility and patience are essential in overcoming a child's past neglect or harm that lead children to disrupt at mealtimes.

CHAPTER 6

Foster Care and the 'Body'

She just loves being cuddled now. Suzanne was never like that but now I often give her a cuddle. I tug her hair a little bit, playful you know and she loves it.

Introduction

In this chapter we examine the domestic world of fostering with particular regard to the body, the boundaries around it and related aspects of intimacy in foster home settings. We use the term 'embodied' in this chapter to denote a focus upon the physical body and the way this impinges upon relationships, particularly in regard to physical care, nurturing, touch, cleanliness, privacy and personal territory in the families we studied. In short, we aim to illuminate key elements of the embodied world of fostering, a topic not much researched to date. There has been an increased focus by social scientists on body matters relating to children in recent years and the importance of embodiment is now increasingly recognised as a means to discover much more of the ways in which children actively participate in social life (Aitken 2001; Morgan 2011; Prout 2000; Shilling 2013). Indeed, the emphasis within much contemporary social science is on children as active creators of social life and of childhood itself as full of transformations and reversals, rather than being some linear progression towards an ever closer copy of adulthood (James and James 2004).

By contrast, notions of the body and embodiment seem rarely explicated in social work assessment materials and debates, nor much invoked in social work's professional standards and procedures. Yet the body and related areas were prominent in most of our interviews and audio diaries in this study, particularly those involving the children. In examining this data and analysing its relevance for our understanding of foster care we have drawn upon sociological sources (Douglas 1989; Shilling 2013) as well as on social work literature (Chase *et al.* 2006; Piper *et al.* 2006) to draw out additional themes around the body in relation to gender, appearance, boundaries and bodily transgressions.

Usually in foster care, the child as a stranger becomes a family intimate in a relatively short time. It is often taken for granted that the child as stranger can enter a family with relative ease and quickly come to understand the nuances of household relationships and negotiate the boundaries of interpersonal living in the confined space of the average family home. This settling into the family is rarely straightforward and much depends upon carers and their birth children being able to respond to the child and their often complex needs in ways that allow a trusting intimacy to develop. It is this recognition and careful consideration by the foster family of ways of dealing with intimacy and body issues that contributes to a successful placement (Holland and Crowley 2013). We start by looking at the everyday ways in which basic aspects of bodily comfort and care can mean so much to the fostered child.

Bodily comfort and nurturing

The symbolic nature of bodily care appeared to be very important for the children in our study, particularly for girls, and often arose in interview and diary data (see also Cameron and Maginn 2008). The ordered routine of personal, physical care provided by the families was both comforting and reassuring for the young people and they valued the nurturing aspects of this care. Whilst the physical care, protection and nurturing of children by parents or carers is fundamental to their wellbeing (Christensen 2000), it can be debated that not all children need intensive nurturing. That said, we would argue that foster children in particular are likely to need much nurturing and this may also mean they need to *learn* that they can be nurtured and to enjoy it. In turn they can then develop self-nurturing capacities as well as learning to nurture others. This much was evident from the data which revealed the critical importance of bodily care as a basic indicator of warmth and inclusion in the family. Family 1 provided a clear demonstration of this. The family home contained three girls (fostered, birth, adopted) and a male and female foster carer. Examples from the girls' audio diaries reflect the significance of bodily caring and a child's sense of security and comfort:

> Had a bath, now I'm going to sort out my clothes for tomorrow...I straightened my hair and it looks nice. I changed my belly bar.
>
> (Audio diary, Melonie, foster child, Family 1)

> My food was warm and delicious and the hot bath was lovely, especially when I lie listening to the rain. Thank you.
>
> (Audio diary, Helen, birth child, Family 1)

> Now I'm in bed and after dinner we had some chocolate chip ice cream. Then I went up for a nice warm bath and washed my hair. Then I done my teeth and went downstairs to say goodnight to my dad and then I jumped in bed and my dad and mum came up and said goodnight I am going to have a very nice sleep. Night, night.
>
> (Audio diary, Carla, adopted child, Family 1)

> Greg always puts Carla to bed on a Wednesday. He puts her cream on. Carla puts her own E45 on most of the time, but when her skin is bad we have to use steroids and she is not allowed to put this on. On a Wednesday Greg puts her to bed and I pop in and give her a kiss...
>
> (Audio diary, Liz, foster carer, Family 1)

As suggested in these diary extracts, it was the individualised and embodied routines of care for each of the girls that, irrespective of their being fostered, adopted or birth child, demonstrated to them a sense of warmth and belonging within a nurturing family environment. Similarly in another family a foster child talked about the organisation of washing routines and bodily care:

> He [foster carer] always makes us wash our hair and have a bath or a shower. We don't get out until we've done it, which is different

[from own family experience] really... I go in the bath first, then Libby gets in, then Jake. They are really strict about that.

(Nadia, foster child, Family 2)

Carers felt that boys also appreciated physical comfort and nurturing and the concern this expressed. Below a foster carer demonstrates her care for the young person, regardless of his recent difficult behaviour, by putting his physical needs first:

He returned [after running away] and he hadn't washed or anything... I said have a hot shower, look after yourself and go to bed because it looks as if you haven't slept for days.

(Hazel, foster carer, Family 8)

There were similar accounts from other carers about their emphasis upon physical care as a display of affection and concern despite worrying behaviour outside the home. Their emphasis on bodily care served far more than to maintain the body but acted as a clear indication of positive reassurance, as well as providing physical wellbeing and comfort – the underlying emotional message being that the child's needs were the prime interest.

Gender

Interviews, observation and audio diaries revealed frequently the salience of gender in the way that care was shaped and individualised. Some families tended to foster girls and preferred to do this; other families offered care mainly to boys. Families therefore provided what could be seen as a 'specialist' service in which 'gender fit' was very important. For example, the girls in this study clearly valued physical caring, especially that which enhanced their appearance, and this was recognised and built upon by the carers. It has long been known that clothing and gender are inextricably linked (Barnes and Eichler 1992) but we know relatively little about the way clothing in foster care impacts upon a child's sense of identity, worth and belonging.

Our study noted how carers consciously used clothing to demonstrate care but within the normative bounds of what they deemed appropriate from a traditional gendered perspective. For example, the carer below made particular reference to gender and the need for the female body to reflect a particular notion of femininity. Whilst this could of course be seen as some unreflective stereotyping by the carer, it has to be understood in the context of care giving within a family steeped in a culture, place and time that disposed them to such a view. The carer described a girl who arrived wearing 'scruffy, boyish' looking clothes, with her head shaved and with 'pitifully few belongings in a plastic bag'. The carer perceived a need for the girl to re-define herself and her appearance so that she could begin to find a secure and positive identity and to value herself. Promoting a sense of femininity and a feminine identity was for this carer an essential starting point:

> We grew her hair, we went out, we bought her new clothes, pinks and lilacs and, we got rid of everything from before and we went out and fitted her out in all the girl colours. I mean, we couldn't do anything with her hair, so we bought some slides and one thing and another and slowly she came to be this little girl.
>
> (Sally, foster carer, Family 3)

The girl, according to the carer, had made much progress whilst with the family and was looking to remain with them for the foreseeable future. Sally recounted a time when one rushed morning she had tried to get the young girl to wear a brown 'boyish looking coat' to school, when they could not find her usual one:

> ...she couldn't find her coat, sorry but maybe she had left it in school, so she needed a proper coat on to go to school and I took out this brown one and I said to her, 'there you are you can put this on', she said 'no!' I saw it in her face, 'put it on please, it won't hurt, it's only to go to school', she said 'no I don't like it...I don't want to go back to being a boy, I don't want to be a boy, I'm not a boy, am I? I'm not a boy'. I must say she was dreadful [upset], so I put that in the bin that day, let her see me put it in the bin, it must have reminded her of something in that anorak, reminded her of the past and all of a sudden she was going to turn back into what she was before, whatever that was.
>
> (Sally, foster carer, Family 3)

While we have no access to the child's history that may give us clues to her needs or her sense of gender preference before arriving with this foster family, it is clear however that carers can exert considerable influence over a child's unfolding identity, particularly in regard to gender and related matters of appearance. Thus there is an example here of embodied interventions by a carer which had allowed the child to acquire a sense of 'girlness' to which she was now attached. Similarly, a young person talked at length about the importance to her of a foster carer who understood her desire to be 'girly' and who provided a home setting for intimate encounters that helped create a preferred sense of gendered self. The following brief extract reveals something of the taken-for-granted nature of gender – of being a 'girl' – and the considerable reinforcing power that carers have in simply sharing particular gender conventions and attitudes:

> I always wanted a girly mum to share make-up and clothes, and to be able to talk to but I can't [with my mum]. Like with Dawn [carer] she really likes make-up.

> (Nadia, foster child, Family 2)

Children who are looked after in fostering or residential care need sound and regular advice about their emotional, physical and sexual wellbeing and there are useful examples of the sorts of issues they need help with (Minnis and Walker 2012). In our study, most of the girls were at the onset of puberty and menstruation where the need for a private, feminised space with a significant female role model (in the absence of a positive birth mother) was vital. Prendergast (2000, p.103), in her study of girls at the start of menstruation, found that they looked to their own mothers at this time. She observed how menstruation marks for girls '…an end to childhood and the re-mappings of bodily experience, meaning and value'. Such mappings are often done by girls alone, in isolation from their peers or other adult women, except for the mother. It is often an intense phase in the acquisition of gender and difference for girls and occurs in a world of mindfulness and closure as it is rarely discussed openly. Prendergast goes on to assert that girls feel quite different at this moment and often feel that they want to be quiet and alone. Mothers are the main source of information about menstruation and this time acts as an opportunity for 'protective discourse between mothers and daughters' (Prendergast 2000, p.103). Many young girls will be in the care system at the time of the onset of menstruation and will need this important personal discourse with a significant female whom they feel comfortable with; this might be the female carer or a female residential worker. Thought and preparation are required to enable a foster family to provide a young woman with the support required to handle this intimate embodied experience (Aitken 2001). Meanwhile at the same stage boys are growing in physical prowess, building strength and publicly demonstrating their changes and will also need a significant adult male to whom they can relate (see Fostering Network 2011). It was notable that none of the young people or carers spoke about aspects of their sexuality in interviews or in audio diaries. However, we know that young lesbian and gay people may face more difficulties with how others perceive their sexual orientation and attracting and supporting carers to meet their needs is essential (Cocker and Brown 2010; Cosis Brown 2014; Hind 2010). As noted earlier, our foster families assumed fairly traditional gendered identities and oriented their family practices accordingly.

Bodily adornment

The carers and their families in this study all put much store in providing clothing for the children placed with them. It was important to them that the children had clothing about which they could feel proud. Carers were particularly aware of how few garments some children had in the past, and the importance of promoting a positive self-image through appearance:

> He [arrived and] sat in the arm chair and he brought his stuff in a black bag. His stuff was junk. His clothes were rags. I thought I've got better rags than this. I felt sorry for him.
>
> (Hazel, foster carer, Family 8)

The conceptual division between the inside and the outside of the body so marked in social science literature (Simpson 2000) was mirrored in a way by the carers in that they saw their roles as divided between caring for the outer body through clothing, cleaning, grooming, touching, observing and monitoring and also nurturing the inner emotional and often vulnerable psyche. An (adult) birth daughter demonstrated this in her account of a foster child trying on new clothes:

She tried it on [a blouse] and liked it. One pair of jeans had to go back. She had a trouser suit but the trousers did nothing for her. She looked beautiful, gorgeous but I couldn't say it [that the trousers didn't suit her]. If she was more secure I could have said 'don't have the trousers'. I don't think she has had stuff [in the past]. I have a cousin who is 12, who I could say different things to her because she is more secure. I still like Suzanne [foster child] for who she is. We've built her up – we don't want to knock her down.

(Katie, adult birth child, Family 7)

Another carer describes the importance of appropriate clothing in the preparation for holidays:

Like we went to Butlins in February, and I took them into town before we went and they chose seven party outfits for the nights, seven different outfits, they choose their own...and Peter chooses all these mosher jeans, he wants to be a mosher now...he thinks he's cool...and the girls choose something that they wanted.

(Sally, foster carer, Family 3)

Choice and freedom to select clothes were not seen by carers as 'spoiling' foster children but as positive status-enhancing experiences. Boys too were appreciative of attention to the outer body through clothes, especially when their birth parents had not been able to provide much for them. The provision of clothing appeared to symbolise to the individual child that they were cared for:

They were the things that meant the most. I don't know I'd come home one day and there would be a new jumper or a hooded top or a pair of jeans on my bed if she knew I'd had a bad day...and clothes... Clothes tend to cheer me up. Just little gestures like that. It is always nice to feel wanted.

(Callum, foster child, Family 8)

One carer spoke of a foster child visiting their birth parent who would then sell the child's new clothes in order to raise money. This resulted in the child visiting home wearing older clothes which had little financial value. Young people talked about their previous experiences of having few and unfashionable clothes or having to share clothing, particularly those from larger families. They stated they enjoyed ownership of their own clothes in foster care and could choose what to wear. It made them feel independent and valued. This aspect of acquiring a more developed sense of self, of having choice and control, can be discerned in the following interview extract:

> In the end I was sharing my room with my cousin for about four years...and I get, well the biggest problem was sharing clothes with my cousins and stuff like that. Now I go in my wardrobe, every thing in the wardrobe, in the drawers and on the floor [laughs] is mine. I can wear what I want.
>
> (Callum, foster child, Family 8)

Carers whilst providing clothing also expected the foster children to respect and look after these. Thus attention to the exterior of the body while primarily expressing care and concern can also be a means of social control (Simpson 2000). A carer in his audio diary describes his frustration when a foster child does not comply with expectations about care of clothes and cleanliness:

> I say 'No Chris you can't wear those trousers, you can't wear that shirt, it's dirty. Where is that (other) shirt? Where are all of your clean shirts?' And they are all over the floor in the bedroom or just thrown over the chair.
>
> (Audio diary, Mark, foster carer, Family 5)

Thus for some carers the provision of clothing came with clear assumptions of its respectful upkeep; an intended inculcation of self-care and responsibility within the foster child. It was the provision and physical care of clothing that appeared to symbolise for children a world that was ordered and nurturing, and seemingly much appreciated by children in the study. In that regard, the attention to the exterior of the body can express care as well as social control. Also, the child's visible appearance is acted upon by others as it inevitably exhibits the status of parents (and carers too) and in that sense is a moral statement of adult achievements (Christensen 2000). By contrast, a child's appearance may also reflect the pathology of the family – pathology, in this context, being 'read' from the physical demeanour and clothing of the child. This point is made by Morgan (1996, p.128):

Bodily appearance stands for the social status and standing of the individual while that embodied individual also stands for or reflects the social status of the family from which she or he comes.

Thus it could be said that carers wanted the children to dress in a way which reflected their own sense of status in the community and would reveal to the outside world the sort of care which they were providing for the children in their family (see Finch 2007). However, it was not the status of designer labels on clothing that the participants in this research referred to, nor did carers seem overly acquisitive on behalf of their foster children. Rather, the provision of clothing was understood less as status but much more as representative of thoughtful nurturing and care. For example, one foster carer prided herself on the foster children being indistinguishable from her own in respect of their external appearance and consequently how others would be unlikely to guess who was their birth child and who was not:

> They never ever get it right. People who don't know us very well but know we foster, never ever once have got it right.
>
> (Sally, foster carer, Family 3)

Body boundaries

Rules around uncovering the body were explicit in all of the families in this study. The revealing of the body was often restricted to private space. Bedroom space was clearly delineated for example and all families had a rule that everyone knocked on a bedroom door before entering and in some families nobody entered anyone's bedroom. This was viewed as particularly pertinent when there were both boys and girls living in the home. One carer explained that this rule was so well inculcated within the children that on one occasion when she asked a foster child to go and get something from her bedroom, he was very reluctant to do so and asked for clarification.

Another family who had teenage daughters ensured that if they had a male foster child in the house, he would stay downstairs when the girls were changing or bathing and that the bathroom door would be locked (there had been an incident in the past when a young male foster child had inappropriately watched and tried to touch the girls). Matters of privacy and the gender of the foster child were conscious aspects of how families managed the domestic space. This was raised in different ways by children and adults across all the families:

> For a start you can't walk around in pyjamas like you would with your own child; making sure everyone has their bedroom door shut when they go to bed. It just comes natural; it is just part and parcel of life now…

> (Judith, foster carer, Family 7)

These rules, both explicit and tacit, impacted upon birth children too and inevitably influenced their behaviour in the domestic setting. For example, it is hard to imagine being as mindful of the body within one's home as the young respondent below:

> You can't just lay around in your pyjamas watching telly and eating chocolate.

> (Charlie, birth child, Family 6)

When questioned about this, Charlie stated that it was a basic if implicit rule that birth children did not reveal their bodies when foster children were present. He also stated he would be expected to share his chocolate, if it was seen by one of the foster children! A sense of risk or potential risk lay behind many of these often self-imposed and informal strictures that made the body a self-conscious object in day-to-day domestic arrangements. Another carer who had a young person placed with her, with a history of sexual offending, talked about managing that risk more explicitly, ensuring that even infants did not wander around without clothing:

> …a couple of our friends they've got very young children and they can sometimes go out of the border of safe care and not realise it. Like a year ago we had a little one running around… in the paddling pool and I said [to the infant's mother], 'Now I really think it's best that you put his pants on whilst he's doing that, seeing his bottom and things like that.' So they're the sort of things that you instil…all I can do is guide and watch.

> (Josie, foster carer, Family 4)

In brief, there are observances and practices that constitute a 'curriculum' for the body (Simpson 2000) and detail what kind of embodiment is acceptable within different situations. Some foster families had written rules which were posted in the home prescribing the covering of the body, such as wearing dressing gowns if going to the toilet at night:

> The bathroom, shower room are downstairs, please wear your dressing gown when going to and from the bedroom to those rooms, we don't want to frighten the cat. No worries flushing the loo in the night.
>
> (Excerpt from Josie and Philip's rules, Family 4)

It may be that all families have similar types of expectation at some implicit level, but rarely so clearly delineated as to be encoded and posted on the wall, as in some of the foster homes. In essence, however, schools and families are centres and domains for discipline and structure. Parents and teachers are in that sense experts in body management. Children are told how to dress appropriately and observe basic standards of hygiene within both the home and the school environment. For example, one particular family were caring for a young person who struggled to achieve their minimum requirements for bodily hygiene:

> The constant reference to 'have you cleaned your teeth?' 'Have you washed your face?' I find tiring.
>
> (Audio diary, Mark foster carer, Family 5)

Thus, young people had to learn the rules of engagement in order to fit in with domestic expectations that had accrued over years of family fostering, particularly with regard to the body and its careful management.

Touch

The covering of the body and the heightened sense of privacy in foster homes makes the question of touch an important topic of enquiry. Touch is vital for all people as reassurance and a means of communication. Yet because of the risk of abuse allegations (Minty and Braye 2001; Sinclair *et al.* 2004) and because of the bureaucratisation of the caring role, it may be that some children in foster care are rarely touched; however, this did not appear to be the case in this small study. It is of course important to remember that this is a study of successful fostering and for that reason the nature of touch as physical reassurance and affection was perhaps clearer and less risky. Also, the children themselves will have been judged by carers and birth children as less likely to view touch as an opportunity to allege some impropriety:

> Oh, he did ask for a cuddle after school, which is something that doesn't happen very often, so I gave him a little cuddle.
>
> (Rachael, foster carer, Family 5)

Here Rachael was responding to the child's request for a cuddle and, as for other carers, it was important to judge when such a demonstration of affect would be appropriate and appreciated. Foster children and birth children noted the importance of touch, signifying care and concern over and above that which had been anticipated:

> Just small things she said like um [when he was upset] letting me know that it would be alright, and comforting me and little gestures like hugging me...
>
> (Callum, foster child, Family 8)

The young people in placement were keenly aware that they could expect to be cared for from a physical perspective but were less clear about what to anticipate by way of demonstrations of affection through touch or play – they welcomed this when it occurred but were not sure they had a right to expect this. Those carers who were willing to enact affection in addition to good physical care were deemed by young people to be giving more than expected and to be demonstrating exceptional care. This was the case for boys and girls alike:

> He [foster carer Josh] is a real people-person. He is a very funny person and a very serious person as well. I found living with him he'd mess about 'do you want a fight' just messing around we just got on so well from the moment I came here. He was very hands on, he'd put his arms round me and stuff. Again gestures...

from both Hazel [carer] and Josh…with Hazel embracing…it would be when I needed it whereas with Josh it would often be as a friendly arm around. Hazel would be a motherly hug.

(Callum, foster child, Family 8)

Katie, an adult birth child [Family 7], comments on the development of her relationship with Suzanne:

…during the first 6–8 months, I wouldn't say that Suzanne and I had had a conversation. I tried very hard but nothing at all. Now she has started to talk to me. I don't know what works with her. She never really asks for anything. Some children want this, want that, she is not like that. I don't know what makes it work. She just loves being cuddled now. Suzanne was never like that but now I often give her a cuddle. I tug her hair a little bit, playful you know and she loves it.

(Katie, adult birth child, Family 7)

Above we have an adult birth child reflecting on how a foster child's sense of security and belonging has grown sufficiently to find physical touch safe and acceptable, and to learn to like the emotional nurturance that accompanies touch. By contrast, the social work profession has become much less likely to view touch as a means of reassurance to children within social care relationships. Piper *et al.* (2006) see this anxiety over touch as part of an occupational culture of fear about the body and about risk of allegation of impropriety.

Current social work practice can be viewed as inhibited by fear of accusation and litigation, rather than an over-riding concern for a child's emotional wellbeing (see Piper *et al.* 2006; Wilson *et al.* 2000). Gilligan (2000, p.67) too noted this fear of allegation when undertaking focus groups with male foster carers and observed that 'the risk of allegations being made against male carers was a frequently cited concern. It can rob the male carers' role and relationship of spontaneity'. Likewise, Inch (1999) in his study of male foster carers observed that fear of allegation led to a more limited physical contact with foster children. A few carers and notably one birth child in our study expressed similar concerns and referred to accusations made against them by foster children:

I've learnt from past experience never to touch or cuddle or anything with children. That came from the last placement when he was in one of his mad rages he decided to say that I'd restrained him.

(Sara, birth child, Family 5)

Many child-related settings have become 'no touch' zones, in case touch is misinterpreted or misunderstood. Touching is still nonetheless regarded as vital to children's emotional and physical development (Powell 2001). The discourse of fear in social work, the focus of which is often on abusive touch, may well distort fostering practice in that it diminishes the full potential of a nurturing intervention. Many children in the care system have come not to expect physical contact with their carers and this makes it difficult for them to express emotion. Indeed, one carer recollected when a child actually asked her 'why do people hug each other?'

Of course many of the children within the care system have experienced physical and sexual abuse and thus may be more anxious about touch, or, conversely, they may be in even more need of positive, physical touch and reassurance. Within foster care a young person may have been the victim of abusive touch and therefore vulnerable; a young person may also have been the 'abuser'. Thus, it would not be difficult to conceive of some fostering scenarios as arenas of mutual distrust and surveillance, whereby both child and carer warily suspect the motives of the other. This aspect of 'suspicious care' could potentially be very damaging in inhibiting a healthy approach to physical expressions of warmth. Much depends on experience and the 'learning' of others' motives and behaviours, both subtle and obvious. Within three of the families in our sample a fostered child was described as an actual or potential abuser, physically or sexually. In such a context, Sara (birth child, Family 5) saw her role as one of watchfulness and was keenly aware of risk:

You can't afford to take your eyes off John (the foster child), really...because of what can happen...I think with John I was the second pair of eyes for my mum, because he didn't have quite the same attachment to me as he did to Mum. I guess I learnt the skill of watching and I could read his face 'cos with him you could tell whether something bad had happened 'cos you could read his facial expression…just changes in facial expression because he could be so violent. You were always on guard really…

(Sara, birth child, Family 5)

Whilst this particular birth child had come to the view she should not touch or cuddle foster children, this was not typical as all of the carers (including her birth mother), and most birth children, had provided physical comfort and hugged foster children, despite previous unsubstantiated allegations having been made against some of them. Carers acknowledged the need to be selective with whom and when they would cuddle, thus, as ever, offering a tailored and individualised response to the children in their care. While positive touch can be beneficial it remains a challenging everyday aspect of care to be navigated albeit against a backdrop of official recognition that touch can be therapeutic (DfES 2002), yet at the same time it is widely perceived to be an area of uncertainty and potential risk (Piper et al. 2006). This problematic duality (touch or no touch) in regard to the body in foster care is explored further below.

Pets

Children in care may have been limited in their experiences of intimate touch for the reasons outlined above. It may be however that children had access to a different form of physical intimacy, that which can be derived from interaction with pets. It was interesting to note that nine out of the ten families interviewed had pets in the home. One family had photos of some of their pets included in the information about the family given to foster children when they first came to stay (the pets were anthropomorphised by speech bubbles introducing themselves and saying things like 'I love sleeping on Philip's chair'). Another carer, Rachael, when completing similar information, returned it with a cat's paw prints across the page which were circled and 'Foot marks by Ena' written alongside. Triseliotis et al. (2000), when describing the background and lifestyle characteristics of foster carers and their families, noted that as a group they tend to 'have more pets' than other families. Some of the children chose to place the pets in their eco-maps and they clearly played an important part in their affections. The significance of human–pet relationships in children's creation of family has been noted by Mason and Tipper (2006). Gilligan's (2007) analysis of the range of factors potentially increasing a young person's resilience included learning to care for a pet.

Children in foster care may have more physical contact and intimacy with pets in the home than with humans, as there are fewer boundaries around this type of touch and intimacy. Details about family pets will be important to be included along with the information about family members when matching a child with a family. Gabb (2007, p.6) notes that 'cross-species (human–pet) relationships remain on the periphery or are typically excluded altogether from intimacy research especially within the terrain of social theory'. She continues: 'pets join in and shape exchanges of affection'. This may not be the same kind of love one has for a person 'but it is nevertheless experienced as love and as such should remain within the intimate equation' (Gabb 2007, p.9). Cats, for example, sit on laps and sleep on beds, whilst dogs snuffle intimate places that would be out of bounds for anyone else. Data from interviews and observation would suggest that where physical touch and intimacy is restricted for a child, the presence of a pet takes on an even greater significance and many lessons can be learnt by children about the care of pets (Gabb 2008).

Likewise, carers have learned from experience that the presence of pets may not be without its difficulties and that some children may first need to learn about nurturing other living things before they can be given responsibility for looking after an animal:

> Yeah but the sunflowers, you see, what I'd done in the past was, you let one of these children have a pet, they don't look after them, so you end up looking after the pet, or they hurt it. So, what I tell them that they have to do, is grow a plant from a seed and then when the plant has got a flower it will mean that they're learning how to look after something, then they're allowed to have a small pet, so those are Chris' sunflowers that he's growing from a seed. They're teddy bear sunflowers and they're not well developed yet but when they come to plants, he's allowed to have a fish...
>
> (Rachael, foster carer, Family 5)

The emotional value of pets was self-evident in a number of the families and afforded intimate contact between the fostered child and another being. Burgon (2014) too has written much about the importance of the therapeutic relationships between young people at risk and animals. But often this physical comfort and intimacy could not be continued when a child leaves placement, leaving a significant gap in their lives. While there is much to discuss with regard to human–pet relationships we return briefly to our core focus on the body and its management in foster care.

Dirt and taboo

The use of the body within the foster home can be a means to express rebellion, rejection, or achieve some desired outcome (Simpson 2000). However, in dealing with difficult bodily matters most interviews with carers revealed their reluctance or inability to cope with those fairly rare behaviours that defiled the home. Social order is ultimately concerned with regulation and restraint of individual and collective bodies. For example, dirt essentially represents disorder (Prout 2000). Our notions of dirt and defilement are revealed through our conventions around hygiene and our respect for these conventions (Douglas 1989). Sacred things and places (such as our homes) are to be protected from defilement which would constitute a significant transgression. Such transgressions, or their potential, could be detected in the way carers often struggled with the dirt and lack of hygiene that some children exhibited. One described her difficulties when a young person in her care started to urinate inappropriately:

> His personal hygiene had gone down and with other things as well, he started wetting himself. He had hidden them – I picked them up, cups and cups of urine. It was terrible…he had hidden them, cups and cups of urine, and faeces as well. We had to redecorate afterwards…
>
> (Kerry and Mervyn, foster carers, Family 9)

Dirt exerts pressure on socially defined boundaries. Bodily orifices, together with the matter that may issue from them, are potent symbols of danger, pollution and taboo (Prout 2000). Simply by inappropriate production or lack of control over bodily fluids, people have transgressed the expected boundaries of the body (Grosz 1994). In fostering, such transgressions can severely test or break the normally resilient bonds of care and commitment:

> ...I won't take them if they do that, the smearing (of faeces), because my stomach won't take it and if my stomach won't take it, then I can't deal with myself to be able to deal with them. If a child had been here for a while and then started, then I would have to find a mode of help really for myself to be able to deal with it. ...I had one that used to, used to do it in bags and hide it under the bed...no, no I don't like that, I'm not up for that.
>
> (Rachael, foster carer, Family 5)

On the one hand, our bodies are inherently ordered and organised; on the other hand bodily seepages and discharge can create horror and disgust. Thus the body is always subject to surveillance, regulation and control by ourselves and others (Prout 2000). Indeed, the body of the child in care can be seen to be subject to particular surveillance through records and progress reviews that note achievements around developmental milestones (see Humphries and Kertesz 2012). Furthermore, soiling for example might well be construed by professionals as a sign of unhappiness and a cry for attention (Cohn 2007). Yet such interpretations based on some distanced clinical discourse about therapeutic or developmental need tell us little of how the foster family perceives these issues. Thus while children more generally are subject to a civilising process in which they learn the basic rules of bodily etiquette, some children in foster care may not have been subject to such socialising influences from their birth parents. Some have little understanding of hygiene norms, nor can they always interpret the behavioural codes signalled by foster families, some of whose members may well evince little sympathy for an unfortunate incomer whose bodily emissions are deemed inappropriate:

> You can't imagine what it's like to live with someone who you don't like, who is particularly difficult or smells or pees on the wall or whatever, you just can't imagine it until you actually have to live with them...
>
> (Sara, birth child, Family 5)

Such children whose bodies might be described as 'troublesome agents' in need of control (Christensen 2000, p.67) map well on to social science reflections about children polarised by society as either vulnerable or threatening (Jenks 1996). Such ideas resonate all too well with notions of children in public care, who on the one hand are vulnerable 'abused' children and on the other hand are potential abusers, who may defile the home and are challenging children who may sometimes make unwarranted allegations against the very people that care for them (Minty and Braye 2001; Sinclair *et al.* 2004). Foster children are often at the margins of society and at the margins of families; in this sense their bodily transgressions in respect of hygiene, obscenity, lawlessness and danger symbolise and reinforce their 'difference' and exclusion from the majority (see Douglas 1989). Such foster children are likely to be a small minority but their behaviour mark the limits for many carers about what can be tolerated within the intimate realm of the family.

Conclusion

Carers and birth children demonstrate much resilience in caring for the series of young people entering their homes. Likewise, fostered children too learn to cope and build trust in a home that is not of their making or necessarily of their choice. Central to this is the largely under-researched theme of the body, of the ways in which looked after children reveal themselves, are physically nurtured, touched, acquire identity and learn boundaries and sometimes, for a multitude of reasons, test and break those basic taboos that sustain our more intimate arrangements around shared habitation.

We now move on to examine aspects of space, place and time in the foster setting but from the perspective of the children only. This final chapter gives the last word to the young people – both birth and fostered – about the ecology of the foster home and the way it is understood and occupied by them on a day-to-day basis. This will reveal ways in which the foster child experiences a physical sense of family belonging as well as revealing something of the complicated dynamics that young people must learn and manage within the care setting.

THE BODY, NURTURING AND BOUNDARIES: KEY MESSAGES

- It is important to listen to the gender preferences of foster carers; some families are set up for or have far more experience of either boys or girls.

- Time spent by carers and fostered children doing gendered types of activities is often highly valued; this is especially important as young people navigate their path through puberty.

- Clothes and a choice of clothing is highly valued by foster children, to develop their individuality or to help them fit in. This is especially important where children have experienced neglect.

- Explicit boundaries and rules (for example, around the body) are seen as helpful by young people, to help ensure that they are not breaching the conventions of the family around privacy and intimacy.

- Touch is a vital aspect of human development and it is important that whilst we focus on safe care and risk reduction we do not as a result become touch averse. Guidance on touch can be found in Fostering Network's *Safer Caring: A New Approach* (2012).

- All the foster children in this study valued being given a cuddle and physical reassurance (touch) and saw this as a distinctive and valued aspect of the care experience.

- Having pets is as an opportunity for children to care for and nurture another living thing. This may well have therapeutic potential. Pets are also a means to generate positive touch and for the building of relationships and responsibility.

CHAPTER 7

Space and Place in the Foster Home

Views from the Young People

Now I go in my wardrobe, everything in the wardrobe, in the drawers and on the floor is mine.

Introduction

Space and place are very real and practical elements of daily living for all families but particularly so for the children in foster homes and this quickly became apparent during interviews and from analysing audio diaries. In this chapter we concentrate on the young people's experiences and ways of dealing with space. Aspects of space are particularly critical given that the fostering relationship necessitates the acceptance of an outsider into the very private confines of the home. This means that families need to create space both literally and emotionally for the 'strangers' coming into the home. Likewise, foster children too must quickly come to terms with the idea of moving into the private space of strangers, a daunting prospect as Nadia observed:

> If we had a choice to move in...er none of us would have. It's really hard to move in with strangers...
>
> (Nadia, foster child, Family 2)

Similarly, the experience for the birth child in a foster family can be challenging. They have to share their belongings, their space, their time, possibly their identity and indeed their parents with the incomers. Whilst many children have new infant siblings arriving in their families (usually after a pregnancy), they will often have time to emotionally prepare for the newcomer. Similarly with a reconstituted family, there may well have been a period of getting to know each other and the incoming children will be accompanied by their own birth parent and possibly their own siblings too. What we have in the foster family is a unique situation whereby a formerly unknown individual or group of siblings is incorporated into a household which will have its own distinct family practices within which the newcomer(s) will be expected to fit. Generally there is little time, if any, for extended introductions in order to get to know each other before a child moves in.

In this chapter we explore how the foster children in this study together with the birth children sought to live together harmoniously and with mutual regard. The foster child may have had a range of negative experiences in their own birth home and from other care settings and will likely be anxious in navigating yet another transition into the new foster family. In addition there is the likelihood that the child is not going to become a 'forever' bona-fide member as a birth or adopted child (Erera 2002). That said, some long-term foster children do become 'de facto' and 'as if' family members, deeply attached and accepted and in some instances adopted (see Biehal *et al.* 2010). Some foster children because of their personal histories may themselves pose a threat to members of the family and this risk needs to be managed. Much of the management of risk involves creating space – both physical and emotional – in order to reduce the opportunity for contest or conflict, as we shall see shortly.

For the most part, the young people being fostered did not see themselves as unwanted or as the object of suspicion or pity. Nor did most of them wish to be seen as some unhappy victim of circumstance which 'we' as carers and professionals might readily assume to be the case. For example, a foster child when asked during interview 'what are the important things that I should know about you?' replied 'I'm not sad!'. Another young person (finding himself at last in a safe and supportive environment) replied 'I've landed on my feet really!' Thus as George *et al.* (2003, p.356) note:

Foster care children are not merely statistics, or victims and thus objects of pity to be ministered to by individuals and organisations. They are also protagonists in their own right… It is for this reason alone that their views, as well as those who are close to them, should be taken on board in decision making about their lives and future.

The importance of the child's view in our grasping the quality of foster care cannot be underestimated (Wilson *et al.* 2004). Sinclair *et al.'s* (2000) study of young people in foster care revealed that their preoccupations were focused around five broad themes:

- the care they received from foster carers
- their sometimes conflicted feelings for the foster carers and for birth parents
- contact with and prospect of return to birth family
- the predictability of their care career and their own say in it
- the ordinariness of their lives or lack of it.

Sinclair *et al.* (2000) concluded that in order for services to respond to these sorts of concerns there is a need for clear, individual and flexible planning which promotes children's individuality and choices. An obvious example is where young people want to remain part of a foster household past the age of 18 and not have to leave the home and try to become fully independent until they are ready (see Boddy 2013; Munro *et al.* 2011; Rees *et al.* 2014; Welsh Government 2014). Indeed, most young people we interviewed were concerned to varying degrees about life stability linked to staying within the foster families until they were at least 18. The reasons for this are of course not difficult to discern. It is within our most intimate associations of kin and peers that we develop and sustain our sense of self and derive emotional security. For example, research by the Children's Society (2009) involving some 8000 young people found that the most common words used when asked about what constitutes a good childhood were 'family' and 'friends'. In essence, their responses pointed to the familiar but fundamental notion that relationships and connectedness to others are critical to our overall wellbeing (Boddy 2013). The Children's Society study also noted that being loved and being treated with fairness and respect by others were frequent themes.

Similarly, Smart *et al.* (2001) found that children whose parents had separated rated highly four interlinked factors in their dealings with significant others – fairness, trust, care and respect. In brief, children value love, care, support, mutual respect and being trusted as key elements of 'family' life (Happer *et al.* 2006; Morrow 1998). We can see from these several sources that children have a well-developed sense of the moral nature of family life whereby love and care is bound up in the way fairness, respect and trust underwrite their most intimate of relationships with others in the household. These relationships however occur over time and in particular places and spaces within the home and outside, as we discuss next.

Time and space from a child's perspective

The home is often thought of in static terms whereas the reality is that it is typically constituted by movements in and out of the physical setting (Sibley 1995). Children's understandings of themselves are informed through the movement in, out and around the home as a material space and a fixed locality (Christensen 2000). Children's understanding of the house and their 'border work' with friends and neighbours in and around the home are foundational in developing social skills and competences (Thorne 1993). Children become navigators and negotiators in the public realm of the neighbourhood, community and within friendship circles (see Evans and Holland 2012; Holland *et al.* 2011). Foster children must 'learn' the home setting and locality quickly given that many are placed short term. Some children may well have become proficient at such navigating by virtue of their repeated experiences of foster care. By comparison, other children may only have to do this once or twice in their childhoods and will have experienced a more gradually evolving and perhaps deeper sense of connectedness to their everyday world.

Research by Matthews *et al.* (2000) into children and youth playing 'on the streets' stressed the importance of the local environment for children, enabling them to move away from the surveillance of adults and from the constraints of a supervised childhood. Matthews *et al.* suggest that any decline in the use of the 'street' reduces opportunities for identity construction, for it is in this external environment of peers and public that young people explore and come to understand their present and prospective social roles. Yet, as more families become dual earners and mothers go out to work, so children's experiences are becoming more institutionalised in a variety of forms of child care and supervised leisure in which an adult-defined curricula of appropriate activities and attitudes is inevitably conveyed (Ennew 1994; James and Prout 1997). Notably, for the birth and foster children in this study, all had at least one carer/parent at home for the duration of their out-of-school hours. All of them were given regular access to outside play and were allowed to go out unattended by adults and all had the opportunity to explore and construct an 'outdoors' identity with friends and peers (see also Holland *et al.* 2011; Matthews *et al.* 2000). They (birth children, foster children and adopted children) all spoke of going out alone or playing out and how important this was for them. Playing out with other local children is particularly important in developing capacities for negotiation and independence. The foster children sometimes 'rated' a placement by the opportunity to play out with other children of a similar age in the locality. Thus when asked about the things she liked about her foster home, Suzanne immediately referred to her friends in the neighbourhood and playing outside:

> I like living round here because I have a lot of friends around here to play out with. I like to hang out with friends on the streets.
>
> (Suzanne, foster child, Family 7)

Playing with local peers gives foster children the opportunity to mix with others who are not being looked after and so they are not confined in their choice of who they mix with, as may be the case for some children in a residential care setting positioned away from the streets and avenues that most families occupy. Research has shown that having friends and peer contact outside of the care system and being able to sustain these relationships is a useful barometer of emotional health and very important in helping to stabilise a placement (see Schaffer 2008). Playing outside also helps children to understand and become part of the local community. Birth children were often helpful in facilitating the process of introducing the foster child to the new neighbourhood and to local friendship circles. The children spoke of these events and the examples below, taken from their audio diaries, describe how a birth child and foster child walked home from Guides together, which neither had ever done before. The mother/foster carer revealed her reaction to this event and noted its importance in terms of the girls building a sense of independence as well as both gaining experience in safe navigation of their local environment:

> I went to Guides tonight and we played a game called, I can't remember but we had to dress up in loads of different costumes. Then me and Melonie [foster child] walked home so I've enjoyed it today. Hopefully it will be a good day tomorrow. Bye.
>
> (Audio diary, Helen, birth child, Family 1)

> Me and Helen went to Guides. We walked home from Guides 'cos Greg had the car to watch the football over the pub.
>
> (Audio diary, Melonie, foster child, Family 1)

> The girls came home and they walked home on their own, it's the first time they have ever done that but it was a nice evening, good weather, nice and light. I wasn't worried but I couldn't wait for them to get in but they came home safe and sound. They came in quite grown up! They had actually been offered a lift but refused it because they wanted to walk home on their own.
>
> (Audio diary, Liz, mother/foster carer, Family 1)

Implicated in the above account is the trust that the foster carer/ mother placed in the two children and their reciprocation of this by coming home in good time. As ever, these small but not insignificant events reveal something of the interdependencies involved in growing up whereby children test in relative safety the boundaries of their own agency and control – of working out what it means to be trusted, of learning the limits of negotiation, and understanding where lines are not to be crossed. Much of this learning occurs in the local community and at school as we discuss next.

Neighbourhood and school – continuity or change?

O'Brien (1996) states that children live in the 'local' and hence the quality and safety of the local environment is paramount. The incorporation into growing up in the UK of a regular autonomous outdoor life is most apparent from the age of 11 years when children go to secondary school often using public transport. Many foster children continue to attend their old school in order to preserve their educational stability but do so from a different home location (Jackson and Sachev 2001). This continuity also sustains much of their friendship and peer networks.

Transport from foster household to school is often by taxi (paid by the local authority) and often necessary due to the distance or travel complications involved or absence of local transport due to the location of the new home. This diminishes their opportunity for more autonomous movement and for the companionship to and from school with other pupils. Taxis were often the source of much frustration for carers and children as they seemed to have limited influence over the precise timing and frequency of the service, despite their communications with social workers about this issue. This often left them feeling that the service was purely a bureaucratic arrangement which could have worked much better and with less cost had the families been allowed to negotiate directly. Taxis also made the foster children feel they stood out as 'different' to other children, something that many foster children are concerned about (Madigan *et al.* 2013).

Community for children tends to be located in a sense of belonging that resides primarily in relationships with other people rather than the place itself, although the latter is of course important. Morrow (1996) demonstrates that peer friendships as well as other relationships within school and with local kin are central to building up children's sense of trust and security in their neighbourhood. According to this perspective, there are evident tensions for some fostered children in seeking to sustain their friend and kinship networks in their former home and environment, and investing time and emotional energy in creating relationships in their new home and neighbourhood. Much has to be weighed against the benefits of children remaining in their old school whilst balancing this against the needs of the child to move on and engage with a new future. This needs to be individually assessed; a short-term placement might assume some continuity of school. In a long-term placement it might be that remaining in the same school is counterproductive in encouraging a child to commit to the new locality and a new friendship circle.

Geographies of anxiety?

Foster carers (as with parents more generally) often share anxieties about the world outside the home as a potential source of moral and physical danger, a place where older children or adults are likely to prey on younger children (see Christensen and O'Brien 2003; Furedi 2008). In this context, foster children may face different expectations from the different localities of family home and foster home. The customs and practices within these two localities, particularly around what constitutes risk and harm and who to seek help from, may be very different and the foster child often has to negotiate both (see Holland et al. 2011). Their sense of what is danger, and how to be protected from this, may well be different to those of both carer and birth parent. Take for example the case of Melonie, a child fostered because of serious neglect and sexual abuse by her mother's former boyfriend. The female carer perceives risk in the guise of the spectral preying male paedophile, whereas the birth mother is more concerned about local youth in her neighbourhood. However, Melonie believes she herself is a suitable judge of where harm may lie. The carer Liz, living in what she perceives as a safe home and neighbourhood, views danger thus:

> ...paedophiles, you know, they don't, they haven't got a neon sign over their head, saying I'm a bad man. You have to judge individuals [outside]. This is a safe place here this is home... The home is a secure environment where they feel safe, that's the biggest [thing] and that's what we, we try to create that. I don't sit down and lecture them but I put it into my words that you're safe here. We can't stop people harming you outside but we can stop it in here.
>
> (Liz, foster carer, Family 1)

Liz recently had let 13-year-old Melonie walk home from a leisure activity for the first time without an adult but with clear expectations about returning without delay. Yet when staying with her birth mother that same week Melonie described a very different set of freedoms to be out in the neighbourhood than Liz might permit, albeit Melonie misjudges the discretion she is allowed by her birth mother. The source of threat perceived by the birth family is also very different – older local boys. Melonie's audio diary describes her take on events:

> On Friday it [staying with birth family] went on well but I come in a bit late. I didn't listen to my mum. But I regret that. Saturday it went quite well, 'cos then my brother came to my house and slept for the night. Then Sunday my brother was going to go home and my mum's fiancé, well boyfriend, told me to come in about half past four and I never got in until seven o'clock and my mum's boyfriend told me that he was looking for me and my brother, Keith. Then he [Mum's boyfriend] was going mad and my mother was worrying just in case I sleep around and all that but I'm not going to do that at my age. OK then Alyson. Got to go. Bye.
>
> (Audio diary, Melonie, foster child, Family 1)

Interestingly, the birth family seemed to view Melonie as the source of risk in carelessly exposing herself to the external danger of older boys by staying out too long, whereas the harm to Melonie in the past had come from within the home. For some foster children, adapting to differing perceptions of risk and danger is part of the care experience (Gill 2007; Valentine 2004). Thus Melonie while viewed by her birth family as the 'problem' is cast by her carer as an innocent potential victim of some external paedophile threat. Yet Melonie herself claims some moral understanding and control of events in stating she would view it as unacceptable to 'sleep around' at her age. In essence, everyday risk management by children, parents and carers is informed by a range of local information, 'vicarious and personal experiences, all of which are interpreted and made sense of within the context of local communities, producing subtly different geographies of fear' (Valentine 2004, p.100). In addition, a virtual and infinite 'geography' that is our digital world combines with a highly sexualised culture to unsettle the boundaries of childhood and adulthood, and undercuts the supervisory control of adults, particularly over social media (NSPCC

2013). Cyber-based bullying, easily accessible pornography and images of abuse, internet predators, child traffickers, and child sexual exploitation gangs are just some recent examples of new threats that generate perplexing challenges for parents, carers and professionals alike. In this context, home becomes ever more important in sheltering children from the dangers outside, even if some of those dangers such as abusive social media can accompany the child anywhere. Indeed the belief in home as a safe sanctuary may exist as a comforting ideal only if we ignore the long-known fact that it is the locus of abuse for many children (Morgan 1996) and this is likely to have been the case for many children in foster care. In such circumstances it may be hard for foster children to understand and accept the security of both the physical and emotional family home when they have been abused within their birth families, as Callum describes:

> My mum was violent towards us. My cousins used to live with us and they put themselves into care and they made allegations against us [Callum and siblings] as well! And I was very angry! I was angry with my cousin for doing it. Now I know he did the right thing. I'm glad to be here and I'm glad to be away from my mum… She went to prison for her violence against us.
>
> (Callum, foster child, Family 8)

This young person was only able to move on and feel safe with his foster carers once he had ended contact with his mother and stopped visiting the family home. Developing a sense of belonging to a long-term foster home takes time and can be hostage to the demands and attachments to the birth family home and neighbourhood (see Biehal et al. 2010; Christiansen et al. 2013). These tensions over competing loyalties and affections are not easily resolvable, if at all. Nor should it be the case that children abandon their past and significant people in it in order to put down roots in the foster home. Rather, the point being made is that the child in adapting to a new and safer environment needs to develop confidence in operating within it. Moving away from a home or community in which threats, harms and chronic unhappiness for children are commonplace does not lend itself to some easy trusting transition into the foster home. Navigating and settling into this new physical and emotional world takes time and much depends upon the way the foster child can gradually come to understand domestic arrangements in the home while having the opportunity to retreat to a more private sphere which is theirs alone. It is the use of space in the foster home that we explore next.

Children's rooms and children's space

All of the children in this study valued their own space. Only one of the foster children was sharing a room with another (fostered) child; all the others had their own rooms. This was very important for them as it gave them the opportunity to enjoy privacy and seek separation from the foster family when they felt like doing so. Many of the children took great pride in the orderly arrangement of their rooms which seemed to help them create a sense of control and stability. For some of the children it was the first time they had a room of their own and this lent them a new sense of self-esteem, as Nadia discusses:

> We used to share a room in here but we found it too close together; now we've got our own room… I'm upstairs on the far end; a big narrow room; I got two windows, one at each end. I've got my own sink and a computer. I chose the colour, it's purple with pink curtains. I've got loads of pictures. You can see it if you want.
>
> (Nadia, foster child, Family 2)

In the audio diaries many of the children talked about spending time away from other people in the household by using their own bedrooms. This was the case for birth children and foster children. While they enjoyed choice over furnishings and could customise their space they also had to keep their rooms tidy and put dirty washing in the appropriate place. This was a clear requirement across all the households:

> They have to keep their own bedrooms tidy. They have to pick their washing up from the floor and put it in the laundry basket.
>
> (Sally, foster carer, Family 3)

The foster children typically had their own rooms not least because regulations prescribed the limited circumstances in which rooms could be shared with another child. This meant that it was often the birth children who ended up sharing a room or having a room that due to design or location was deemed less desirable than that occupied by the incomer (see Sinclair *et al.* 2004). Clearly this could be an issue likely to cause bad feeling between birth children and foster children. One adopted child stated that her enduring wish was to have:

> ...my own room. I have to share, as foster girls and boys have to have their own room.

> (Carla, adopted child, Family 1)

This child in giving an unequivocal view did so without rancour towards the foster children within her home, and acknowledged that she herself had moved from being a long-term foster child to a permanent member of the family. The two foster children who shared a room would have liked their own space. One of these, while otherwise happy in what was a long-term placement, ruefully observed:

> We argue a lot. We get on each other's nerves! We share a room and she likes to talk when I'm trying to go to sleep.

> (Lilly, foster child, Family 10)

Foster carers of course recognised that this could be an area of friction between their own children and the foster children. One carer discussed how she sought to ensure that the birth children were not overly inconvenienced by these arrangements by building an extension to the house that would become a bespoke bedroom:

> I wouldn't say they [birth children] made a huge fuss over it, but they did say, why do we have to move [room], and we said, because we can't keep the kids long term if we don't move you, but we will build for you what you want. So you tell us the sort of thing that you want for the bedroom and we'll do it.

> (Sally, foster carer, Family 3)

Rooms became places of safety and refuge for some young people, particularly in the initial stages of care, to the extent they became protective of their own space and rarely allowed anyone into their room. One carer noted that it had taken a young person several months to invite a school friend to the foster home and that it was a sign of feeling secure and settled when the fostered child felt able to let the visitor enter their bedroom:

> That was a real coup because he doesn't let anyone into his bedroom; he is very sacrosanct with his bedroom.
>
> (Josie, foster carer, Family 4)

Belongings

Having their own rooms allowed the foster children to have their own belongings around them. Likewise, many of the birth children felt that it took time for foster children to begin to respect their (birth children) property and having separate rooms helped to deal with this. Several birth children mentioned that the foster children at the beginning of a placement would unthinkingly take their property (such as toys and games) but that this would resolve itself once the child realised who owned what, and also when they acquired belongings of their own:

> When they first come in they don't know that our property is ours and they just go and take it, but after a while they learn that their property is theirs…they take like things that are in my room, games and things. But they are fine now.
>
> (Megan, birth child, Family 3)

Carers also noted the importance of private space and individualised belongings for foster children that would affirm their own sense of self; of being just like other children:

> I think it's really important that they have their own friends, their own space, their own toys. I think it is really important to have their own property.
>
> (Dawn, foster carer, Family 2)

Several of the carers spoke about how foster children arrived with little in the way of personal belongings:

> Jade and Candice both moved into here at the age of six, with a black bag, not two, one black bag! Imagine! They've been in the care system since the age of three and have so few possessions.
>
> (Sally, foster carer, Family 3)

Carers found it difficult to understand why some children came with barely any clothes when previous foster carers would have received allowances for this. Several carers recollected that children had in past years arrived with meagre belongings in black bags and were relieved that policies had been implemented by local authorities to stop this unacceptable practice. One carer recalling such an incident, stated that the first thing she did was provide the foster child with a 'holdall with their name on it'. This modest gesture was not without significance in communicating to the child their importance and worth. It is not easy for most of us to imagine being a child with so few possessions, arriving at a foster home perhaps still upset about separation from their family and feeling insecure and uncertain about the future. In such circumstances the clear demarcation of space (bedroom) and the acquisition of clothes and belongings might, over time, help a foster child recover (or indeed develop for the first time) a sense of self-esteem as enjoyed by other children who take for granted home comforts and personal possessions. Key to this building of self-regard is the part played by birth children. It is towards their experiences of fostering that we move next.

Birth children as temporary 'siblings'?

We have known for some time that birth children enjoy fostering and obtain various benefits from their encounters with the children they help care for (see Part 1993, 1999). For example, Pugh (1999) identified positives such as companionship, looking after younger children and feeling good about helping others. Negatives included having to share bedrooms with their own siblings, dealing with difficult behaviour and coping with professionals who did not always recognise their value or involve them in decisions and training. Farmer (2002, 2010) concluded that many carers received informal support from their own birth children and where this was forthcoming there were fewer disruptions in placement. Over a decade ago Fox (2001, p.45) noted that:

> Consideration of the significance of natural children in foster families…would ensure a more holistic approach which would ultimately lead to quality, safe and total care for all involved.

In fostering, the birth children have new temporary 'siblings' entering their family on a regular basis. Surprisingly, there is limited research into full sibling relationships compared to most other kinds of family ties (Jackson 2006) and even less research into the relationships between foster and birth children. What we do know from sibling research (Punch 2004) is that sibling interaction often occurs in what might be termed 'backstage' areas of the family, often hidden from parental view. Backstage activity occurs when an individual loosens control over their actions and appearance and where the social rules of politeness and etiquette are not always observed. Punch (2004, 2008) found that most siblings spoke of 'being who you wanted to be' when with siblings backstage; they felt more relaxed in not 'performing' expected niceties in front of parents and other adults. Backstage can also be a tense, irritable place where anger is easily vented.

Thus the home can be a double-edged environment where people can relax and be themselves but also a place for conflict to emerge. This duality does not easily translate to foster families where strangers become a sort of surrogate sibling but with whom one cannot necessarily act in a free or unrestrained 'backstage' manner. This was mentioned by several of the birth children who noted that they were not always able to fully relax when foster children were around. This might make for a very different home environment where perhaps one's guard may never be truly dropped. Certainly the birth children in our study were aware of this and some noted the difference in the relationship between themselves and the foster child compared with their siblings.

Charlie (birth child, Family 6) discussed this aspect during interview, stating with some insight that it was not always possible to argue with foster children in the way he could with his own brothers and sisters. This was because sibling relationships, deepened by time and attachment, might prompt forgiveness and understanding over some disagreement, yet this may not be so easily rendered to the foster child as newcomer. As Charlie reflected: '…if something happened you would not necessarily be able to make up…'. It could be argued that living in a home where one cannot fully relax places undue tensions upon the birth children who, in this study and elsewhere, utilised their bedrooms as areas of protective 'seclusion' from the family (Twigg and Swan 2007). Alternatively, being concerned about another's welfare, attending to the needs of others and learning how not to initiate or respond to conflict are important capacities for all young people to acquire.

Sibling relationships have been characterised as either involving rivalry or being supportive, or a mixture of both. These relationships are typically played out in the child's need for parental love, affection and approval (Sanders 2004). Positive sibling relationships are important preparation for friendship and family building in later life (Cossar and Neil 2013; Ottaway 2012). However, children can also experience divisive and troubled relations with siblings (Sanders 2004) and often have to find their own niche within the family pecking order (Sulloway 1996). The same may occur in foster families. For example, for the birth child in foster families, they may have a child coming to the family who is close in age or the same age and thus the birth child could feel their positioning within the family to be less secure or in some cases usurped (Twigg and Swan 2007). Younger children could become middle children, by virtue of having younger children placed with them (Holmes and Silver 2010). Clearly, this may present some difficulties for birth children understanding their role and position in the family, as was noted by carers such as Liz (Family 1):

> Yeah, well I'm glad Melonie [foster child] is in the middle. You know, they're too close, because they're both thirteen now [Melonie and Helen], but at least Helen [birth child] just stays the oldest, Carla [adopted child] stays the youngest and they both stay in their position.

> (Liz, foster carer, Family 1)

Children too similar

An additional but infrequent complicating factor can occur when the foster child is not only close in age to a birth child but also has the same name. An adult birth child in this study recalled the deep discomfort of feeling displaced by a child of a similar age with the same name:

> Yeah. Well the first one we had was older than me so it was before they went into independent living and I got on really well with him. The girl that came after him, she was quite difficult but the younger ones that would come then you'd start to notice more that you were sharing like your parents more than with the older ones I think… My parents would have to do more for the younger children depending on their problems as to how much time they would have to spend… You know they did actually place someone [who was a year younger] with the same name which was horrible. It was really horrible. I was big Sara and she was little Sara. That was awful… Well I didn't like being big Sara [laughs]. I'm not big, I'm little. Um and the name shouldn't come into it, but it is difficult… I don't know what it was really. It's hard to imagine what it's like to have someone else there the same [as you]. I guess it's a bit of role removal as well… I hated them copying. I remember with Sara, the one with the same name, Mum was taking me clothes shopping and it was quite a rare thing 'cos I always had hand me downs from my older cousins. And my mum had taken me clothes shopping and then Sara had, had her clothing money through and she went out and bought just exactly the same thing and that was like uhhh, the copying especially at like fourteen, fifteen years of age.
>
> (Sara, birth child, Family 5)

As an adult it is perhaps difficult to imagine how it would feel as a child to have another person of the same gender, age and name moving in to your home, especially when they then started to mirror appearances. Yet birth children are sometimes expected to cope with such discomforts and do so with good grace. For example, Josie and Philip (foster carers, Family 4) recalled that their youngest son, Stuart, found it difficult to accept a foster child who had the same name and was of a similar age. Interestingly, they viewed their son's reluctance to accept the foster child as an act of selfishness and were unpersuaded about Stuart's fears of a loss of positioning in their affections and attention:

> He [Stuart] fronted us and I suppose he wanted us to, to [drop] the thought of fostering because he wouldn't then be the youngest in the family, he wouldn't have all the attention or whatever but because we sort of stood firm and we had time together to think the thing through, it sort of took its own natural level in the system, didn't it. When we met Stu [foster child] for the first time there was no animosity...
>
> (Philip and Josie, foster carers, Family 4)

The family managed the matter of the name by calling the foster child 'Stu' and the birth child Stuart. Of note in this home was that Josie was stepmother to the birth children, hence there had already been some experience of integrating an 'outsider' within this reconstituted family. Josie stated that she was well placed to understand how a foster child might feel as an incomer because she too had to establish her own position *vis-à-vis* her new partner and his children. Another carer felt that her now adult son may have experienced feelings of displacement, not for himself, but in respect to his own infant children (the carer's grandchildren), when young foster children were placed with his parents. Sally (Family 3) discussed something of the complex interplay of generational expectations that fostering can bring to the surface. She noted how two young boys, of a similar age to her two grandsons, were placed with her:

> That did cause jealousy in a way, Harri [grandson] used to be so jealous. He [son, Paul] used to find it hard to see the two little ones that we had, the foster children on our laps, and not the grandchildren... My son probably thought you've waited all this time for grandchildren and you are not making a massive fuss over it because you've got someone else's kids! Yet he [son, Paul] never behaved like that when we fostered kids and he was living at home... We had the caravan and quite often we would take the boys, the two little ones down to the caravan and maybe Paul [son] thought that we should be taking his [children], but there wasn't enough room in the car and he may have thought if we didn't have them [foster children], we could have taken his...
>
> (Sally, foster carer, Family 3)

Such insights reinforce the importance of anticipating the impact on the birth children and grandchildren when arranging a foster care placement and matching needs.

Choice of placement by birth children: 'it's my home too'

Whilst all of the birth children in this study believed that they had been informed when a prospective foster child was coming to the family, it is possible this process might have been perceived more as a matter of intention than one of consultation or negotiation. They could not think of scenarios when they might have been allowed to veto a proposed placement. Nonetheless some, like Helen below, felt they had been approached meaningfully about a new child coming to stay:

> My mum wouldn't accept a person into the house without asking, 'cos it's my home too and she would want me to feel safe as well as my parents. Mum would know about the problems and tell me, so I would then know what my safety is... [she would tell me about] what type of home they have come from so I know what type of things I could help them with. My mum don't tell me the really secretive ones because they are confidential.
>
> (Helen, birth child, Family 1)

By contrast, Sara felt that she was told rather than consulted:

> When Chris was coming Mum said it's another little boy, but you don't really get a choice. When we were getting approved we, Mum specified the type of child and they asked what Dad and I thought too. I have never said no to a child and cannot think of any circumstances when I would say no.
>
> (Sara, birth child, Family 5)

Sara said that she would never say 'no', despite recalling problems with certain foster children and their behaviour in the past. In practice, the opportunities to object to a placement are limited in a world of adult decision-making (Thomas 2001), and consultation more generally is curtailed by the shortage of time for matching and preparation that often occurs before placements are set up.

Positives of fostering for the birth child

The foster carers, as in other studies (Triseliotis *et al.* 2000; Twigg and Swann 2007), felt that, with a few exceptions, fostering had been a positive experience for their own children. Most believed that their offspring had learned from their encounters with foster children about troubled lives and difficult experiences, and did so vicariously without having to experiment or engage in risk-taking activities themselves. Most carers thought that fostering prompted their children to contrast their lives with those fostered, and in so doing appreciate much more their home comforts and security. This exposure to children much less fortunate than themselves seemed to lend the young people a capacity for empathy:

> Charlie [teenage birth child] is a kind of father figure. He is very, very good with children younger than himself. He has a hell of a lot of time for people, very intelligent, very compassionate so I knew that he would get on with Carl...
>
> (Steve, foster carer, Family 6)

In most instances, the birth children described how they enjoyed being in a helping role and how they appreciated the social contact (play and company) that fostering provided. Helen, for instance, spoke of helping and protecting foster children, and gave an example of how she engaged with Melonie (foster child):

> Like when sometimes when Melonie says 'I am going to have a fight today'...so you're like trying to help them and stopping them from getting hurt and like protecting them at the same time, which is really helpful to them... It makes you feel warm hearted and kind and considerate when you are doing it. It makes me feel good about myself...
>
> (Helen, birth child, Family 1)

Like other birth children, Helen spoke about the importance of welcoming the foster child to the home and, in the example below, of providing support and protection as an almost routine part of her engagement with the vulnerable strangers that from time to time joined her family:

> When [foster child] came and we all went to [shops in town] to buy her a few things to get her nice and settled in, I went up into her room to help her settle in. I was just helping her to relax and unpack so she would feel more welcome and everything. We went into Church Road to buy her more stuff so she would feel more welcomed into this home. And she goes 'Oh my Aunty lives down by Church Road'. I go 'Oh that's nice' and she says 'I'll run away or something'!! But I talked her through it to stop her from running away. I told her all the bad stuff that would happen, like the police would be after her, maybe she'd have to get moved to another home after another. Then I told her all the good stuff, like if you stay, the foster people [i.e. professionals] might think you are getting better and you go home to your parents more sooner than you think. And as soon as I started to put all them good ideas into her head, she started to come round to the idea that she was getting more welcomed into the home and that was starting to secure her and that I wouldn't let anything bad happen to her if she ran away.
>
> (Helen, birth child, Family 1)

Here, Helen (aged 13 when interviewed) reveals something of her caring skills that assisted the child settle in the placement and she also alludes to her 'insider' knowledge of fostering which she shared with the new arrival and which gave some authority to her advice and support. Indeed, other mainly older birth children used phrases associated with the professional terminology of care, particularly in regard to aspects of behaviour and to therapeutic interventions. For example, Sara, aged 20 and living at home, talked about the care experience and skills required to foster a particular child:

> Sara: There is a lot of stress [from challenging behaviour] I think, and a lot of people don't understand about the way to er...like different behavioural techniques of managing behaviour.

Researcher: Do you ever use such techniques?

Sara: I do if I need to, like the child we had before, we had him for so long, it was effective that, that I did use them.

(Sara, birth child, Family 5)

Sara was the only birth child in the sample to have undertaken training with her parents in behaviour management techniques to help in caring for sexually abused children. She had found the training useful and believed it assisted her in contributing to a more consistent family approach. She had also briefly attended support groups for birth children run by the local authority. The occasional use by Sara and other young people of phrases and terms drawn from a welfare vocabulary implied some acquisition of formal knowledge and interpersonal skills. This aspect of birth children's skills has not been the subject of much research and we know little about the capacities and competences that they develop over time and the impact of this in the home. For our part we gained no sense that the birth children were somehow proto-professionals or junior social workers in the making; rather their caring impulses seemed just that – an authentic wish to help others and that sharing their home with children less fortunate than themselves was quite simply the 'right thing to do'. That they both gave and gained much was evident throughout the study and like their parents they too felt a sense of loss or bereavement when a foster child left them (see Twigg and Swan 2007). It is towards the welcoming of the foster child and also to her or his often sad departure that we now turn.

Foster children: choosing and being chosen

The care journey of some children may well expose them to different family settings, including their own and those of their kin and friends. In this respect their experiences may well have taught them what they do and don't like about living in families (Holland 2007). However, all foster children have to negotiate the difficult period of settling in and need time to do this in order to come to terms with what has happened, to stabilise, and to then invest in their new circumstances (Cairns 2006; Schofield and Beek 2009). Yet fostering often does not allow this, and particularly does not facilitate a process whereby carers and the child test the arrangement and then choose to continue the placement after an initial short-term trial. During interviews only one foster child could recollect making a choice to come to a foster family. All the others were clear that they had few other options if they turned down the placement:

> Not much [choice] if I hadn't come here I'd have gone into a home.
>
> (Chris, foster child, Family 5)

In our small study it was apparent that little matching, testing and actually 'choosing' to continue had happened before a child was placed in a home for any length of time. Choosing to stay and also knowing that a carer has chosen to keep a child after an initial trial are important dynamics in the early stages of settling in a placement (see Sinclair *et al.* 2005a). Take for example the experience of Lilly who quickly decided she wished to remain long term with Julie as a 'forever family'. Julie was happy for such an arrangement to continue but Lilly, against her wishes, was taken from Julie for adoption. When the adoption failed she was returned to Julie for the foreseeable future:

> Lilly: I've always felt at home here… I didn't like the other one [adoptive parent]. I like Julie. She is like my mother.
>
> Researcher: How is she like your mother?
>
> Lilly: Cos she treats me good.
>
> (Lilly, foster child, Family 10)

Julie recalled that when Lilly returned to her the local authority stated they would not place other children with her if she kept Lilly long term. Julie described how this was potentially very difficult for her as a single parent with limited income and who wanted to foster more than one child. She believed it was inconceivable that moving Lilly again after the failed adoption would have been in her best interests and insisted the child should remain with her:

> I had to wait to go to panel. I was told that if I was going to take her [foster Lilly long term] then I wouldn't be having any other placements. I said 'fair enough, if I can get one out the system,

carry on!' At least I knew she [Lilly] wanted to be here and she was happy... She had been here two years and it is a long time in a child's life... It was just the way it was put over to me. I think they thought that I would say OK I'm not going to take her on then, but I wanted to make it work. They didn't want to lose me as a short term carer basically...since then I have been passed for, actually I could take two long term and a short term now! So, things can change drastically! [laughs]

(Julie, foster carer, Family 10)

Julie's commitment to Lilly, to publicly and insistently articulate her wish to keep the child, was a very powerful message for Lilly, who for the first time felt wanted and cared for. Callum (foster child, Family 8) too perceived it as highly significant that Hazel *chose* to keep him and vice versa, demonstrating a mutual commitment that cemented the young man's sense of belonging:

I didn't think I was ever going to settle down here and I had only been told that I was coming here for two weeks until they could find me a place...and two weeks came and went and then I went on to a couple of months and then I started school and I just fell in love with them...with the place and the area. I got moved from placement to placement and I never settled anywhere and then they dragged me away from everything I knew, my family and...I was told get into the car you are going to a place down in [current placement] and I got in the car and I got here about half past nine bonfire night [4 years before] and I never left [laughs] and it was supposed to be a two week temporary thing because Hazel was only a carer for temporary for six months so she had to go back to panel so that I could stay... They realised that they didn't want me to go, and I realised that I didn't want to go and I felt [it was] a real big gesture by Hazel when she went back to the panel to ask if she could be a long term foster carer, just for me and I thought that was really, really... I really felt wanted by Hazel... After that six months they could have said OK the six months is over take him away but they didn't. That was when I felt wanted...

(Callum, foster child, Family 8)

Callum, an articulate young man, felt settled for the first time in his life and was able to stabilise emotionally and physically and put down roots in the local area. He had made attachments to the foster family, the locality and to the local people; thus if he (or any other child in a similar context) was to move, then more would be lost than just the immediate foster family (see Farmer 2010). This ecology of care and attachment often provides the lasting stability needed for children to remedy lost opportunities over their education (see Osborne *et al.* 2010). Callum for example undertook a literacy scheme in school, much reinforced by carer Hazel, and began to succeed academically, achieving GCSEs and commencing an employment training course. He was starting to lay the foundations for his adult life. It is difficult to see that he could have done this without settling long term with this family that chose to keep him, and particularly so after a childhood of maternal cruelty and rejection. Hazel, the carer, recalls a critical turning point for Callum:

> But when [Callum's] mum went to prison it was a different story. He seemed to think Mum pleaded guilty to a crime and he no longer wanted to protect her, because she admitted what she had done to them. He realised that there was more to life than what Mum was doing. He didn't have to stand there and be the battering ram. He didn't have to be hit. She went down for GBH on them and his cousins.
>
> (Hazel, foster carer, Family 8)

Given these sorts of childhood experiences it is perhaps not surprising that some carers might only be asked to offer a single placement in order to devote the time and energy needed to care for a child exposed to harm and adversity. Being in placement alone or with others is therefore an important aspect of planning as well as a key dynamic in the child's care experience, as we note next.

Alone and with others

Several of the foster families had only one foster child placed with them. This was because it was felt better for the foster child to be placed alone to meet his or her substantial needs, or because the foster child presented challenging behaviour that might be difficult to deal with if more than one foster child was in the home. Three of these 'singleton' placements occurred where there were no birth children under 18 years in the home (Stu, Family 4; Chris, Family 5; Suzanne, Family 7). Two of these were in rural locations (Stu and Chris). For Stu this was not an issue as he was older and going out to work, but for Chris, still at school, this was problematic. Chris and Suzanne were also transported some distance to school, and so it was potentially more difficult to make friends in the neighbourhood. Suzanne was not in a rural location and very much enjoyed going out to play on the streets of a large housing estate and was able to tap into the local children's social network. However, Chris found his rural isolation difficult:

> I'm having a rubbish day. Every day is a rubbish day. It's because there is nobody here to play with. [I do play with the boy down the road] but not very often; I don't really know him... I can't play board games. They are for two players. I haven't got anyone to play with! I'm on my own all of the time. I would like to be with my brother [who he had not seen for many years and was in prison].

> (Audio diary, Chris, foster child, Family 5)

Whilst Chris did see the foster carers' nephews and nieces on a regular basis, he found not having any local opportunities over friendships difficult. It can be difficult to balance the needs of the foster child for company with any risk they may pose to other children. Being with others was appreciated by many of the foster children and they compared this favourably to times when they had been placed without other local children being around:

> Well if you are on your own, you get left out and upset but where we live we have lots of friends.

> (Candice, foster child, Family 3)

In five of the ten families there was more than one child in placement and this seemed to be appreciated by the foster children as supportive and helpful. This has long been noted by Berridge and Cleaver (1987) who found that sibling and peer support are vital in sustaining placements. There were children in four placements in this study who had siblings elsewhere in care but only one foster family in our sample had a sibling group. Their shared placement was a matter of deep importance to them in that it kept them together and in touch with other siblings:

> I think it's that we [siblings] are all here together and Dawn and Ian are our friends more than just a carer...here we go out a lot and do a lot of things. Going out together and doing things together. We all go and see my other brothers and sisters.
>
> (Nadia, foster child, Family 2)

It is of course the case that keeping in touch can be promoted in many ways, not least through social media which has transformed the way that young people and families communicate, and we briefly consider its relevance to fostering next.

Communication and technology

The view that new information technology, computers and television weaken the interdependency and links between adults and children has been around for some time (see Wyness 2006), yet it is the case that most young people are both conversant and comfortable with new social media such as Facebook, Twitter and instant messaging together with the multi-media and internet facilities of the mobile phone and laptop computer. It has been recognised for some time that the computer and the internet have profoundly shifted the boundaries of our domestic world and people now spend considerable time and emotional investment in maintaining virtual contact with friends and kin across time and space. It was not surprising therefore to find the foster children in our study, like others, enthusiastic about the internet as a means of keeping in touch with family and friends to whom they no longer lived near (Facer et al. 2001; see also Gilligan 2001). The social and technical characteristics of new information technologies reveal distinctive generational patterns in frequency of use and uptake of applications and which give children access to an external world beyond the 'cocoon of the family' (Lee 2001, p.159).

Given that foster children often feel that many of the decisions about their lives are taken out of their hands, their ability to take control over the contacting of friends and sharing information via social media was important to them (Simpson 2013). All of the foster homes had internet which facilitated this possibility. Madinou and Miller (2012) note the benefits for transnational families of keeping in touch via mobile phones and new media and this is not dissimilar to the world of fostering where children and their birth family and friends can use the internet to keep alive particular relationships and affections, despite there being no physical presence to enact close bonds and feelings. It is evident that many contacts with kin and friends that were once managed by social workers and carers are now accessible via social networking and whilst there are benefits to this there may be risks too that need to be understood and minimised (Fursland 2011). Whilst we should not judge a child negatively simply for wanting to be in contact with their family, it is the case that there may be drawbacks to this as well as advantages. Professionals and carers need to become knowledgeable (and adept) about new technologies in order to assess both benefits and the not inconsiderable risks that children can be exposed to through the internet and social media (see Simpson 2013).

Dodsworth *et al.* (2013) examined the impact of internet technology on relationships between foster carers and social workers. They found that, whilst useful, it was a supplement to rather than a replacement for traditional methods of communication. However, its potential to promote national and international links between foster children that may facilitate support and a more visible presence to influence policy makers was noted over a decade ago by George *et al.* (2003). More research is needed to establish if internet contacts and support networks play a significant role in improving self-esteem for foster children which in turn can help develop resilience, a theme we return to next.

Resilience

Much has been written about promoting resilience in children and this has been noted in earlier chapters. Here we address from the child's perspectives a range of interests and skills that are thought to contribute to resilience (see Gilligan 2001, 2007, 2009). These include various extra-curricular activities and sporting events about which children were highly appreciative. For some, their participation stood in some contrast to that made available to them in their birth home, as Nadia highlights:

> I'm learning German… I used to do Theatre Craft but now I just want to do singing. I like activities! I've been to Germany. I go to Romarts [arts centre] to do art… I'm staying here [foster home]. I don't want to go home. I aint got enough activities to do there. I want to start driving lessons next year; I've been saving up already, I got my money. I won't be able to earn nothing there [birth family home]. I'd have nothing! Here I've got so many more options.
>
> (Nadia, foster child, Family 2)

Initially, Nadia found it difficult to accept that she was worthy of having special things of her own or money spent on her. Both Nadia and the carers commented on this and the confidence that being involved in community activities had given her:

> Like I'm always worried about finances and I don't like asking for things, but they have taught me to be able to ask for anything. I come first with them [carers]… I have done so many activities now, I think well my attitude has changed. Now I think I can try anything… I feel every activity I've done is where my confidence has come from.
>
> (Nadia, foster child, Family 2)

Other children spoke about the new opportunities available to them that would have been very unlikely to occur in their birth family:

> I am in a band at the moment, called [names a then popular 'horror' film after which the band is named]… My friend chose that name [laughs] he is a little bit more weird than I am… I wanted it to be a mellow band you know with significant guitar solos and stuff. But he wanted it all this, a lot of heavy, almost violent lyrics and stuff and we just came about it. We were talking about the film and he thought it would be a good name [for the band]… We are hoping to have a concert in the Queens Hall

[local community hall] and that would be around 250 people... It's only been in the last months that I have been interested. I had a guitar for Christmas off Hazel [carer], an acoustic. At the moment it doesn't sound like anything, but I'm starting to put things together.

(Callum, foster child, Family 8)

It was the pride that these children, like others in our sample, took in their new activities that was striking. Nadia noted how her foster carers, like others (see Gilligan 2001; Gilligan 2007) were effective role models who inspired her and boosted her confidence:

Dawn and Ian are so active; they are really confident people. Living with confident people makes you confident. They are always doing things...

(Nadia, foster child, Family 2)

Foster carers were not only facilitating events and pastimes for the children but also modelling a positive approach to activities. This contrasted markedly with some children's limiting childhoods in which parents seemed to do little for their offspring, indeed were exploitative of their energies and dependency, as Nadia notes:

When I lived there [family home] I used to be the mother. I used to feed her [sister] and look after her. I was making bottles [for the other children) at five [years of age]. I was changing nappies at six [years of age].

(Nadia, foster child, Family 2)

Nadia had no wish to return home and like other fostered children was profoundly affected by exposure to a new way of living in which all manner of new interests and activities had given her confidence and self-esteem. Similarly, the carers gained much from sharing in the child's discovery of new hobbies and saw this as something that contributed to the enjoyment of the family. For example, Steve described how a foster child had brought a fishing hobby into the home and how gradually all the males in the family had acquired this interest. Steve's brother Jason had joined them too:

If you said to me last year, to me how anyone can sit all day long in the freezing cold and not catch anything all day long – got to be stupid, bored out of my head but what it is – it's meditation. It's time and space. The time goes like that! Carl [foster child] initiated us into it. He is passionate!

(Steve, foster carer, Family 6)

Promoting and sharing sporting activities with fostered children seemed to be a male province for the most part, and one which involved other male family members too. Ian comments:

We have always said that whatever child comes along our focus is around finding out what makes them tick. And you do. You will find something [i.e. sport]…there will be something. So we throw ourselves into different activities all of the time. Something clicks. Which is rather wonderful for us.

(Ian, foster carer, Family 2)

Sport and supporting teams was of much importance for nearly all the males fostered. Spectators and participants in sport have the opportunity to move from an individual interest to a collective membership that binds people together (see Willams and Bendelow 1998). Such a binding together around a sport or specific team often occurred between young people and those in the extended family of the foster carers. Carl enjoyed a range of sporting interests with the males he was connected to through the foster home. Indeed, Carl talked only of sport during a lengthy interview:

[My name is] Carl Lord and I support Chelsea at football… My birthday party is this Saturday… It's a football party…I like football, I like playing rugby, I like going fishing, coarse fishing. I like catching fish, I like golf and swimming…

(Carl, foster child, Family 6)

Bonding, particularly for the male foster children, appeared to be developed strongly through sport and the supporting of team games. This seemed to give children a sense of identity and belonging: 'it is the emotional engagement with the team that makes it so gripping and inspires this loyalty. And to really feel that you need a strong sense of tribal loyalty and attachment to place' (Baggini 2007, p.15). Their allegiance to sports teams seemed to bolster a sense of affiliation and self-esteem and was something they were able to take with them in the course of their care careers that for some had involved moves to different families and different regions of England and Wales.

Extended family and local community

As with other foster children, the young people in this study highly valued the part played by the extended family (adult birth children and their families, grandparents, aunts and uncles) in supporting the care agenda (Farmer 2010; Happer *et al.* 2006). For example, Callum exemplified the sentiments of other foster children about the importance of the extended family in confirming a sense of belonging and identity:

> We went to [an outdoor community event] and I carried him on my shoulder. He is still my little nephew. I was so happy because of it. Little Sophie, his sister is the same, she comes up sits on my knee and I read to her. She is a darling. She means a hell of a lot to me. As far as I am concerned they are my relatives, that's why I call them my niece and nephew. I asked Fran [adult birth child] if she minded me calling them that and she was quite flattered by it. They mean a lot to me. It's a shame they support Man United though.
>
> (Callum, foster child, Family 8)

Likewise, the local community too was seen as an important source of relationships that play a part in a child's developing sense of stability and identity (see Ungar 2008). We draw again on Callum as an example of others in the sample who spoke with enthusiasm about being part of the community and being recognised and affirmed by local people:

> Well most of the people know me. I say 'Hi' to everybody but a lot of the people I do know. There is the occasional person who will say 'Hi' and I don't know them...
>
> (Callum, foster child, Family 8)

This ecology of care and connectedness (family, extended family and community) is likely to contribute significantly to a child's gathering resilience (see Boddy 2013; Howe *et al.* 1999). Thus we can see that support networks can spread wider than the family unit (Ciarrochi *et al.* 2012; Williams 2004). Even when children had left these foster families there was for many the offer of continued support and care:

> It's funny how they [past foster children] pop out of the woodwork. One girl visits and she brings her son and we baby sit for her. She is a friend really too. We help out whenever we can.
>
> (Dawn, foster carer, Family 2)

What we see within most of the foster families is an ecology of care that embeds the child in the foster family, extended kinship network and local neighbourhood. This amalgam of care and place, of being accepted, of feeling they belonged meant that over time the children became, and crucially believed themselves to be, authentic members of the family (Biehal *et al.* 2010; Christiansen *et al.* 2013).

Conclusion

This chapter has sought to give children in this study a 'voice' and to place them centre stage in order to recognise and affirm their status and rights, as should be the case in any research with children and young people (see Minnis and Walker 2012; Woodhead 2003). The children in this study did not want to be seen as passive victims of circumstance but overall saw themselves as fortunate to have found some stability in their lives via foster care. All valued their own bedroom space, and took sanctuary in the seclusion of their own rooms. This private realm gave the fostered children something to take pride in, as did accumulating and establishing their belongings around them. The birth children were seen to play a pivotal role in fostering, although they were rarely included in placement planning or foster training. They nevertheless had, in their own way, become 'experts' by experience in assisting foster children settle and mediating their engagement in the home and local area. Where children were placed with birth children of the same age and gender this sometimes proved difficult and was exacerbated in some instances when a foster child shared the same first name. The extended relatives of the foster family were seen to be significant in their capacity to deepen the bonds of belonging and attachment, especially adult birth children who no longer lived at home and who took on the mantle of trusted 'uncles and aunts'.

The children very much valued the opportunity to play in the neighbourhood with other children and the opportunity this gave to engage outside of the home independently of adults. First, however, the foster children had to navigate the new home and new community into which they had moved. They had often come from geographies of distrust and risk because of a lack of safety and stability in their home lives and localities but quickly adjusted to the new cultures and communities that they joined via the foster family (see Valentine 2004; Reiner 2010; Evans and Holland 2012).

Resilience and self-esteem are critical aspects of child development and this was acquired to some degree by foster children's involvement in a range of extra-curricular activities and interests. Participation in sports and allegiance to teams engendered a sense of identity and esteem. Foster carers who encouraged and participated in activities and acted as role models in such pastimes were particularly valued by the young people. Foster homes that offered warmth and acceptance and which connected the child to affirming relationships with extended kin and to positive activities in the community provided an invaluable ecology of care, reinforcing the child's sense of worth and belonging.

SPACE AND PLACE IN THE FOSTER HOME: KEY MESSAGES

- Foster children value having their own space to enjoy seclusion and to spend time apart from the family.

- Foster children value having a say in the décor and furnishings of their bedrooms, so that these are individualised and allow the child a sense of belonging and not to feel they are just another child 'moving through'.

- Birth children should be recognised for the important part they play in fostering and should be involved in information sessions and (age-appropriate) training.

- Birth children should be more readily and meaningfully consulted about the implications for them and the family of prospective placements.

- Support groups should be more available to birth children; see, for example, the *Thrive* newsletter published by Fostering Network.

- Extended family can play a significant role in fostering and it may be appropriate for some of them to be involved in training and information sessions.

- Neighbourhoods play a big part in foster care and carers should have a good working knowledge of the resources available to support foster children, e.g. sports facilities, leisure and activity opportunities.

- Resilience can be bolstered by being involved in a range of activities and interests outside the home that engender achievement and self-esteem.

- Foster children may find it particularly helpful when their carers join in with these activities, modelling the expected performance and enthusiasm.

- Watching and supporting sport together can promote a sense of occasion, shared allegiance and membership and may be an important aspect of bonding with a family and its kinship network.

- Activities and interests are rarely cost neutral and funding for such opportunities should be factored into fostering allowances.

- Foster homes that offer warmth and acceptance and which connect the child to affirming relationships with extended kin and to positive activities in the community provide an ecology of care that reinforces a child's sense of worth and belonging.

- Social media can play an important part in keeping foster children connected to their birth families, although this may need to be monitored.

- Social media offers the possibility for foster children to connect together to become a mutually assistive community and to share their voice with policy makers.

- Social media can help children connect with foster families after they have moved on by keeping alive caring networks across distance and time.

- Social media could be useful in linking up birth children who foster, giving them more voice and support.

Final Comments

Research in foster care has often drawn upon a quantitative and outcomes-based approach based upon large data sets such as the classic studies by Triseliotis *et al.* (2000) and Sinclair *et al.* (2000). Quantitative studies, whilst hugely valuable, do not always uncover the everyday practices and the meanings ascribed to them by people in families, which this study has sought to reveal. The early chapters noted the small number of studies in the UK that have deployed a qualitative social science approach to foster care drawing upon sociology, psychology and social work (see Berridge 2007; Holland and Crowley 2013; Winter 2006). Hence we have sought to add to this slender body of work through our multi-method qualitative design that included interviewing, diary completion, eco-maps and occasional observation of adults and children in the foster household. Our research was informed by a social constructionist perspective in that we focused on activities, meanings, participation, rules, settings and relationships. In this way we attempted to grasp how foster carers and children create and understand their day-to-day domestic world. In doing this, we have placed children and their needs as the starting point for our study and have tried to keep their voice centre stage throughout (see also Clark 2014; Kehily 2004; Minnis and Walker 2012; Woodhead 2003).

We have also sought to avoid dwelling on the all too familiar negative aspects associated with being looked after and have taken a strengths-based perspective, focusing on capacities and skills and on what is being done well. In brief, we have attempted to unpick key elements of foster care success from the lived experiences of children and their carers. Central to our enquiry has been the notion of an 'ethic of care', of reciprocal interdependent relations of affect and attachment (Beck 2012; Evans and Holland 2012; Williams 2004). Care is fundamental to all our lives, but particularly so in our formative years. Indeed, studies undertaken with children have revealed their strong moral understanding of care and that 'love, care, support and mutual respect were the key characteristics of family that they valued' (Morrow 1998, p.112). Williams (2004, p.51) too observed that 'children value fairness, care, respect and trust' and Happer *et al.* (2006) note the importance to children of relationships and trust in social care.

Our study has drawn upon these and other key sources (Beck 2012; Featherstone 2010; Orme 2002; Parton 2003; Pithouse and Rees 2011) in order to explore how an ethic of care in fostering reveals itself in the countless minutiae of daily events within the intimacy of the home and the warmth of extended kin and other friendships. Thus we looked at care as constructed within activities such as mealtimes, at moments when clothes and belongings are provided, when touch and closeness are made normal and safe, when place and privacy become understood, when play and interests are encouraged and jointly pursued with carers. These came to the fore as pivotal experiences in signifying, over time, mutual commitment and acceptance. Clearly, the symbolic importance of such activities in revealing both the nuance and the 'ordinariness' of care are unlikely to be captured if research focuses solely upon the regulatory and formal processing of care arrangements and the more 'visible' indicators around placement disruptions and the child's outcomes in regard to education and health – imperative though these are.

In earlier chapters we noted that much has been made of the globalised shift to a more individualistic ethos in advanced societies and the consequent erosion of traditional family or communal life. We do not rehearse those arguments again (see Bauman 2003, 2007; Smart 2007; Williams 2004), nor would we ever assert that our study refutes such claims. Instead we follow Smart (2007, p.9) who argues that 'qualitative studies cannot prove or disprove the grand theories (such as individualisation), they can only bolster or chip away at their credibility'. Accordingly, we suggest that our study 'chips away' at 'the decline in the family' thesis insofar as our small sample revealed kinship continuity across generations and localities. The families and their networks of friends and kin provided significant support and anchorage for foster children (see Boddy 2013). These were not entities in decline; rather they were highly adaptive systems engaged in a range of emotional and practical exchanges that sustained daily a notion of 'us' the 'family'. Their internal and external connectedness provided a rich context of support for birth and foster children alike. The private yet profound function of these families and their networks in providing care cannot easily be 'measured' without losing sight of their unique meaning to the people involved (see Smart 2007). At best we have been able to offer some useful insights into the nature of care as constructed within the mundane world of 'ordinary' homes occupied by some very special families who care because they care. Their unassuming motives in offering to foster – because people *should* care about disadvantaged children – belie virtues and qualities that we far too easily take for granted.

Key messages for practice

Listen to the stakeholders

There are a number of implications for practice from this study. The first is that some excellent work takes place by fostering families and their views should be listened to with more regard around matching. Their expertise is often unacknowledged or not even recognised. Many children have found permanence, security and stability from foster care that they had never previously experienced. In fostering, children and families have the chance to 'try each other out', providing an obvious opportunity to consider longer-term possibilities. If the child and the foster family wish to become part of a long-term care arrangement this must be listened to and taken seriously unless it is not in the child's interests. Long-term arrangements must not be rejected simply because professionals may wish to free up carers as a future resource or to implement some prior care plan regardless of new preferences around long-term care. 'Forever' families are not found easily by children, and should be cherished not jeopardised. Adoption by carers should be encouraged as advocated by Sinclair (2010) and more research is needed into the impact of concurrent planning whereby those wishing to adopt can foster the child first while awaiting approval (see Borthwick and Donnelly 2013).

This study suggests, as have others (Sinclair *et al.* 2005b), that notions of short-term and long-term care are not always helpful. Placements that are only intended as short term but where the child and family 'click' and display signs of meaningful attachment should be allowed to continue where feasible, as alternative plans may be unsuccessful. Our participants, adults and children, cited instances where it seemed that sometimes organisational policy took precedence over individual needs and choices (see Minnis and Walker 2012). As Berridge (2001, p.172) rightly observed, 'organisations owe it to the people that they serve to keep in mind their key overall objective of improving the quality of life of children and families'. Choosing and being chosen was a vital ingredient in the success stories of both the fostered children and the fostering family. Choosing is essential for participants to demonstrate their self-determination, their commitment to care and to display acceptance (Boddy 2013). Financial support should be put in place to facilitate adoption or residence orders to further increase the likelihood of long and lasting care.

Parenting style and assimilation into the family

Throughout we have attempted to map the day-to-day informal family practices that underpin successful fostering and the lessons that can be learned from this. The vital aspects of effective parenting that surfaced from our study were acceptance and warmth, blended with an authoritative style. Parenting style was highly significant in helping vulnerable young people whose sometimes difficult behaviour was moderated by caring that was consistent, warm and empathetic. This approach to parenting and care was often tested, but in most instances carers were able to absorb some extreme expressions of distress and challenging conduct until the children began to assimilate and stabilise.

Foster families need to have clear rules that are reasonable, not oppressive, and are tailored to the needs of the foster child. It is the accessibility of the rules and the ability of the child to understand, digest and interpret the rules that allows the child to settle in the home. Our study noted how some carers more readily 'click' with particular children than might other carers. However, where the 'click' or 'chemistry' did not occur or had not yet happened, it was evident that fostering was quite a laboured and stressful experience for some families. It is difficult to know whether parenting style in foster care can be 'taught', but workshops discussing attachment, resilience, different approaches to parenting and dealing with challenging behaviour which are jointly facilitated by foster carers and professionals can help demonstrate the importance of parenting style and encourage carers to see themselves as beacons of good practice.

Carers and therapists can be instrumental in helping a fostered child move through loss and ambivalence towards adaptation and assimilation into a foster home (Cairns 2006). It was notable that a therapist was more readily available via the independent agencies than in the local authorities in our study. It would of course be beneficial if this service could become more accessible to all looked after children given what we know about their sense of anxiety, loss and consequent attachment needs on entering foster care (Aldgate and Jones 2006). Foster carers and birth children may also need ongoing support to cope with a placement; it is also the case that foster families experience loss when particular children leave them and some may need help in dealing with their sense of bereavement (see Blythe *et al.* 2012).

Physical care and emotional warmth

The provision of physical care in fostering can be overlooked because incorporating this into service standards and outcomes is not straightforward. However, physical nurturing and bodily comfort featured prominently in accounts from the children. Attention to physical appearance and grooming and its impact upon self-esteem should not be under-estimated and should be actively encouraged. Touching and hugging were valued highly by the fostered young people who often had limited experiences of positive and in some instances non-sexual intimacy. This aspect of touch in care settings remains a topic of ongoing debate. Touch poses risk as well as therapeutic potential. Occupational opinion differs and the matter always calls for careful reflection by foster families and professionals. Pets proved to be significant in offering foster children the possibility of physical comfort and nurturing as well as providing opportunities for learning to be responsible and to give and receive affection. To repeat, emotional warmth and physical touch were highly valued by children with little positive warmth previously in their lives. Rather than being touch-averse as part of a risk minimisation strategy, touch should be placed firmly back on the agenda and highlighted as an important tool in the repertoire of interpersonal skills held by carers and their children too.

Individualised placements that provide 'time', 'space' and 'play'

Some placements in our study could be described as gender specific and the 'gender fit' of a family should be considered when the initial explorations for a placement are being made. The impact of individualised placements for young males and females as a means to optimise effective care was evident throughout the study. Some families could provide more feminised spaces for children, whereas others offered more masculine-oriented settings. Where the gender preferences of carers are not met by foster agencies it is more likely that a placement will disrupt (Farmer 2010). Aspects of gender and sexuality, particularly the needs of gay and lesbian young people, need to be factored into planning (Cosis Brown 2014). Foster children may have been exposed to harmful sexual practices before entering care and may in any event be sexually active. Hence, training in matters of sex and sexuality will be important topics for carers, particularly so given that many foster children will be reaching puberty.

Time needs to be prioritised for private and intimate engagements between carers and children to promote attachment and belonging. Foster children also need their own clearly understood space (bedrooms in most instances) and personalisation of their own belongings. This in turn allows the young people to respect the space and belongings of others. Space also enables foster children, birth children and carers to enjoy much-needed seclusion within the home. Space for play and leisure (for example, outdoor space, leisure centres, parks and caravans) were seen as important environments which created further opportunities for fostered young people to develop their skills in handling different situations and people. The Fostering Network (2013) note the benefits of camping and caravanning and have an outdoor adventures website which aims to provide practical advice, resources and activities that carers and foster children can undertake together. Similarly, the charity Learning Through Landscapes (2014) offers many examples of how parents and carers can become involved in creative outdoor play activities that provide educational value for children.

In our study, the children wanted and needed safe places in their own neighbourhoods (see Evans and Holland 2012). Their feelings of connectedness and being part of a peer group and the benefits this offered were facilitated by access to playing out in the locality. This independence from adult supervision allowed for a sense of autonomy, essential for the development of resilience. Similarly, autonomy over maintaining family links and promoting friendship networks for young people was also assisted by the use of internet and social media sites. These technologies carry potential risks as well as benefits for child wellbeing, and carers and professionals need to be well informed and adept in dealing with both (Simpson 2013).

Self-esteem is an aspect of resilience and developed through a range of interests. Foster children should be encouraged to access a range of extra-curricular activities. Whilst seemingly obvious this could be more actively encouraged by carers; resources and payment for this should be made available to the placement. Promoting activities should be given greater prominence within the fostering role, rather than being seen more the job of an external mentor, youth worker or voluntary project. Many parents spend money and time on supporting their children to undertake evening, weekend and holiday activities and looked after children should also have access to these same 'ordinary' opportunities. The willingness of carers to try out new interests or hobbies jointly with the child should be encouraged as a means by which fostered children can learn to engage positively with the wider community (Gilligan 2007). Participating in activities and sports and shared allegiance to sporting teams offered a sense of connectedness and belonging for fostered young males in particular, and appeared to bolster their self-esteem and thereby potentially increase their resilience.

Family network, siblings, and culture

Young people were supported by extended foster family members including grandparents, uncles, aunts and adult birth children which allowed them to feel connected, related and part of a wider family support network. This connectivity and density to family membership may be under-recognised in fostering research. Children in this study benefited from being placed with other foster children and the reciprocal care that it afforded. They sometimes did not appreciate being the sole child in the home. Rural locations could exacerbate these difficulties and the impact of this needs to be considered. Only one sibling group was placed together in this study and this was experienced as supportive and helpful, yet all the other foster children had siblings but no others had been placed with them. More emphasis needs to be placed on keeping siblings together and more carers trained and allocated for this role – for example, those carers who do not have birth children living in the home. All of the carers in this study were White UK citizens although there were six Black British children fostered with them. Notably, this was not raised as a matter of interest or concern by any of the young people or carers during interviews nor in their audio diaries. While the vexed question of ethnic, cultural and linguistic matching continues to tax service providers, for the children and carers in this study there seemed no obvious discomforts arising from their different ethnic backgrounds.

To reiterate, the foster children valued relationality, feeling connected and part of a greater whole. The importance of the carers' family networks to the foster children has been highlighted in this study and if this were more fully recognised by professionals it might lead foster agencies to extend some of their training to extended family members. The positive feelings of the foster children with regard to their connection to the immediate community would suggest the need for more emphasis in placement planning to be focused on their taking part in local activities and groups.

Birth and foster children – care and reciprocity

Birth children were a key element of placement success. In some cases they made significant sacrifices in terms of space and opportunities for undivided parental attention. The needs of birth children did not automatically override those of the foster child who often took priority in the home setting. But there was an exchange of sorts; the birth children benefited from a deeper understanding of the complexities and difficulties of other children's lives and learnt vicariously about the social worlds of those fostered. On occasion birth children were put in challenging situations, including having allegations made against them. Placing foster children with birth children of a similar age (especially with the same name) can give rise to tensions and consideration of this needs to be factored into placement planning.

Birth children in fostering contexts have the same rights to protection, participation and self-determination as foster children. Our study suggested there should be more access to training and support for birth children and more meaningful involvement when planning the placement and matching the foster child. More group-based support is needed for birth children, possibly via virtual communities where birth children can share, learn from and assist each other. Not only are birth children valuable contributors to fostering arrangements, but evidence suggests that some of these young people may also become the foster carers of tomorrow (Twigg and Swan 2007).

Birth, adopted and foster children all displayed notable strength and resilience. All were able to locate and develop their abilities and achievements through extra-curricular activities in and out of the home. This offered significant potential to improve self-esteem. None of the foster children felt sorry for themselves and the majority felt appreciative of the opportunities that they were being given and viewed themselves as active participants in the fostering process. The foster children reciprocated too through their communing and sharing in the home, and through the care they returned which they demonstrated in a number of small but significant daily acts that enhanced family life.

Food, family and time

Food of course is fundamental to the lives of children but can be seen also as a potential therapeutic device, which merits more thought in the training and child development workshops that carers attend. The eating of communal meals and the joint preparation of food and table were seen as highly significant by the young people. The symbolic and practical importance of preparing good nourishing food and the regularity of mealtimes should not be under-estimated as part of physical, emotional and cultural wellbeing. Family life is seen to be enacted through such routines; their regularity and constancy become taken-for-granted structures in which foster children locate themselves in the home and its membership. Likewise, having time to spend together as a distinctive 'group', for example through the Sunday lunch routine, was an important ritual by which families and often their extended kin could be enacted and displayed to the foster children.

More recognition is needed of the importance to successful fostering of sitting together to partake of family meals and its significance as a vehicle for communication. The young people valued food not just as sustenance but something to be enjoyed and shared. The adaption of daily menus to the 'food personae' (Brannen *et al.* 1994) of the children was a symbolic gesture which allowed the young people to feel special and cared about; it also encouraged some reciprocity in foster children preparing and cooking food. A more nuanced grasp of food should be placed on the training agenda of foster service providers.

It is important that time is freed up to be spent with foster children in order to help them come to terms with separation from their families and to create meaningful attachments in the foster home (see Aldgate and McIntosh 2006). In our study this was assisted by at least one carer in each family being dedicated solely to the role of fostering. This also enabled them to attend a range of related commitments – for example, school meetings, health appointments, external activities. There were many child-related demands on carers' time overall and opportunities to engage in activities without any children seemed extremely limited.

Limitations of the study

This study is based upon a small sample of successful placements and does not seek to be representative of foster care more generally. The carers and children are however 'representative of themselves and worthy of study in their own right' (Thomas 2001, p.200). We were only able to gather data about what the participants chose to share verbally in interviews or audio diaries or to display in their behaviour during our research visits. We did not seek to interview professionals, the aim instead being to focus exclusively on the home setting and the perceptions of children and carers about family life and fostering. Had time and cost permitted, it would have been useful to compare these families with those generating less successful outcomes, revealing more insights into the rarely glimpsed processes of care in the foster home.

There were areas of interest that, counter-intuitively, did not surface in the study. For example, while not directly solicited in interviews, matters of ethnicity, sexual activity or sexuality were rarely brought up if at all by the carers or the young people. Similarly, only a few of the foster children volunteered any reflections about their own parents and seemed to draw a veil over this aspect of their lives. Education and related themes about school life were rarely, if ever, highlighted within the responses of most fostered young people. While all of these areas would have been interesting to delve into, it was a principle of the research to allow the young people to filter out areas of sensitivity rather than permit the research methods to become overly intrusive. As Thomas notes (2001, p.102) when researching with children 'it may be necessary to make space for children's own ideas about what is relevant, interesting or important'.

Areas for future research

Further studies into cross-cutting aspects of identity and maturation (e.g. gender/sexuality/ethnicity/disability) of young people and their 'fit' with different types of foster arrangements (e.g. solo carer, same-sex couples, male and female couples, carers with and without birth/other children) could be illuminating and may help improve matching and stability. The complex and contested realm of 'touch' in care settings would benefit from much more careful evaluation to elucidate the skills needed to manage risk and yield therapeutic gains. More research into the use and impact of the internet and social media upon foster care settings would be timely and valuable. A comparative study into extra-curricular activities promoted by carers or by external agencies might generate useful insight into their relative impacts upon self-esteem and resilience. Additionally, further studies that examine the skills and capacities of birth children and the training or support they might require would help ensure their contribution is properly understood and their need are met. The value of concurrent planning arrangements – fostering to adopt – needs further exploration to identify its full potential.

REFERENCES

Aitken, S. (2001) *Geographies of Young People: The Morally Contested Space of Identity.* London: Routledge.

Aldgate, J. and Hawley, D. (1986) *Foster Home Breakdown.* London: BAAF.

Aldgate, J. and Jones, D. (2006) 'The Place of Attachment in Children's Development.' In J. Aldgate, D. Jones, W. Rose and C. Jefferey (eds) *The Developing World of the Child.* London: Jessica Kingsley Publishers.

Aldgate, J. and McIntosh, M. (2006) *Time Well Spent: A Study of Well-being and Children's Daily Activities.* Edinburgh: Social Work Inspection Agency.

Arthur, S., Mitchekk, M., Lewis, J. and McNaughton Nicholls, C. (2014) 'Designing Fieldwork.' In J. Ritchie, J. Lewis, C. McNaughton Nicholls and R. Ormiston (eds) *Qualitative Research Practice* (2nd edition). London: Sage.

Ashley, B., Hollows, J., Jones, S. and Taylor, B (2004) *Food and Cultural Studies.* London: Routledge.

Ashley, C., Featherstone, B., Roskill, C., Ryan, M. and While, S. (2006) *Fathers Matter – Context and Recommendations.* London: Family Rights Group.

Atkinson, P., Coffey, A., Delamont, S., Lofland, J. and Lofland, L. (2001) *Handbook of Ethnography.* London: Sage.

BAAF (2012) *The Law.* Available at www.baaf.org.uk/res/law, accessed on 12 February 2014.

BAAF (2014) *The Law.* Available at www.baaf.org.uk/res/law, accessed on 12 February 2014.

Baggini, J. (2007) 'My life in every town.' *The Guardian*, 7 March, pp. 12–15.

Barnes, R. and Eichler, J. (1992) 'Preface.' In R. Barnes and J. Eichler (eds) *Dress and Gender: Making and Meaning.* Oxford: Berg Publishers.

Bauman, Z. (2003) *Liquid Love: On the Frailty of Human Bonds.* Cambridge: Polity Press.

Bauman, Z. (2007) *Liquid Times: Living in an Age of Uncertainty.* Cambridge: Polity Press.

Beck, S. (2012) *Care in Everyday Life: An Ethic of Care in Practice.* Bristol: Polity Press.

Beck, U. and Beck-Gernsheim, E. (1995) *The Normal Chaos of Love.* Cambridge: Polity Press.

Beck-Gernsheim, E. (2002) *Re-inventing the Family: In Search of New Lifestyles.* Cambridge: Polity Press.

Bell, D. and Valentine, G. (1997) *Consuming Geographies: We Are Where We Eat.* London: Routledge.

Berridge, D (1999) *Foster Care Part 1 and 2, Research Highlights.* London: The National Children's Bureau.

Berridge, D. (2001) 'Foster Families.' In P. Foley, J. Roche and T. Tucker (eds) *Children in Society: Contemporary Theory, Policy and Practice.* Basingstoke: Palgrave.

Berridge, D. (2002) *The Importance of Stability. Research Briefing Number 2.* London: Nuffield Foundation.

Berridge, D. (2007) 'Theory and explanation in child welfare: Education and looked after children.' *Child and Family Social Work* 12, 1, 1–10.

Berridge, D. and Cleaver, H. (1987) *Foster Home Breakdown.* Oxford: Blackwell.

Berridge, D., Biehal, N. and Henry, L. (2012) *Living in Residential Homes,* Research Report. London: DfE.

Best, S. (2012) *Understanding and Doing Successful Research.* London: Pearson.

Biehal, N. (2005) *Working with Adolescents. Supporting Families: Preventing Breakdown.* London: BAAF.

Biehal, N. (2014) 'A sense of belonging: meanings of family and home in long-term foster care.' *British Journal of Social Work 44,* 4, 995–971.

Biehal, N., Ellison, S., Baker, C. and Sinclair, I. (2010) *Belongings and Permanence: Outcomes in Long-term Foster Care and Adoption.* London: BAAF.

Blythe, S., Halcomb, E., Wilkes, L. and Jackson, D. (2012) 'Perceptions of long-term female carers: I am not a carer, I'm a Mother.' *British Journal of Social Work 43,* 6, 1056–1072.

Boddy, J. (2013) *Understanding Permanence for Looked After Children: A Review of the Research for the Care Enquiry,* available at www.scie-socialcareonline.org.uk/understanding-permanence-for-looked-after-children-a-review-of-research-for-the-care-inquiry/r/allG0000000189471AA, accessed on 24 February 2014.

Borthwick, S. and Donnelly, S. (2013) *Achieving Early Permanence for Babies and Young Children.* London: BAAF.

Bowlby, J. (1951) *Childcare and the Growth of Love.* Harmondsworth: Penguin.

Bowlby, J. (1969) *Attachment and Loss.* London: Hogarth Press.

Brandon, M., Belderson, P., Warren, C., Howe, D., Gardner, R. Dodsworth, J. and Black, J. (2008) *Analysing Child Deaths and Serious Injury through Abuse and Neglect: What Can we Learn? A Biennial Analysis of Serious Case Reviews, 2003–2005.* London: DCSF.

Brannen, J., Dodd, K., Oakley, A. and Storey, P. (1994) *Young People, Health and Family Life.* Buckingham: Open University.

Brannen, J. and Moss, P. (2003) 'Some Thoughts on Rethinking Children's Care.' In J. Brannen and P. Moss (eds) *Rethinking Children's Care*. Maidenhead: Open University Press.

Brannen, J. and Nilsen, A. (2006) 'From fatherhood to fathering: transmission and change among British fathers in four-generation families.' *Sociology 40*, 2, 335–353.

Brannen, J., Parutis, V., Mooney, A. and Wigfall, V. (2011) 'Fathers and intergenerational transmission in social context.' *Ethics and Education 7*, 6, 155–170.

British Sociological Association (2002) *Statement of Ethical Practice for the British Sociological Association (March 2002)*. Available at www.britsoc.co.uk/about/equality/statement-of-ethical-practice.aspx, accessed on 12 February 2014.

Buehler, C., Cox, M.E., and Cuddeback, G. (2003) 'Foster parents perceptions of factors that promote or inhibit successful fostering.' *Qualitative Social Work 2*, 61–83.

Buehler, C., Rhodes, K., Orme, J. and Cuddeback, G. (2006) 'The potential of successful foster family care; conceptualising competency domains of foster carers.' *Child Welfare 85*, 3, 523–558.

Bullock, R. (2002) *Two Influences on the Effectiveness of Foster Care; the Needs of Children and Families and Arrangements for Leaving*. London: Nuffield Foundation.

Bullock, R. (2012) 'Crisis? What crisis?' *Adoption and Fostering 36*, 2, 2–3.

Bullock, R., Courtney, M. Parker, R., Sinclair, I. and Thoburn, J. (2006) 'Can the corporate state parent?' *Adoption and Fostering 30*, 4, 6–19.

Burgon, H. (2014) *Equine Assisted Therapy and Learning with At-risk Young People: Horses as Healers*. Basingstoke: Palgrave Macmillan.

Bywaters, J. and Jones, R. (2007) *Sexuality and Social Work*. Exeter: Learning Matters.

Caballero, C., Edwards, R., Goodyer, A. and Okitipi, T. (2012) 'The diversity and complexity of the everyday lives of mixed racial and ethnic families: Implications for adoption and fostering practice and policy.' *Adoption and Fostering 36*, 3, 9–24.

Cairns, K. (2002) *Attachment, Trauma and Resilience*. London: BAAF.

Cairns, K. (2006) *Attachment, Trauma and Resilience*. London: BAAF.

Cairns, K. and Fursland, E. (2007) *Trauma and Recovery*. London: BAAF.

Cameron, C. and Petrie, P. (2011) *Social Pedagogy and Foster Care: A Scoping Study*. London:Thomas Coram Research Unit.

Cameron, R., Maginn, C. (2008) 'The authentic warmth dimension of professional childcare.' *British Journal of Social Work, 38*, 6, 115–172.

Carroll, J. S., Olsen, C. and Buckmiller, N. (2007) 'Family boundary ambiguity: A 30 year review of theory, research and measurement.' *Family Relations 56*, 2, 210–230.

Chambers, D. (2001) *Representing the Family*. London: Sage.

Chang, G. and Foley, L. (1994) *Mothering Ideology: Experience and Agency.* New York: Routledge.

Chapman, T. (2004) *Gender and Domestic Life: Changing Practices in Families and Households.* Basingstoke: Palgrave.

Chase, E., Simon, A. and Jacson, S. (2006) 'Towards a Positive Perspective.' In E. Chase, A. Simon and S. Jackson (eds) *In Care and After: A Positive Perspective.* London: Routledge.

Cheal, D. (2002) *The Sociology of Family Life.* New York: Palgrave Macmillan.

Children Act (1948) London: HMSO.

Children Act (1989) London: HMSO.

Children's Society (2006) *Good Childhood? A Question for Our Times,* www.goodchildhood.org.uk.

Christiansen, O., Havnen, K., Havik, T. and Anderssen, N. (2013) 'Cautious belonging: Relationships in long-term foster-care.' *British Journal of Social Work* 43, 4, 720–738.

Christensen, P. (2000) 'Childhood and the Cultural Constitution of Vulnerable Bodies.' In A. Prout (ed.) *The Body, Childhood and Society.* Hampshire: Macmillan Press.

Christensen, P. and O'Brien, M. (2003) 'Children in the City: Introducing New Perspectives.' In P. Christensen and M. O'Brien (eds) *Home, Neighbourhood and Community.* London: Routledge Falmer.

Ciarrochi, J., Randle, M., Miller, L. and Dolnicar, S. (2012) 'Hope for the future; identifying the individual characteristics of people who are interested in and intend to foster-care.' *British Journal of Social Work* 42, 1, 7–25.

Clark, A. (2014) 'Undertaking Research with Children.' In T. Maynard and S. Powell (eds) *Introduction to Early Childhood Studies* (3rd edition). London, Sage.

Clark, H. (2009) *The Age of Foster Care.* London: Fostering Network.

Cocker, C. and Brown, H.C. (2010) 'Sex, sexuality and relationships: Developing confidence and discernment when assessing lesbian and gay prospective adopters.' *Adoption and Fostering 34,* 1.

Cohn, A. (2007) *Constipation, Withholding and Your Child; A Family Guide to Soiling and Wetting.* London: Jessica Kingsley Publishers.

Collier, F. (1999) 'Independent Agencies.' In A. Wheal (ed.) *The Companion to Foster Care.* Lyme Regis: Russell House Publishing.

Collis, A. and Butler, J. (2003) *Fit to Foster: A Profile of Foster Care in Wales.* Cardiff: Fostering Network.

Colton, M., Roberts, S. and Williams, M. (2008) 'The Recruitment and Retention of Family Foster Carers: An International and Cross-Cultural Analysis.' *British Journal of Social Work* 38, 5, 865–884.

Colton, M. and Williams, M. (1997) 'The nature of foster care: International trends.' *Adoption and Fostering 21,* 1, 44–49.

Compas, B., Hinden, R. and Gerhardt, C. (1995) 'Adolescent development: Pathways and processes of resilience and risk.' *Annual Review of Psychology 46*, 265–293.

Cossar, J. and Neil, E. (2013) 'Making sense of siblings; connections and severances in post adoption social work.' *Child and Family Social Work 18*, 67–76.

Cosis Brown, H. (2014) *Social Work and Foster Care*. London: Sage.

Cousins, J. (2009) 'Disabled Children: Pathways to Care.' In C. Burns (ed.) *Disabled Children Living Away from Home in Foster Care and Residential Care*. Chichester: Wiley.

Craik, J. (1989) 'The Making of Mother: The Role of the Kitchen in the Home.' In G. Allan and G. Crow (eds) *Home and Family: Creating the Domestic Sphere*. Basingstoke: Macmillan Press.

D'Cruz, H. and Jones, M. (2014) *Social Work Research in Practice* (2nd edition). London: Sage.

Dance, C., Rushton, A. and Quinton, D. (2002) 'Emotional abuse in early childhood: Relationships with progress in subsequent family placements.' *Journal of Psychiatry 43*, 3, 395–407.

Daniel, B. and Wassell, S. (2002) *The Early Years – Assessing and Promoting Resilience in Vulnerable Children*. London: Jessica Kingsley Publishers.

Davey, D. and Pithouse, A. (2008) 'Schooling and looked after children: Exploring contexts and outcomes in standard attainment tests (SATS).' *Adoption and Fostering 32*, 3, 60–72.

De Sousa, S., Roach, R. and Lawrence, J. (2011) 'Successful fostering of black and ethnic minority children.' *Community Care Inform*, 23 August, pp.32–33.

Department of Education (2010) *The Children Act 1989 Guidance and Regulations. Volume 2: Care Planning, Placement and Case Review*. London: HMSO.

Department of Education (2011) *The Children Act 1989 Guidance and Regulations. Volume 4: Fostering Services*. London: HMSO.

Department of Education and Skills (2002) *Birth to Three Matters: A Framework to Support Children in Their Earliest Years*. Norwich: HMSO.

Department of Education and Skills (2007) *Care Matters: Consultation Response*. Norwich: HMSO.

Department of Health (1988) *Protecting Children: A Guide for Social Workers Undertaking a Comprehensive Assessment*. London: HMSO.

Department of Health (2000) *Framework for the Assessment of Children in Need and Their Families*. London: Department of Health.

Dodsworth, J., Bailey, S., Schofield, G., Cooper, N., Fleming, P. and Young, J. (2013) 'Internet technology: An empowering or alienating tool for communication between foster carers and social workers?' *British Journal of Social Work 43*, 4, 775–795.

Dolan, P. (2008) 'Prospective Possibilities for Building Resilience in Children, their Families and Communities.' *Child Care in Practice 14*, 1, 83–91.

Doobar, P. (1996) *We're Here Too: The View of Natural Children of Foster Parents*. Hants: Hampshire Foster Care Federation.

Douglas, M. (1984) *Food and Social Order.* New York: Russell Sage Foundation.

Douglas, M. (1989) *Purity and Danger: An Analysis of the Concepts of Pollution and Taboo.* London: Ark.

Douglas, M. (1998) 'Coded Messages.' In S. Griffiths and J. Wallace (eds) *Consuming Passions: Food in the Age of Anxiety.* Manchester: Manchester University Press, pp 103–109.

Edwards, A. and Talbot, R. (1999) *The Hard Pressed Researcher.* London: Longman.

Eichler, M (1997) *Family Shifts: Families, Policies and Gender Equality.* Ontario: Oxford University Press.

Elden, S. (2013) 'Inviting the messy: Drawing, methods and "children's voices".' *Childhood 20*, 1, 66–81.

Elgar, F., Craig, W. and Trites, S. (2013) 'Family dinners, communication and mental health in Canadian adolescents.' *Journal of Adolescent Health 52*, 4, 433–438.

Emond, R., McIntosh, I. and Punch, S. (2013) 'Food and feelings in residential care.' *British Journal of Social Work*, doi: 10.1093/bjsw/bct009.

Ennew, J. (1994) 'Time for Children or Time for Adults?' In J. Qvortrup, M. Bardy, G. Sgritta and H. Wintersberger (eds) *Childhood Matters: Social Theory, Practice and Politics.* Aldershot: Avebury Press.

Erera, I. P. (2002) *Family Diversity. Continuity and Change in the Contemporary Family.* London: Sage.

Erikson, E. H. (1968) *Identity: Youth and Crisis.* New York: Norton.

Evans, R. and Holland, S. (2012) 'Community parenting and the informal safeguarding of children at neighbourhood level.' *Families and Relationships and Society 1*, 2, 173–190.

Facer, K., Forlong, J., Furlong, R. and Sutherland, R. (2001) 'Home is Where the Hardware is.' In I. Hutchby and J. Moran-Ellis. (eds) *Children, Technology and Culture: The Impact of Technologies in Children's Everyday Lives.* London: Routledge Falmer.

Farmer, E. (2002) *Factors Related to Stability in Foster Care for Adolescents: Evidence from a Recent Study.* London: Nuffield Foundation.

Farmer, E. (2010) 'Fostering Adolescents in England: What Contributes to Success?' in E. Fernandez and R. Barth (eds) *How Does Foster Care Work? International Evidence and Outcomes.* London: Jessica Kingsley Publishers.

Farmer, E., Moyers, S. and Lipscombe, J. (2004) *Fostering Adolescents.* London: Jessica Kingsley Publishers.

Featherstone, B. (2010) 'Ethic of Care.' In M. Gray and S. Webb (eds) *Ethics and Value Perspectives in Social Work.* Basingstoke: Palgrave.

Fernandez, E. and Barth, R. (2010) 'Introduction: Reviewing international evidence to inform foster care policy and practice.' In E. Fernandez and R. Barth (eds) *How Does Foster Care Work? International Evidence and Outcomes.* London: Jessica Kingsley Publishers, pp. 20–28.

Finch, J. (1989) *Family Obligations and Social Change.* Cambridge: Polity Press.

Finch, J. (2007) 'Displaying families.' *Sociology 41*, 65–68.

Finch, J. (2008) 'Naming names: Kinship, individuality and personal names.' *Sociology 42*, 4, 709–725.

Finch, J. (2011) 'Exploring the Concept of Display in Family Relationships.' In E. Dermott and J. Seymour (eds) *Displaying Families: a New Concept for the Sociology of Family Life*. Basingstoke: Palgrave Macmillan.

Finch, J. and Groves, D (eds) (1983) *A Labour of Love; Women, Work and Caring*. London: Routledge.

Finch, J. and Mason, J. (1993) *Negotiating Family Responsibilities*. London: Routledge.

Fisher, M. and DeBell, D. (2007) 'Approaches to Parenting.' In D. DeBell (ed.) *Public Health Care Practice and School-age Population*. London: Hodder Education.

Flynn, R., Ghazal, H., Legault, L., Vandermeulen, G. and Petrick, S. (2004) 'Use of population measures and norms to identify resilient outcomes in young people in care: An exploratory study.' *Children and Family Social Work 9*, 1, 48–65.

Fonagy, P., Steele, M., Steele, H., Higgitt, A. and Target, M. (1994) 'The theory and practice of resilience.' *Journal of Psychology and Psychiatry 35*, 2, 231–257.

Forrester, D., Goodman, K., Coker, C., Binnie, C. and Jensch, G. (2009) 'What is the impact of public care on children's welfare? Review of the research findings from England and Wales and their policy implications.' *Journal of Social Policy 38*, 3, 439–446. Available at www.fostering.net/news/article, accessed on 24 February 2014.

Fostering Network (2007) *Most Foster Families in Wales Struggle on a Low Income*. London: Fostering Network.

Fostering Network (2010) *Men Who Care*. London: Fostering Network and Glamorgan University.

Fostering Network (2011) *Men are Good Foster Carers Too*. London: Fostering Network.

Fostering Network (2012) *Safer Caring: a New Approach*. London: Fostering Network.

Fostering Network (2013) 'Call for more foster carers to improve stability as campaign begins.' London: Fostering Network.

Fostering Network (2014) Fostering Adventures. Available at http:// fosteringadventures.com/ outdoors/lets-go-on-a-picnic, accessed on 24 February 2014.

Fox, W. (2001) *The Significance of Natural Children in Foster Families*. Social Work Monograph 184. Norwich: University of East Anglia.

Fraser, M., Richman, J. and Galinsky, M. (1999) 'Risk, protection and resilience: Toward a conceptual framework for social work practice.' *Social Work Research 22*, 3,131–143.

Fratter, J., Rowe, J., Sapsford, D. and Thoburn, J. (1991) *Permanent Family Placement: A Decade of Experience*. London: BAAF.

Furedi, F. (2008) *Paranoid Parenting* (3rd edition). London: Continuum.

Fursland, E. (2011) *Foster Care and Social Networking.* London: BAAF.

Gabb, J. (2007) *Stretched to the Limits: Accounting for Contemporary Intimate Relationships.* Paper presented at Centre for Research on Families and Relationships Conference 'Extended and Extending Families', Edinburgh, June 2007.

Gabb, J. (2008) *Reframing Relationality in Families and the Sociology of Intimacy.* Paper given to Cardiff University Children's Research Group, June 2008.

Gaskell, C. (2010) 'If the social worker called at least it would show they cared: Young care leavers' perspectives on the importance of care.' *Children and Society* 24, 2, 136–147.

George, S., Van Oudenhoven, N. and Wazir, R. (2003) 'Foster care beyond the crossroads: Lessons from beyond an international comparative analysis.' *Childhood* 10, 3, 343–361.

Gill, T. (2007) *No Fear: Growing Up in a Risk Averse Society.* London: Calouste Gulbenkien Foundation.

Gillies, V. (2007) *Marginalized Mothers: Exploring Working-Class Experiences of Parenting.* London: Routledge.

Gillies, V., Ribbens McCarthy, J. and Holland, J. (2001) *Pulling Together, Pulling Apart: The Family Lives of Young People.* London: Joseph Rowntree Foundation.

Gilligan R. (2000) 'Men as foster carers; a neglected resource?' *Adoption and Fostering* 24, 2, 63–69.

Gilligan, R. (2001) *Promoting Resilience.* London: BAAF.

Gilligan, R. (2007) 'Spare time activities for young people in care: What can they contribute to educational progress?' *Adoption and Fostering 31*, 1, 92–99.

Gilligan, R. (2009) *Promoting Resilience: Supporting Children and Young People Who Are in Care, Adopted or in Need.* London: BAAF.

Golding, K., Dent, H., Nissim, R. and Stott, E. (2006*) Thinking Psychologically about Children Who Are Looked After and Adopted. Space for Reflection.* Oxford: Wiley.

Golding, K. and Hughes, (2012) *Creating Loving Attachments.* London: Jessica Kingsley Publishers.

Greig, A., Taylor, J. and MacKay, T. (2007) *Doing Research with Children* (2nd edition). London: Sage.

Greishaber, S. (2004) *Rethinking Parent and Child Conflict.* New York: Routledge Falmer.

Grosz, E. (1994) *Volatile Bodies: Towards a Corporeal Feminism.* Bloomington: Indiana University Press.

Guerney-Smith, B., Granger, C. and Fletcher, J. (2010) 'In tune and in time – the Fostering Attachments Group: capturing sustained change in both care giver and child.' *Adoption and Fostering 34*, 4, 50–60.

Haggerty, R., Sharrod, L., Garmezy, N. and Rutter, M. (1996) *Stress, Risk, and Resilience in Children and Adolescents: Processes, Mechanisms and Interventions* (2nd edition). Cambridge: Cambridge University Press.

Hallett, S. (2013) *Child Sexual Exploitation.* Doctoral Thesis, Cardiff University.

Hamil, J. (2007) *The Symbolic Significance of Food in the Treatment, Care and Recovery of Emotionally Damaged Children.* London: Fostering Network.

Happer, H., McCreadie, J. and Aldgate, J. (2006) *Celebrating Success: What Helps Looked After Children Succeed.* Edinburgh: Social Work Inspection Agency.

Harber, A. and Oakley, M. (2012) *Fostering Aspirations: Reforming the Foster Care System in England and Wales.* London: Policy Exchange.

Harwin, J. and Owen, M. (2003) 'Stability in Foster Care', Nuffield Seminar paper, Centre for Research on the Child and Family, University of East Anglia.

Head, A. and Elgar, M. (1999) 'The Placement of Sexually Abused and Abusing Siblings.' In A. Mullender (ed.) *We are Family.* London: BAAF.

Held, V. (2006) *The Ethic of Care: Personal, Political and Global.* Oxford: Oxford University Press.

Helgar, R., (2005) 'Sibling placement in foster care and adoption: An overview of international research.' *Children and Youth Services Review, 27,* 717–739.

Hidden Lives (2014) *Hidden Lives Revealed: A Virtual Archive of Children in Care 1881–1981.* Available at www.hiddenlives.org.uk, accessed on 24 February 2014.

Hill, A. (2007) 'How Friday saved the Sunday Roast.' London: *The Observer* 19.8.07.

Hill, M., Stafford, A., Seaman, P., Ross, N. and Daniel, B. (2007) *Parenting and Resilience.* University of Glasgow: Joseph Rowntree Foundation.

Hind, T. (2010) 'Supporting lesbian, gay and bisexual young people in the foster care families of faith beliefs.' *Community Care,* 23 June.

Hojer, I. (2004) 'What happens in the foster family?' *Adoption and Fostering 28,* 1, 38–48.

Hojer, I., Sebba, J. and Luke, N. (2013) *The Impact of Fostering on Foster Carers' Children: An International Literature Review.* Oxford: Rees Centre Publications.

Holland, S. (2007) *Looked after Children; Unique Perspectives on Family Practices.* Conference paper presented at Centre for Research on Families and Relationships (Extended and Extending Families), Edinburgh, June 2007.

Holland, S. (2010) 'Looked after children and the ethic of care.' *British Journal of Social Work 40,* 4, 1664–1680.

Holland, S. (2011) *Child and Family Assessment in Social Work Practice* (2nd edition). London: Sage.

Holland, S. and Crowley, A. (2013) 'Looked after children and their birth families: Using sociology to explore changing relationships: hidden histories and nomadic childhoods.' *Children and Family Social Work 18,* 57–66.

Holland, S., Tanner, S. and Collicott, H. (2011) 'Everybody's business? A research review of the informal safeguarding of other people's children in the UK.' *Children and Society 25,* 5, 406–416.

Holmes, B. and Silver, M. (2010) 'Managing behaviour with attachment in mind.' *Adoption and Fostering 34,* 1, 65–76.

Howe, D., Brandon, M., Hindings, D. and Schofield, G. (1999) *Attachment Theory, Child Maltreatment and Family Support: A Practice and Assessment Model.* Basingstoke: Macmillan.

Humphries, C. and Kertesz, M. (2012) 'Putting the heart back in to the record: Personal records to support young people in care.' *Adoption and Fostering 36,* 2, 27–39.

Inch, L. J. (1999) 'Aspects of foster fathering.' *Child and Adolescent Social Work Journal 16,* 5, 393–412.

Ironside, L. (2004) 'Living a provisional existence: Thinking about foster carers and the emotional containment of children placed in their care.' *Adoption and Fostering 28,* 4, 36–48.

Ironside, L. (2012) 'Meeting of minds: Using the Tavistock model of child observation and reflective group work in the advanced training of foster carers.' *Adoption and Fostering 36,* 2, 29–42.

Jackson, S. (2006) 'Looking after children away from home, past and present.' In E. Chase, A. Simon and S. Jackson (eds) *In Care and After: A Positive Perspective.* London: Routledge.

Jackson, S. and Martin, P. (1998) 'Surviving the care system: Education and resilience.' *Journal of Adolescence 21,* 569–583.

Jackson, S. and Sachev, D. (2001) *Better Education, Better Futures.* Ilford: Barnardo's.

James, A. and James, L. (2004) *Constructing Childhood: Theory, Policy and Social Practice.* Basingstoke: Palgrave Macmillan.

James, A. and Prout, A. (1997) 'Re-presenting Childhood: Time and Transition in the Study of Childhood.' In A. James and A. Prout (ed.) *Contemporary Issues in Sociological Studies of Childhood.* London: Falmer Press.

Jenks, C. (1996) *Childhood.* London: Routledge.

Jensen, A. and McKee, L. (2003) 'Theorising Childhood and Family Change.' In A. Jensen and L. McKee (eds) *Children and the Changing Family: Between Transformation and Negotiation.* London: Routledge Falmer.

Kehily, M. J. (2004) 'Understanding Childhood: An Introduction to Some Key Themes and Issues.' In M.J. Kehily (ed.) *An Introduction to Childhood Studies.* Maidenhead: Open University Press.

Kellett, M. and Ding, S. (2004) 'Middle Childhood.' In S. Fraser, V. Lewis, S. Ding, M. Kellett and C. Robinson (eds) *Doing Research with Children and Young People.* London: Sage.

Kelly, G. (1995) 'Foster parents and long term placements: Key findings from a Northern Ireland study.' *Children and Society 9,* 2, 19–29.

Kelly, G. and Gilligan, R. (2000) 'Introduction.' In G. Kelly and R. Gilligan (eds) *Issues in Foster Care.* London: Jessica Kingsley Publishers.

Kirton, D., Beecham, J. and Ogilvie, K. (2007) 'Still the poor relations? Perspectives on valuing and listening to foster carers.' *Adoption and Fostering 31,* 3, 6–17.

Kjedsen, C. and Kjeldsen, B. (2010) 'When family becomes the job: Fostering in Denmark.' *Adoption and Fostering 34*, 1, 52–64.

Lawton, K. and Thompson, S. (2013) *Tackling In-work Poverty By Supporting Dual-Earning Families.* York: Joseph Rowntree Foundation.

Laybourne, G., Anderson, J. and Samuel, J. (2008) 'Fostering attachments in looked after children; further insight into the group-based programme for foster carers.' *Adoption and Fostering 32*, 4, 64–76.

Learning Through Landscapes (2014) Available at www.ltl.org.uk, accessed on 18 March 2014.

Leathers, S. (2006) 'Placement disruption and negative placement outcomes among adolescents in long term foster care.' *Child Abuse and Neglect 30*, 307–324.

Lee, N. (2001) *Childhood and Society: Growing up in the Age of Uncertainty.* Maidenhead: Palgrave Macmillan.

Leith, P. (1998) 'Cooking with Kids.' In S. Griffiths and J. Wallace (eds) *Consuming Passions: Food in the Age of Anxiety.* Manchester: Manchester University Press.

Lietz, C. (2006) 'Uncovering stories of family resilience: A mixed methods study of resilient families.' *Families in Society 87*, 4, 575–582.

Lipscombe, J., Moyers, S. and Falmers, E. (2004) 'What changes in "parenting" approaches occur over the course of adolescent foster care placements?' *Child and Family Social Work 9*, 347–357.

Looked After Children Strategic Implementation Group (2013) *National Foster Care Review* Scotland (2013) Final Report. London: Department for Education.

Macdonald, G. (2002) *Helping Foster Carers to Manage Challenging Behaviour: An Evaluation of a Cognitive-Behavioural Training Programme for Foster Carers.* London: Nuffield Foundation.

Madigan, S., Quale, E., Cossar, J. and Paton, K. (2013) 'Feeling the same or feeling different? An analysis of young people in foster care.' *Adoption and Fostering 37*, 4, 89–403.

Madinou, M. and Miller, D. (2012) *Migration and New Media: Transnational Families and Polymedia.* London: Routledge.

McDermid, S., Holmes, L., Kirton, D. and Signoretta, P. (2012) *The Demographic Characteristics of Foster Carers in the UK: Motivations, Barriers, Messages for Recruitment and Retention.* London: Childhood Wellbeing Research Centre.

McVeigh, T. (2012) 'Forty years of feminism but women still do most of the housework.' *The Guardian*, 10 March, p. 7.

Mason, J. and Tipper, B. (2006) *Children, Kinship and Creativity.* Available at www.esrc.ac.uk/my-esrc/grants/RES-000-23-0271-A/outputs/read/90c0ac88-2ecc-4cc8-87c5-3790383e8230, accessed on 8 January 2009.

Matthews, H., Limb, M. and Taylor, M. (2000) 'The Street as Third Space.' In S. Hollway and G. Valentine (eds) *Children's Geographies.* Oxford: Routledge.

Mayall, B. (2002) *Towards a Sociology for Childhood.* Buckingham: Open University.

Mehmet, M. (2005) *What the Standards Say About Fostering.* Lyme Regis: Russell House Publishing.

Mennell, S., Murcott, A. and van Otterloo, A. H. (1992) *The Sociology of Food: Eating, Diet and Culture,* London: Sage.

Minnis, M. and Walker, F. (2012) *The Experiences of Fostering Adoption Processes – the Views of Children and Young People: Literature Review and Gap Analysis.* Slough: National Foundation for Educational Research.

Minty, B. and Braye, S. (2001) 'Allegations against foster carers: An in-depth study.' *Child Abuse Review 10,* 336–350.

Morgan, D. (1996) *Family Connections: An Introduction to Family Studies.* Cambridge: Polity Press.

Morgan, D. (2011) *Rethinking Family Practices.* Basingstoke: Palgrave Macmillan.

Morrow, V. (1996) 'Improving the Neighbourhood.' In P. Chrisensen and M. O'Brien (eds) *Children in the City: Home, Neighbourhood and Community.* London: Taylor & Francis, pp. 161–181.

Morrow, V. (1998) *Understanding Families: Children's Perspectives.* London: National Children's Bureau.

Mullender, A. (ed.) (1999) *We are Family.* London: BAAF.

Munro, E. R., Lushey, C., Ward, H. and National Care Advisory Service with Soper, J., McDermid, S., Holmes, L., Backhelling, J. and Perren, K. (2011) *Evaluation of the Right2BCared4 Pilots: Final Report.* DfE Research Report DFE-RR106. London: Department for Education.

Murcott, A. (1980) *Women's Place: Technique and Technology in the British Kitchen.* Cardiff: Working Paper, Department of Sociology, Cardiff University.

Murcott, A. (1983) 'It's a Pleasure to Cook for Him: Food, Mealtimes and Gender in South Wales Households.' In E. Gamarnikow, D. Morgan, J. Purvis and D. Taylorson (eds) *The Public and the Private.* London: Heinemann.

National Foster Care Association (1997) *Foster Care in Crisis,* London: NFCA.

Newstone, S. (1999) 'Men Who Foster.' In A. Wheal (ed.) *The Companion to Foster Care.* Lyme Regis: Russell House.

Norgate, R., Warhurst, A., Hayden, C., Osborne, C. and Traill, M. (2012) 'Social workers' perspectives on placement instability of looked after children.' *Fostering and Adoption 36,* 2, 4–18.

NSPCC (2013) Available at www.nspcc.org.uk/Inform/resourcesforprofessionalsbullying/bullying_statistics_wda85732.html, accessed on 12 March 2014.

Nutt, L. (1998) *Public Care in a Private Place? The Paradoxical Situation of Foster Carers and the Issue of Payment.* Paper given to Social Policy Association Annual Conference, Loughborough.

Nutt, L. (2002) *Foster Carers: The Dilemmas of Loving the Bureaucratised Child.* PhD, Oxford Brooks University.

Nutt, L. (2006) *The Lives of Foster Carers: Private Sacrifices and Public Restrictions.* Abingdon: Routledge.

Oakley, A. and Ashton, J. (1997) 'Introduction.' In R. Titmuss (1970) *The Gift Relationship: From Human Blood to Social Policy.* Reprinted, London: New Press.

O'Brien, M. (1996) 'Children in Families.' In P. Christensen and M. O'Brien (eds) *Children in the City: Home, Neighbourhood and Community.* London: Taylor & Francis.

O'Connor, G. and Scott, B. (2007) *Parenting Outcomes for Children.* York: Joseph Rowntree Foundation.

OFSTED (2011) Fostering Agencies and Fostering Data Set. London: Ofsted, available at www.ofsted.gov.uk/resources/fostering-agencies-and-fostering-services-dataset-201011, accessed on 12 February 2014. O'Leary, Z. (2014) *The Essential Guide to Doing Your Research Project* (2nd edition). London: Sage.

OFSTED (2012) *Children's Care Monitor 2011: Children on the State of Social Care in England Reported by Children's Rights Director for England.* London: Ofsted (online). Available at www.ofsted.gov.uk/sites/default/files/documents/surveys-and-good-practice/c/Children%27s%20care%20monitor%202011.pdf, accessed on 28 February 2014.

Oosterman, M., Schuengel, C., Slot, N., Bullens, R. and Doreleijers, T. (2007) 'Disruptions in foster care: A review and meta-analysis.' *Children and Youth Services Review 29*, 1, 53–76.

Orme, J. (2002) 'Social work: Gender, care and justice.' *British Journal of Social Work 32*, 3, 799–814.

Orme, J.G. and Buehler, C. (2001) 'Foster family characteristics and behavioural and emotional problems of foster children: A narrative review.' *Family Relations 50*, 1, 3–15.

Osborne, C., Alfonso, J. and Winn, T. (2010) 'Paired reading as a literacy intervention for foster children.' *Adoption and Fostering 34*, 4, 17–26.

Owen, C. and Statham, J. (2009) *Disproportionality in Child Welfare: The Prevalence of Black and Minority Ethnic Children within the Looked After and Children in Need Populations and on Child Protection Registers in England.* London: Thomas Coram Research Unit.

Owen, L. (1989) *Professional Foster Care. A Client Perspective Study.* Social Work Monographs. Norwich: University of East Anglia.

Padbury, P. and Frost, N. (2002) *Solving Problems in Foster Care.* London: The Children's Society.

Parker, J. and Bradley, G. (2010)*Social Work Practice: Assessment, Planning, Intervention and Review* (3rd edition). Exeter: Learning Matters.

Part, D. (1993) 'Fostering as seen by the carers' children.' *Adoption and Fostering 17*, 1, 26–31.

Part, D. (1999) 'Fostering as seen by the carer's children.' In M. Hill (ed.) *Signposts in Fostering.* London: BAAF.

Parton, N. (2003) 'Rethinking professional practice: The contributions of social constructionism and the feminist ethics of care.' *British Journal of Social Work 33*, 1, 1–16.

Peake, L. (2009) *Caring for Children with Disabilities: The Results of a Consultation in the Learning and Support Needs of the Foster Care Work Force.* Northampton: The Fostering Network.

Perez-del-Aguila, R., Holland, S., Faulkner, A., Connoll, D. and Hayes, S. (2003) *Overview and Survey of Effectiveness of Interventions to Promote Stability and Continuity of Care for Looked After Children.* Cardiff: National Assembly for Wales and Cardiff, University School of Social Sciences, University of Wales.

Petrie, P., Boddy, J., Cameron, C., Wigfall, V. and Simon, A. (2006) *Working with Children in Care: European Perspectives.* Milton Keynes: Open University Press.

Piper, H., Powell, J. and Smith, H. (2006) 'Parents, professionals and paranoia. The touching of children in a culture of fear.' *Journal of Social Work 6*, 2, 151–167.

Pithouse, A., Hill-Tout, J. and Lowe, K. (2002) 'Training foster carers in challenging behaviour: A case study in disappointment.' *Child and Family Social Work 7*, 3, 203–215.

Pithouse, A. and Rees, A. (2011) 'Care as regulated and care in the obdurate world of intimate relations: Foster care divided?' *Ethics and Social Welfare 5*, 2, 196–209.

Powell, J. (2001) 'Making contact: Sometimes when we touch.' *Community Care*, 19–25 July.

Prendergast, S. (2000) 'To Become Dizzy in Our Turning: Girls, Body Maps and Gender as Childhood Ends.' In A. Prout (ed.) *The Body, Childhood and Society.* Hampshire: Macmillan.

Prout, A. (2000) 'Childhood bodies: Construction, agency and hybridity.' In A. Prout (ed.) *The Body, Childhood and Society.* Hampshire: Macmillan.

Prout, A. (2005) *The Future of Childhood.* Oxford: Routledge Falmer.

Pugh, G. (1999) 'Seen But Not Heard? Addressing the Needs of Children Who Foster.' In M. Hill (ed.) *Signposts in Fostering.* London: BAAF.

Punch, S. (2004) *'You can do Nasty Things to Your Brothers and Sisters Without a Reason': Time, Space and Siblings.* Paper given to British Sociological Annual Conference, Loughborough.

Punch, S. (2008) 'You can do nasty things to your brothers and sisters without a reason. Siblings' "backstage" behaviour.' *Children and Society 22*, 5, 333–344.

Quereshi, H. and Alborz, A. (1992) 'Epistomology of challenging behaviour.' *Mental Handicap Research 5*, 130–145.

Quinton, D., Rushton, A. Dance, C. and Mayes, D. (1998) *Joining New Families: A Study of Adoption and Fostering in Middle Childhood.* Chichester: Wiley.

Rees, P., Forbes, N. and Holland, S. (2014) *Outcomes for Young People Leaving Foster Care: A Review of Literature and Data Review on the Affects of Age of Exit.* Wales: Action for Children.

Reimer, D. (2010) 'Everything was strange and different: Adults' recollections of transition in to foster care.' *Adoption and Fostering 34*, 2, 18–33.

Resilience Research Centre, Canada. (2014) Available at www.resilienceproject.org, accessed on 10 February 2014.

Rhodes, K., Orme, G. and McSurdy, M. (2003) 'Foster parents' role performance responsibilities: Perceptions of foster mothers, fathers and workers.' *Children and Youth Services Review 25*, 12, 935–964.

Ribbens McCarthy, J., Edwards, R. and Gillies, V. (2000) *Parenting and Step-Parenting: Contemporary Modern Tales.* Oxford: Centre for Family and Household Research , Oxford Brooks University, Occasional Paper 4.

Ribbens McCarthy, J., Edwards, R. and Gillies, V. (2003) *Making Families: Moral Tales of Parenting and Step-Parenting.* Durham: Sociology Press.

Riggs, D. and Willsmore, S. (2012) 'Experiences of disenfranchised grief arising from unplanned termination of a foster placement: An exploratory South Australian Study.' *Adoption and Fostering 36*, 2, 57–66.

Roberts, L. (2011) 'Ending care relationships: Carer perspectives on managing 'endings' within a part-time fostering service.' *Adoption and Fostering 35*, 4, 20–27.

Roberts, L. (2014) *Supporting Families in Need: A Qualitative Case Study of the Support Care Intervention.* Doctoral thesis. Cardiff: Cardiff University.

Rock, S., Michelson, D. and Day, C. (2013) 'Understanding foster placement instability for looked after children: A systematic review and narrative analysis of quantitative and qualitative evidence.' *British Journal of Social Work*, doi:10.1093/bjsw/bct084.

Rose, W. (2006) 'Children's Perspectives.' In J. Aldgate, D. Jones, W. Rose and C. Jefferey (eds) *The Developing World of the Child.* London: Jessica Kingsley Publishers, pp. 287–311.

Rowe, J., Hundleby, M. and Garnett, L. (1989) *Child Care Now: A Survey of Placement Patterns.* London: BAAF.

Rowe, J. and Lambert, L. (1973) *Children Who Wait: A Study of Children Needing Substitute Families.* London: BAAF.

Rushton, A. (2003) *The Adoption of Looked After Children: A Scoping Review of Research.* London: SCIE.

Ryan, M. (2012) *How to Make Relationships Matter for Looked After Young People: A Handbook.* London: National Children's Bureau.

Saga (2013) Available at www.saga.co.uk/newsroom/press-releases/2013/may/OVER-50s-DESPAIR-AS-KIDS-STILL-AT-HOME-AGED-27.aspx, accessed on 12 September 2014.

Saleeby, D. (1996) 'The strengths perspective in social work practice.' *Social Work Education 41*, 3, 296–305.

Saleebey, D. (ed.) (2006) *The Strengths Perspective in Social Work Practice* (4th edition). Boston: Allyn and Bacon.

Sanders, R. (2004) *Sibling Relationships: Theory and Issues for Practice.* Basingstoke: Palgrave Macmillan.

Schaffer, D. (2008) *Social and Personality Development* (6th edition). USA: Cengage Learning.

Schofield, G. (2002) 'The significance of a secure base: A psychosocial model of long-term foster care.' *Child and Family Social Work 7*, 4, 259–272.

Schofield, G. and Beek, M. (2005) 'Risk and resilience in long term foster care.' *British Journal of Social Work 35*, 8, 1283–1301.

Schofield, G. and Beek, M. (2008) *Achieving Permanence in Foster Care*. London: BAAF.

Schofield, G. and Beek, M. (2009) 'Growing up in foster care; providing a secure base through adolescence.' *Child and Family Social Work 14*, 255–266.

Schofield, G. and Beek, M. (2014a) *Promoting Attachment and Resilience: A Guide for Foster Carers and Adopters*. London: BAAF.

Schofield, G. and Beek, M. (2014b) *The Secure Base Model: Promoting Attachment and Resilience in Foster Care and Adoption*. London: BAAF.

Schofield, G., Beek, M., Sargent, K. and Thoburn, J. (2000) (re-printed 2005) *Growing Up in Foster Care: Long Term Foster Care as a Resource for Children in Need of Care and Protection*. London: BAAF.

Schofield, G., Beek, M., and Ward, E. (2012) 'Part of the family: Planning for permanence in long-term family foster care.' *Children and Youth Services Review 34*, 244–253.

Schofield, G., Beek, M., Ward, E and Biggart, L. (2013) 'Professional foster carer and committed parent: Role conflict and role enrichment at the interface between work and family in long term foster care.' *Child and Family Social Work 18*, 1, 46–56.

Seaburg, J. R. and Harrigan, M. P. (1997) 'Family functioning in foster care.' *Families in Society 78*, 5, 463–470.

Sebba, J. (2012) *Why do People Become Foster Carers: An International Literature Review on the Motivation to Foster*. Oxford: Rees Centre.

Sellick, C. (2002) *Foster Care Services in the Independent Sector*. London: Nuffield Foundation.

Sellick, C. (2011) 'Commissioning permanent fostering placements from external providers: An exploration of current policy and practice.' *British Journal of Social Work 41*, 3, 449–466.

Sellick, C. (2013) 'Foster care commissioning in an age of austerity; the experiences and views of the independent provider sector in one English region.' *British Journal of Social Work*, doi:10.1093/bjsw/bct046.

Sellick, C. and Connolly, J. (2002) 'Independent fostering agencies uncovered: The findings of a national survey.' *Child and Family Social Work 7*, 2, 107–120.

Selwyn, J., Saunders, F and Farmer, E. (2010a) 'The views of children and young people cared for by an independent foster-care provider.' *British Journal of Social Work 40*, 3, 696–713.

Selwyn, J. Quinton, D., Harris, P., Wijedasa, D., Nawaz, S. and Wood, M. (2010b) *Pathways to Permanence for Black, Asian and Mixed Ethnicity Children*. London: BAAF.

Shanahan, S. (2007) 'Lost and found: The sociological ambivalence toward childhood.' *Sociology Annual Review 33*, 407–428.

Shilling, C. (2013) *The Body and Social Theory* (3rd edition). London: Sage.

Shotton, C. (2010) 'The experience of foster/adoptive carers in carrying out memory work with children; telling different stories.' *Adoption and Fostering 34*, 2, 61–69.

Sibley, D. (1995) 'Families and Domestic Routines: Constructing the Boundaries of Childhood.' In S. Pile and N. Thrift (eds) *Mapping the Subject*. London: Routledge, pp.94–118.

Simpson, B. (2000) 'The Body as a Site of Contestation in School.' In A. Prout (ed.) *The Body, Childhood and Society*. Hampshire: Macmillan.

Simpson, J. (2013) 'Managing unregulated contact in the age of new technology: Possible solutions.' *Adoption and Fostering 37*, 4, 380–388.

Sinclair, I. (2005) *Fostering Now: Messages from Research*. London: Jessica Kingsley Publishers.

Sinclair, I. (2008) *Stability and Wellbeing in the Care System*. Available at http://php.york.ac.uk/inst/spru/pubs/1459, accessed on 12 February 2014.

Sinclair, I. (2010) 'What Makes for Effective Foster Care: Some Issues.' In E. Fernandez and P. Barth (eds) *How Does Foster Care Work? International Evidence on Outcomes*. London: Jessica Kingsley Publishers.

Sinclair, I., Baker, C., Lee, J. and Gibbs, I. (2007) *The Pursuit of Permanence: A Study of the English Care System*. London: Jessica Kingsley Publishers.

Sinclair, I., Baker, C., Wilson, K. and Gibbs, I. (2003) *What Happens to Foster Children? Report Three*. York: York University.

Sinclair, I., Baker, C., Wilson, K. and Gibbs, I. (2005b) *Foster Children: Where They Go and How They Get On*. London: Jessica Kingsley Publishers.

Sinclair, I., Gibbs, I. and Wilson, K. (2000) *Supporting Foster Placements: Report One and Two*. York: Social Work Research and Development Unit.

Sinclair, I., Gibbs, I. and Wilson, K. (2004) *Foster Carers: Why They Stay and Why They Leave*. London: Jessica Kingsley Publishers.

Sinclair, I. and Wilson, K. (2003) 'Matches and mismatches: The contribution of carers and children to the success of foster placements.' *British Journal of Social Work 33*, 7, 871–884.

Sinclair, I., Wilson, K. and Gibbs, I. (2005a) *Foster Placements: Why They Succeed and Why They Fail*. London: Jessica Kingsley Publishers.

Slater, N. (2004) *Toast: The Story of a Boy's Hunger*. London: Harper Perennial.

Small, J. (1991) 'Ethnic and racial identity in adoption within the United Kingdom.' *Adoption and Fostering 15*, 4, 61–68.

Smart, C. (1999) 'The "New" Parenthood: Fathers and Mothers After Divorce.' In E. Silva and C. Smart (eds) *The New Family*. London: Sage.

Smart, C. (2007) *Personal Life: New Directions in Sociological Thinking*. Cambridge: Polity Press.

Smart, C., Neale, B. and Wade, A. (2001) *The Changing Experience of Childhood: Families and Divorce*. Cambridge: Polity Press.

Smart, C. and Shipman, B. (2004) 'Visions in monochrome: Families, marriage and the individualisation thesis.' *British Journal of Sociology 55*, 4, 491–509.

Smith, C. and Carlson, B. (1997) 'Stress, coping and resilience.' *Children and Youth. Social Services Review 71*, 2, 81–93.

Smith, F., Brann, C., Cullen D. and Lane, M. (2004) *Fostering Now: Current Law including Regulations, Guidance and Standards.* London: BAAF.

Social Care Institute for Excellence (2004) *SCIE Guide 7: Fostering* (November). London: SCIE.

Spears, W. and Cross, M. (2003) 'How do children who foster perceive fostering?' *Adoption and Fostering 27*, 4, 38–45.

Stein, M. (2012) *Young People Leaving Care: Supporting Pathways to Adulthood.* London: Jessica Kingsley Publishers.

Sulloway, F. (1996) *Born to Rebel: Birth Order, Family Dynamics and Creative Lives.* London: Little, Brown and Company.

TACT (2011) Care to Cook Recipe Book. Available at www.Tactcare.org.uk/support-us/care-to-cook-recipe-book/, accessed on 1 March 2014.

Tapsfield, R. (2007) *Most Foster Families in Wales Struggle on a Low Income.* London: Fostering Network.

Tapsfield, R. (2012) 'The fostering system is on the brink' *The Independent* 7 May 2012.

Testa, M. and Rolock, N. (1999) 'Professional foster care: A future worth pursuing?' *Child Welfare 78*, 1, 108–118.

Thoburn, J., Norford, L. and Rashid, S.P. (2000) *Permanent Family Placement for Children of Ethnic Minority.* London: Jessica Kingsley Publishers.

Thomson, L. and McArthur, M. (2009) 'Who's in our family? An application of the theory of family boundary ambiguity to the experiences of former foster carers.' *Adoption and Fostering 33*, 1, 68–79.

Thorne, B. (1993) *Gender and Play: Girls and Boys.* New Brunswick: Rutgers University Press.

Timms, J. E. and Thoburn, J. (2006) 'Your shout! Looked after children's perspectives on the Children Act 1989.' *British Journal of Social Work 36*, 4, 541–559.

Titmuss, R. (1970) *The Gift Relationship: From Human Blood to Social Policy.* London. Reprinted by New York: New Press, 1997.

Triseliotis, J., Borland, M. and Hill, M. (2000) *Delivering Foster Care.* London: BAAF.

Triseliotis, J., Borland, M., Hill, M. and Lambert, L. (1995) *Teenagers and the Social Work Services.* London: HMSO.

Tronto, J. K. (1994) *Moral Boundaries: A Political Argument for an Ethic of Care.* London: Routledge.

Twigg, R. and Swan, T. (2007) 'Inside the foster family: What research tells us about the experience of foster carers' children.' *Fostering and Adoption 31*, 4, 49–61.

Ungar, M. (2008) 'Resilience across cultures.' *British Journal of Social Work 35*, 2, 218–235.

Valentine, G. (2004) *Public Space and the Culture of Childhood.* Hampshire: Ashgate.

Waerness, K. (1996) 'On the Rationality of Caring.' In S. Gordon, P. Benner and N. Noddings (eds) *Caregiving: Readings in Knowledge, Practice, Ethics and Politics.* Philadelphia: University of Pennsylvania Press, pp.175–186.

Wainright, J. and Ridley, J. (2012) 'Matching, ethnicity and identity: Reflections on practice and realities of ethnic matching in adoption.' *Adoption and Fostering 36*, 3–4, 50–61.

Walkerdine, V. (2004) 'Developmental Psychology and the Study of Children.' In J. Kehily (ed.) *An Introduction to Childhood Studies.* Berkshire: Open University Press, pp.96–107.

Ward, H., Munro, E., Dearden, C. and Nicholson, D. (2003) *Outcomes for Looked After Children: Life Pathways and Decision-making for Very Young Children in Care or Accommodated.* Loughborough: Centre for Child and Family Research.

Wedge, D. and Mantle, G. (1991) *Sibling Groups in Social Work: A Study of Children Referred for Permanent Family Placement.* Aldershot: Avebury.

Welsh Government (2011) *Rights of Children and Young Persons (Wales) Measure 2011.* Available at www.assemblywales.org/bus-home/bus-legislation/bus-leg-measures/business-legislation-measures-rightsofchildren.htm, accessed on 12 February 2014.

Welsh Government (2013) *Adoptions, Outcomes and Placements for Children Looked After by Local Authorities.* Available at wales.gov.uk/statistics-and-research/adoptions-outcomes-placements-children-looked-after/?lang=en, accessed on 12 February 2014.

Welsh Government (2014) *Written Statement – Post-18 Placements for Care Leavers and the Social Services and Well-being (Wales) Bill.* Available at http://wales.gov.uk/about/cabinet/cabinetstatements/2014/8423411/?lang=en, accessed on 12 February 2014.

Whittaker, K. (2001) 'The context of youth.' *Social Sciences Review 75*, 4, 682–683.

Williams, F. (1996) 'Good-enough principles for welfare.' *Journal of Social Policy 28*, 4, 667–687.

Williams, F. (2004) *Rethinking Families.* London: Calouste Gulbenkian Foundation.

Williams, S. J. and Bendelow, G. (1998) *The Lived Body: Sociological Themes, Embodied Issues.* London: Routledge.

Wilson, J. (ed.) (2004) *Taking Care: A Collection of Writings and Drawings by Children in Care and Young Care Leavers.* London: BBC Books.

Wilson, K. and Evetts, J. (2006) 'The professionalisation of foster care.' *Adoption and Fostering 30*, 1, 39–47.

Wilson, K., Fyson, R. and Newstone, S. (2007) 'Foster fathers: their experiences and contributions to fostering.' *Child and Family Social Work 21*, 1, 22–31.

Wilson, K., Petrie, S. and Sinclair, I. (2003) 'A kind of loving.' *British Journal of Social Work 33*, 8, 991–1004.

Wilson, K., Sinclair, I. and Gibbs, I. (2000) 'The trouble with foster care: The impact of stressful events on foster carers.' *British Journal of Social Work 30*, 2, 193–209.

Wilson, K., Sinclair, I., Taylor, C., Pithouse, A. and Sellick, C. (2004) *Fostering Success: An Exploration of the Research Literature in Foster Care.* London: SCIE Polity Press.

Winter, K. (2006) 'Widening knowledge concerning looked after children.' *Child and Family Social Work 11*, 55–64.

Wolin, S. J. and Wolin, S. (1993) *The Resilient Self: How Survivors of Troubled Families Rise Above Adversity.* New York: Villard Press.

Woodhead, M. (2003) 'The Case for Childhood Studies'. Annual Lecture, Children's Research Centre, Trinity College, Dublin.

Wyness, M. (2006) *Childhood and Society: An Introduction to the Sociology of Childhood.* Basingstoke: Palgrave Macmillan.

Wyness, M. (2011) *Childhood and Society: An Introduction to the Sociology of Childhood* (2nd edition). Basingstoke: Palgrave Macmillan.

Young, M. and Wilmott, P. (1973) *The Symmetrical Family.* London: Routledge and Kegan Paul.

Zelizer, V. (2002) 'Kids and commerce.' *Childhood 9*, 4, 375–396.

SUBJECT INDEX

AUTHOR INDEX